LEARNING JOY FROM DOGS WITHOUT COLLARS

a memoir

LAURALEE SUMMER

SIMON & SCHUSTER PAPERBACKS

New York   London   Toronto   Sydney

SIMON & SCHUSTER PAPERBACKS
Rockefeller Center
1230 Avenue of the Americas
New York, NY 10020

The names and other identifying characteristics
of some people herein have been changed.

First Simon & Schuster paperback edition 2004

Grateful acknowledgment is made for permission to reprint: "Theme from a
Summer Place," by Max Steiner and Mack Discant. © 1960 (Renewed)
Warner Bros. Inc. All Rights Reserved. Used by Permission. Warner Bros.
Publications U.S. Inc., Miami, FL. 33014
Lines from "Sketch for a Memoir" by Adam Wazyk, from *Postwar Polish Poetry*
by Czeslaw Milosz. Copyright 1965 by Czeslaw Milosz. Used by permission of
Doubleday, a Random House imprint.
Lines from "The Age of Reason" by Jorie Graham in *Erosion*. Copyright
© 1983 by Princeton University Press. Reprinted by permission of
Princeton University Press.
Lyrics from "I'm Not There." Words and Music by Chris Colbourn, Bill Janovitz,
and Tom Maginnis. © 1994 EMI VIRGIN SONGS, INC. and SCRAWNY MUSIC. All
Rights for Controlled and Administered by EMI VIRGIN SONGS, INC. All Rights
Reserved. International Copyright Secured Used by Permission.

For information about special discounts for bulk purchases,
please contact Simon & Schuster Special Sales:
1-800-456-6798 or business@simonandschuster.com.

Manufactured in the United States of America

1   3   5   7   9   10   8   6   4   2

The Library of Congress has catalogued the hardcover as follows:
Summer, Lauralee.
Learning joy from dogs without collars : a memoir / Lauralee Summer.
p.   cm.
1. Summer, Lauralee, 1976—Childhood and youth. 2. Homeless children—
United States—Biography. 3. Homeless persons—United States—Psychology.
4. Parent and child—United States. 5. Self-actualization (Psychology)
6. Successful people—United States—Biography. I. Title.
HV4505.S86 2003
305.23'092—dc21
[B] 2003042712

ISBN 0-7432-0102-7
      0-7432-5792-8 (Pbk)

Praise for *Learning Joy from Dogs without Collars*

"An accurate and meaningful recounting of a young woman's difficult and inspiring life."

—The Sunday Oregonian

"Readers will feel a connection with this young woman, who solicits neither sympathy nor special favors."

—USA Today

"Summer's memoir is anything but a treacly inspirational work filled with homilies and bootstrap-pulling tales, though she admits that others in her economic circumstances certainly can derive hope from her story. It is, rather, an honest look at one family's experience with homelessness in all its desperate and maddeningly humane forms. It offers no prescription for success. It is a work of literary naturalism, only in reverse—from degradation to acclaim."

—San Francisco Chronicle

"Here is an American story of vulnerability and willful determination—and here, too, is a story of youthful survival and success against great odds. We readers have so much to learn from this writer's life as she tells it."

—Dr. Robert Coles

"As well as telling her story with insight and a remarkable generosity of spirit, Summer quietly but insistently explores the meaning of the word 'home.' . . . A rare memoir of hard times that is both forgiving and perceptive."

—Kirkus Reviews (starred review)

"Summer's tale is memorable as she writes frankly about poverty, shame, and class distinctions."

—Publishers Weekly

ACKNOWLEDGMENTS

THANK YOU to members of my family for their love and support: my mother, Elizabeth Summer; my Aunt Jane and Uncle Ron for treating me like one of their own; my teacher, mentor, and friend, Mr. Charles Maclaughlin; also Joanie Walker and Caitlin and Kimberly Wilson for their encouragement and for welcoming me into their home when I had no place to go; and my father and stepmother, Robert and Dawn Morgan. Thanks too to other family members whom I have not named.

Thank you to the many friends who believed I would finish and that it would be worth reading: Alena Williams, Amanda Lockshin, Bree Cheatham, Courtney King, Diane Hughes, Emily Sweeney, Gayle Ollerhead, my housemates at "the Dorchester house," Melissa Burt, Meghan O'Brien, Nadia Croes, Patrick and Lynda Daly, and Veronica Terriquez. Each of you offered inspiring words to keep me going, and many of you read and helped to make the manuscript better.

Huge thanks to the many mentors who guided and encouraged me: the teachers and staff at Quincy High School, and at Harvard: Natalie Kusz, Margaret Bruzelius, Sandra Naddaff, Eliza Garfield, and Verlyn Klinkenborg; and my agents at Zachary Schuster—Rochelle Lurie, Lane Zachary, and Todd Schuster.

Thanks to my editor, Geoff Kloske, for the many hours spent helping me to improve the book and for believing in it from the beginning.

Thanks to Jay Weiss and my teammates and coaches on the Harvard Wrestling team and to Mr. Louis Venturelli and the Quincy High School Wrestling team.

Additional thanks to Norine Johnson, Kate Stokes, everybody at Wilkins Investment Counsel in Boston, Dorothy Austin and Diana Eck, NASCEHCY, and my writing classes at Harvard Extension School and the New College of California.

Biggest thanks to my mother, for answering the hard questions and loving me unconditionally.

Biggest thanks to Janice Obrzut, for being so beautiful inside and out and for making me laugh through the tears.

This book is dedicated to three
who have taught me joy:
my mother, Mr. Mac, and Jan.

CONTENTS

CONTENTS

we are not lost
we know where we are
but our itinerary is chance and weather
we do not believe in destinations
and we are in no hurry
we have learned patience
from statues in a thousand parks
and joy from dogs without collars.

—Anonymous, homeless youth

LEARNING JOY
FROM DOGS
WITHOUT
COLLARS

PROLOGUE

WHEN I WAS SEVENTEEN, a reporter interviewed me about my family, my mother, and my life. I was unsure why he wanted to write about me, other than I'd won a wrestling scholarship and was going to Harvard. He grew more interested when I mentioned that I had been homeless as a child. I told him about how I moved twenty times before I was twelve, living in four states—Oregon, California, Arizona, and Massachusetts—and that I stayed at most places for no more than six months at a time. These were things I rarely talked about; I didn't want to emphasize my differences from my peers. I felt different enough inside. But to me, my experiences weren't extraordinary, unique, or newsworthy. I accepted them as part of who I was.

The article was put on the Associated Press wire in early June 1994 and was picked up by every major paper in the country, often as a front-page story with a color photograph of me playing the violin in my room with my mother looking on. It appeared on page six of the Saturday *New York Times* and even in a few European papers.

Soon my phone was ringing thirty times a day, and streams of mail came in through the mail slot of my apartment's front door. *Good Morning America, Dateline NBC,* ABC's *Prime-Time Live,* various talk shows, *People* and *Seventeen* magazines, among many others, all called and wrote. People wanted to make movies and write books, people wanted me to write books.

Suddenly I was transformed from just me into something larger, almost mythological. I became the manifestation of everyone's American Dream. Homeless to Harvard—it had a good sound. Maybe Homeless to Brown or even Homeless to Yale would not have worked as well. Harvard was a name already immersed in myth, tradition, and prestige. It is the ultimate dream college and a place of unassailable privilege and tradition. And wasn't this Dream what our country was based on? The Statue of Liberty

cries . . .

With silent lips. "Give me your tired, your poor,
Your huddled masses yearning to breathe free,
The wretched refuse of your teeming shore.
Send these, the homeless, tempest-tost, to me.
I lift my lamp beside the golden door!"

To some, Harvard was the ultimate golden door.

All at once I was forced to see my life in a political way. I was a statue on a pedestal, a model of American success—the efficiency of the American system, in which all were welcome and all things were possible. Homeless children everywhere could read about me in a magazine or see me on TV. They could be assured that they too could be like me. I was a model of Horatio Alger–like hard work and persistence. I was an example for other Americans to point to, a comfort they could rely on as they sat back with sighs of relief in their soft chairs of privilege. They could kick up their feet and rest assured that all was working as it should. The American Dream was still intact and visible.

But being a statue felt uncomfortable—standing with silent lips and bearing the torch of imprisoned lightning. I could not breathe free when I was a statue, and I was still tossed by an inner tempest. My statue seemed to tell the huddled poor to work hard and they wouldn't be knocked flat and broken by the bad things that happen to them. Work hard and the golden door will open.

But there are countless obstacles in the way of that door—undeniable, unworkable facts, like gravity—and these obstacles reveal a darker side of the story.

There was no money, no father, and no car to take me to every soccer game, wrestling match, or art class. As a child, I had no concept of why I didn't have these things, or even that I didn't, or how I would work on getting them. How could I "work on" getting a father? How by "hard work" could I go to an art class that I had no tools to find on my own and no money to pay for? These were physical, tangible obstacles that no amount of intrapsychic energy could entirely bulldoze through.

Poverty is like a gravity that pulls you down to earth. Some obstacles are like laws or scientific facts, the rational, tangible, objective realities that science is so fond of. There's no way to jump high enough to overcome gravity by "hard work." Effort alone won't make you fly.

In the words of Zaphod Beeblebrox, of Douglas Adams's Hitchhiker's Guide to the Galaxy trilogy, "Flying is easy."

"Step One: Throw yourself at the ground.
Step Two: Miss."

This idea is nice in theory, and most theories sound really nice. They can be read in a class, published, expounded upon. But I came to realize that a theory can be nothing more than an opinion written up in a fancy way with a few statistics thrown in to make it sound convincing.

To say "flying is easy" or to suggest "success is easy if you only work hard enough" fails to leave the realm of theory. When it comes to actually missing the ground or flapping your wings in the face of the undeniable reality of poverty, when it comes to launching yourself into the upper stratospheres of economic and intellectual privilege, when it comes to what happens in between Step One and Step Two, there's a tremendous miracle, a hundred thundering, wonderful interventions, and an astonishing pinprick hole in the oh-so-rationally constructed scientific fact of gravity.

Einstein discovered quantum theory and predicted instantaneous nonlocal action——the startling fact that atomic particles once bonded together and later separated by vast distances continue to influence each other instantaneously——and conventional physics was suddenly unmoored. He described this shocking venture into flight: "All my attempts to adapt the theoretical foundation of physics to this [new type of] knowledge failed completely. It was as if the ground had been pulled out from under one, with no firm foundation to be seen anywhere, upon which one could have built." He missed the ground all right.

But he didn't get there by dogged hard work, by formula or method.

Economic and physical laws do have holes in them. Our minds must be open to see these holes, to see new frameworks, ways in which existing theories and myths do not jive with our own personal knowledge. We do not learn to fly by following a strict scientific method.

There's a lot that happens to make missing the ground possible, and it's not all in the leaper. What came in between me and the hard ground were partially chance events, my mother's fanciful whims, her intense care and guidance, her way of engaging my mind in thinking, in education, in reading. There's also a lot that's determined by chance and divine providence, if you want to call it that—and we don't always understand the mysterious boosts we get from being in the right place at the right time.

When I think of the many buffers and boosts I got that landed me at Harvard, in a place of privilege, I know I am unusually lucky. But what about the kids I lived in shelters with? Those dim faces and voices from my childhood? Few of them were my classmates at Harvard. Schools in poor neighborhoods are often lacking in funds and understaffed. Many poor children must make blind leaps that send them crashing, blood covered, into inadequate public schools. They hit the ground and encounter the fists of horizontal violence and despair and the depressing gravity of an unequal public educational system. They live on a planet with a much stronger gravitational field than the earth we privileged ones are used to. For them, gravity's more like the irresistible drawing inward of a black hole—a painful tearing apart at the atomic level. A force that feels as if the skin of your eye sockets is pulled down to your ankles and you can't breathe, you're so compressed.

A story you might hear about a homeless girl who goes to Harvard can tell the truth while also lying. I appeared on a national TV show shortly after the AP article came out. My mother and I were driven to a studio outside of Boston, placed in front of a TV screen on which the hosts in New York asked us questions. We had microphones clipped on and headphone receivers in our ears. The segment was only a few minutes long, so our answers had to be short. They asked me two questions. My mother hardly got to speak at all. I was asked: "What was it like to be homeless?" and "What was the worst thing to happen while you were homeless?"

I think I spoke about a knife fight in the hallway of a welfare motel—witnessed through the chained crack of a door at 2:00 A.M. on a school night. I spoke of not sleeping and feeling tired the next day in school.

I couldn't believe that we were expected to describe the experience of "being homeless" in a short response, a single anecdote.

What I would have liked to answer had I time to reflect: The worst thing about being homeless was the loss of a sense of self, the dispersal of identity without a container to understand oneself in.

If I hadn't been dumbstruck—if I had had more than a twenty-second sound bite to convey the experience of homelessness, this is the story I would have told.

*   *   *

To me, writing this book is like building a home. For my mother, being at home means having a garden. Many of the shelters we stayed in did not have gardens. Everyone needs a home, and some of us do not live in one dwelling for our whole lives. We are always building new ones, to make up for a time when we had not even wood or nails to build with. Please forgive me if I borrow stars to make a ceiling, or clouds for a roof, for I have learned to make do with what I could see and dream of. If my floor's a little dirty, it's only because I've been planting my mother's flowers in here.

1

MOTHER

Keeping all this from them—
when they might have helped

—Adrienne Rich

AFTER FIFTEEN MONTHS of being homeless my mother moved into a new apartment. I stood nervously—hovering in the room's center, not wanting to get too close to the edges—as if I was on a ship. The further to the edges I went, the whole place might shift under my feet, tipping me off the edge. If I went too far to the edge, I might be thrown to the walls or couch or the sink piled with dirty dishes. I might land in the midst of one of her quaint experiments. For Christmas, she placed the tree in a pot full of thousands of pennies, to keep it upright. The pennies are now soaking in water, being cleansed of the Christmas tree's sticky sap.

Broken bits of toys, confiscated from the church nursery, lie in a colorful plastic heap in another corner. As my mother stands in the doorway between the living room and kitchen, she says to me, "They were too small for safety—one and five-eighths inches is the government standard for toys for children under three. One and three-quarters is safer yet." The late afternoon sunlight shines on her hair. She sometimes dyes it black or blond, but the gray always grows back in. My own hair is as straight as uncooked spaghetti, but hers spirals in loose flyaway curls around her face, or is tucked behind her ears with bobby pins. She looks girlish and innocent with her little space-rocket curls, salt and pepper colored.

I do not feel at home here though this might have been one of the homes of my childhood. All I see now is the poverty. The bleak walls are broken by yard-sale finds. My mother tries to fill the space with the contents of two bags she had while in the shelter. The refrigerator and cupboards are bare—only a few items from the food bank: cans, stale taken-off-the-shelf pretzels, a new brand of cereal that didn't sell. All I feel is home's lack.

My mother can spend hours, days, even months on projects of her own devising, projects that utterly absorb her.

There are the three hundred small plants growing in styrofoam cups and egg cartons on her porch. She knows each type of plant and recites its name lovingly. To me they are just plants, although they look beautiful and green in the washed-out yellow sunlight.

In her refrigerator sit row upon row of sprouts: bean, alfalfa; and no food, only half a bottle of flat Pepsi, and some condiments. I worry—this can't be healthy, Mother. She says she eats oatmeal every day, and uses powdered milk. There are Popsicles and vanilla ice cream in the freezer, which she blends together to make "orange crèmes." This was plain poverty, but it was also what she liked.

*

I was a snooty college student, a sophomore. I tried to analyze my mother—distance and detach in an attempt to bring, gather her closer into my understanding. "Mother, do you feel generative or despairing?" I think of Erik Erikson's stages of ego development. The seventh stage, the one my mom should be going through: Generativity versus Stagnation. I sense these feelings pitching back and forth in my mother and I am inadequate to be at home with her. Yet what I have been taught to see as degeneracy (a disorganized house, leaving it only every few days . . .) may be my mom's way of generating new ideas.

Going to Harvard was in many ways a journey away from home for me. At Harvard, one of the favorite buzzwords of academics is *discourse*. A discourse is an ongoing conversation, a talking and listening back and forth. Each discourse is physically and culturally situated in a space. There is the discourse of cognitive psychologists, discourse on literature, sociological discourse on poverty and welfare reform. The word comes from the Latin *discursus*, "to run to and fro." The word *current* also comes from the same Latin root. So when I think of a discourse, I think of a flowing river of words, a current of communication.

With Harvard's discourses, I could categorize and analyze and discuss my mother's life and situation. I could analyze her according to Freudian or Eriksonian discourse; label her with a neurosis or a psychosocial stage of development. In the discourse of sociology, I could place my mother in a chart or a graph with other welfare mothers. I could understand her in a hundred different ways, a hundred different discourses. Yet none of these were satisfactory to me.

This journey—from my mother's thought and speech to what I've learned at Harvard and afterwards—this journey seemed to go in one direction and not the other. When I applied what I learned at Harvard to my mother, she grew farther and farther away from me. No longer a running *to* and *fro*, no longer a bridge, a pathway between two (cultural) locations, instead my education was a running *away from*. I moved away from my mother's thought and speech. I tried to travel back, but I could not find a bridge.

I was told I must not be too at home in the knowledge I created. I must objectively separate it from me as a mother gradually knows her child is separate. If discourses are a running to and fro, then I am left running between my mother's home and the world, out of place (homeless) in both spaces.

Good discourses make it easy to communicate. They increase understanding and clarity. They are like rivers with plenty of water in them, they are like a good steady run, like taking deep long breaths, they flow. There can be rocky parts in a discourse, places you must push through, but you do get from one place to another. As Jeanette Winterson wrote in *Oranges Are Not the Only Fruit*, "I don't know how to answer. I know what I think, but words in the head are like voices under water. They are distorted. Hearing the words as they hit the surface is sensitive work. You will have to be a bank robber and listen and listen to the little clicks before you can open the safe." A discourse may be an imperfect medium but it can help you get from the place inside your head to the place where you can begin to see inside someone else's.

In my mother's apartment, I try to reconcile my two homes, to build a strong bridge, one that will travel between the two (political, class) locations.

Once there was a time when I did not feel distant from my mother's voice. But then I was inside the slippery red warm walls of her womb. Yet it is hard to have been inside the womb of my mother and to know—I can never take her inside of me. My eyes saw more of her wet dark caverns, spaces and limits, than she has ever seen. Although she felt me inside her, now she sees of me only the skin I present. This is difficult for us both.

You and I can judge her from outside, but in her womb, as she read and talked to me, I listened to her voice coming to me not through the wall of stomach muscles but through every inside vibration. I doubled, tripled, became an infinity of the self I was. I grew in nine months more than in the twenty-five years since.

When I was in grade school and high school, I played a violin. The violin's voice was like my mother's was when she read to the unborn me. The violin not only sounded on fingertips but also quivered and spoke within my body. Resounded in my bent elbows, my chin, between my ears, temples. The music spoke in the bones of my foot as it tapped the floor, keeping time. When I heard my mother's voice it was like this. Her voice did not come to me, it was part of me already. Its vibrations peeled me off the womb's walls. I didn't listen with ears because toes could hear as well.

I felt like I would never hear her voice and feel fully separate. I don't want to write only *about* my mother; I also want to write *within*.

One day last fall, I went to visit my mother, hoping to find some answers to questions I had about her life. My mom was a mysterious person. She was thirty-six years old when I was born, had a whole life she'd lived before me. I wanted to understand the hints she gave me about this other life. I knew bits and pieces, but had never heard the full story. I love to get my mom talking about her family before me, her life and her "other" kids. It is important for me to hear about this earlier life, because it helps me to understand how we, she and I, got to the place where we were now, how we had arrived in this apartment, this city, this situation.

My mother will turn sixty-two this year. She lives in her own apartment, in Quincy, Massachusetts, a city of about 90,000 people that borders Boston, where John Adams and his son John Quincy Adams once lived. She took me to see their homes the first spring that we lived in Quincy—the log cabin with no running water where John Adams was born and the large mansion he later lived in where John Quincy was born.

Nothing is clear anymore when I try to understand or write about my mom. My story about her spirals out in a million directions and covers too much material when it needs to be focused and artistic and concise. I feel like since I've grown up so much, I've lost all my great and inspiring truths. My mother seems to stand on the other side of the bank as the river of truth flows past. I search for the bridge that will bring us together again.

She and I know each other well. I hold nothing back from her. Sometimes I must be gentle and slow, when I ask painful questions. I know that because I am her child, she cannot reject me, the bond is too deep. On this fall day, we sit at the kitchen table near the window, with the fading autumn sunlight streaming in. I ask her questions about her life—a few require only dates or one-line answers. I also ask one or two questions that I hope she will not resist.

I have my many theories and interpretations of her. I may know why she is the way she is, perhaps even more than she herself may understand or speak of. But I must ask her the questions, because I tend to write too much into her silences.

In recent years, my mother was diagnosed and treated for a depression that makes it difficult for her to work. She now receives Social Security disability insurance. I asked her why she gets Social Security, or what *she* thinks the reason is. This is a point of sensitivity for her and is something she doesn't like to speak of. I could say simply: She gets Social Security because she is certifiably crazy. I know that this is the easy answer, but I also know that she does not see it that way.

I know my mom, and I am able to reach the places of resistance within her. I am able to call up the most reasonable, deep feeling and thinking, awareness in her. I demand reason of her because I love her and I know her to be a true and truth-seeking person. I want to understand the mystery of my mother, because it is invariably wrapped up with questions about my own identity.

She understands me in a way that few other people do. She is my source and mainspring—to erase her would again leave me alone and blank, wondering if I came only from a place of craziness and strangeness.

As my mother began to tell me the rambling stories of her life, she drifted away, lost in thought. Her mouth quivers when she is thinking hard, or when she becomes upset. As she thought, her mouth opened slightly, as if she were about to speak, and I saw her tongue moving up and down just slightly, inside her mouth.

Here is the story she tells:

My Life and My Viewpoint of It by Elizabeth Summer

I have three siblings—one older brother and sister, Jane and Jimmy, twins, and one younger brother, Tommy. The first time I heard the word sibling *was when I was twenty-seven, and* brought my third child, Kristi, in for her six-week-old checkup. My second child, Bobby, was three years old and sucking his thumb. The doctor said something about sibling rivalry and the middle-child syndrome.

After the doctor's comment, I started thinking about my place amongst my siblings. I was the youngest for three years, until Tommy was born. After that, I was the middle child. But I was "middle" in more than one way.

I was born in the middle of the year (July 7, 1940), grew up midcentury, was the middle child (and lived on the middle of the Pacific Coast in Siletz and Toledo, Oregon. My mother, Savilla Laura Craven, was also born midyear, on July 4, the birthday of the United States, in its heartland, in Russell Springs, Kansas.

I was of average height and weight and fairly average looks. As a middle child, it may be that I was neither as uptight, ambitious, or focused as a firstborn child nor as charming, sociable, and easygoing as a last-born. Rather, I tended to be a steady mediator, to see both sides of a situation, and to attempt to keep the peace or restore it.

When I was a baby, I slept in a dresser drawer. I now have a four-and-a-half-by-two-and-a-half-inch flat spot between the back and top of my head. I think this spot may be from the drawer.

My mother must have been incredibly busy, with twin toddlers and a new baby. She worked like the very dickens. She did not have plastic or paper diapers, and had to wash dozens of cloth diapers each day with a wringer washer.

Our house in Siletz—where I lived until I was almost nine—had no indoor plumbing. Jane and I used to shout to our father when we had to go to the bathroom in the middle of the night, "Daddy, Daddy, turn on the light!" Then we would grope our

way down the stairs and use the pot in the corner of our parents'
bedroom. The outhouse, which we would use during the day,
was an unpainted wood building, three feet by four feet, and was
halfway between the house and the barn.

My earliest memory is of being in the garden with my
mother. A red racer snake was there—about sixteen inches long.
My mother grew raspberries and rhubarb, beans and peas.

Perhaps my love of flowers and plants comes from these
early times spent with Mother. Just today, I looked over the
wildflower seeds at Wollaston Market. There were several more
sweet William and catchfly, but no blanket fly. They had several
kinds that I didn't have: rose mallow, yellow and purple cone-
flowers, rare aster, succulent lupine, scarlet glads, evening prim-
rose, globe gilia, colonial poppies, and yarrow.

I bought rare marjoram, savory, blue flax, a whole package
of flowering kale, corn poppy, Texas bluebonnet, four-o'clocks,
and Drummond phlox. I also bought a package of moonflower;
I'll try again, and maybe have better luck this time.

There are thousands of young whiteflies on my tomatoes and
strawflower. There are none on the white and lavender forget-
me-nots, which I have blooming quite nicely.

When I was a child, we had red, black, and white chickens, some
regular and some bantam, and a brownish red cow, named
Blaze for the white flame-shaped marking on her forehead. Our
mother sold butter and eggs to bring in extra money.

We had an apple orchard of sixteen beautiful apple trees.
The first to get ripe were the transparent apples. I never see
these anywhere anymore. They were little, soft, and yellow.
The Gravensteins ripened next, hard green with red stripes;
they were big and juicy and tasted lovely. There was a crab
apple tree, and other trees with small little hard red apples. The

transparent tree was our favorite tree to climb. The orchard was behind the house and garden, next to Blaze's pasture.

One night, the gate was left open between the pasture and the orchard, and Blaze got into the orchard and choked on an apple and died. I remember the morning when we found out. I was lying in my wooden bunk—built into the wall in the little back area where Tommy and I slept. The area was a walk-through and had unfinished wood walls and one window. It was off of the kitchen, and people walked through to get to the pantry, our parents' bedroom, and the staircase to where Jane and Jimmy slept.

My father came in and told my mother that the cow had died, and I remember lying there under the clean white sheets, pastel yellow blanket, and old quilt, and feeling very sad.

Blaze seemed like such a sweet old cow. She had big brown eyes and long thick eyelashes. When we children went down to the river behind the house, we walked through the pasture, through the dandelions, the cow pies, and all the flies buzzing about. We skirted around the cow, because she was so big. If I hadn't been so afraid of her because I was so small, I might have liked to rub the soft hide of her head, and have her push the flame shape on her forehead into my hand. Now that she had died, I would sit under the transparent apple tree and picture Blaze, all alone in the dark night shadows, choking and convulsing on the pieces of apple and core. I would picture her shaking and falling to the ground.

No tears came to my eyes as I lay there in my bunk. I only looked at the wooden walls, the sun slanting in from the kitchen, and the world felt emptier somehow, for a moment.

I was seven. I suppose my feelings were as resilient as a bouncing rubber ball or the string that pulls a yo-yo, because by that night at the butchering, I was happy again. The cow was hung from the loft from the same rope that we used to swing from, out over the bales of hay, until our mother and father found out and told us to stop. The cow was hung there to be bled out. Our neighbors, the Clarks, Rings, Castles, and the Nelsons, were invited over for the butchering, and it was an exciting and festive occasion. Jane, Jimmy, and I tried to break the bladder by jumping on it and poking it with sticks. Thinking about it now, I get a sad feeling, thinking that it was so easy for me to find freedom from sadness so soon again.

When Jane and Jimmy were in first grade they were invited to a birthday party. I thought that was the best thing and I wanted to go. They had to explain to me that I couldn't go because I didn't know the people and wasn't in school yet.

This may be why my mother had a party for me on my eighth birthday. It was my only birthday party, for we didn't have parties for every year as children do these days. My mother often did special things for me, I think maybe because the oldest were twins and got to do everything first; they had bikes and I didn't. And Tommy was the youngest and got more of her attention. But I was the one she picked to go to California with Uncle Harvey and Aunt Wilma when I was five, and she stayed up all night before I left, sewing gray flannel trousers for me to wear on the train.

At my birthday party, it was summertime. I remember large nests of caterpillars—or tent worms—in the apple tree outside the kitchen.

The party was attended by our best neighborhood friends— Alma and Alton Clark and Irene Nelson; our cousins, Shirley and Clinton; and by my own brothers and sister. We had canned vegetable soup and hot dogs, chocolate cake and ice cream, most likely strawberry. At the time I thought that Irene, an older girl who was about eleven, ruined the party because she didn't like the ice cream and made disparaging remarks about it. But her *gifts are the only ones I remember: a green rat-tail comb and a fifty-cent piece.*

In my ninth year, we left our little "homestead" and apple orchard of sixteen trees on the Siletz River in the town of the same name. We moved to Toledo, Oregon, a larger town not far away. We three older children spent many happy hours on the bank of the stream, "fishing" with string and a safety pin or an old tin can. All we ever saw were tiny fish and crayfish. And— once, we saw eels! They lived in the deep water across the river from our swimming hole, below the Clarks'. We could walk down a steep path about twenty yards and then carefully—yet still slipping and sliding—walk along the muddy, slanted bank of the river to the swimming hole. At one point, there was a one-inch branch that I had to grab on to to keep my balance. One day, there was a fat slug on the other side of the branch. I got a slimy surprise in the palm of my hand. Ugh!

On one occasion, I fell behind the older kids. I got lost and ended up in a garbage dump. I stepped on a rusty tin lid and cut my foot. I remember that as well as I do grabbing ahold of that slug. The wound from the lid was one and a half inches by one inch and a quarter inch deep. I don't remember seeing any blood, but maybe I didn't look at it until Jane and Jimmy had carried me on a "chair" of their arms to the house, which was an eighth of a mile away.

We lived in the house in Toledo for the rest of my growing up years. I went to high school, and even though I got good grades, no one told me I could go to college. My sister, Jane, was vale-dictorian of her class, two years ahead of me, and went to secretarial college. Jimmy also had good grades. He won a baseball scholarship to go to the University of Oregon. He was a sopho-more there and barely twenty-one when he died of leukemia. It's true that no one told me I could go, but I didn't even think of going to college, because when I was young, all I ever wanted to do was get married and have babies. That was my whole life's dream.

I got married when I was twenty-one, in 1961. I had four babies in a row, two boys, and then two girls. My husband and I separated after thirteen years of marriage. He only took the children every Wednesday night for two hours. He and his girl-friend went on vacations often. I was going crazy, alone with four youngsters and their many needs.

I went on a vacation to California. I left a note for him to see when he brought the children home that Wednesday night. "On vacation for a week. Lots of love. See you soon! Mom."

It was January 1976. I packed my bags for California, shut the door, and left the door unlocked so he could get in to feed the cats and dog. I left the dinner dishes undone; I left the bed unmade. I had bought large drums and decorated them for the children to put their toys into, but the toys were still scattered all over the floor. I left them there, for the time being. I left off wor-rying about my son Bobby, whose muscles were deteriorating before my eyes from the Duchenne muscular dystrophy that I felt responsible for giving to him. I left it all behind—for just a week, I thought. Taping the little yellow note to the brown door, I turned and left.

I chose, when I closed the door behind me, but did not know that I had chosen. I thought that I would be allowed to come back to my home in a week, refreshed and ready to begin where I had left. Had I been able to see the future, I might have made the bed, done the dishes, put the toys into the drums. I might not have gone to California at all. I told my ex-husband I needed a vacation. He said, "If you go, I'll . . ." and his voice carried a threat. But how was I to know how he'd finish that sentence?

Who is the mother who has such clarity when she has four chil-dren, one of them handicapped, spinning her mind into tight cir-cles? Before I was Lauralee's mother, I was mother to four others. They were all small and insistent.

The unmade bed, the toys, the pile of dishes, these were important because while I was in California, he (my ex-husband) entered the house and had pictures taken. The pictures were used in court to prove that I was unfit, unable to be a good mother. The bed, the dishes, the toys everywhere, and a half bot-tle of wine left on the counter. Proof, I suppose, that my mind was as scattered as the toys. Proof that I had come uncorked just like that bottle of wine.

I came back the next week, to pick the children up. They were at their grandmother's house. The grandmother was baking cookies, the children were enjoying themselves. It was only Becki, the youngest, six years old, who wanted to go home with me. I went out and started to cross the street, carrying my youngest to the car. But my ex-husband came out and pulled the child away from me.

Becki was the only one who wanted to go with me. But he pulled her back, he took her other arm there in the street, and I had to let go.

I had to leave her. She was saying, "Mommy, Mommy, I want to go with you." She was only six. And she wanted to come with me. I had no choice.

What could I do? I had to leave her there. I had to. He was pulling her one way, in the middle of the street, while I pulled another. She would have been ripped apart. I had to leave her.

He sued for custody, saying I had abandoned my children. He won the case. I was left, in my mid-thirties, with one year of secretarial experience, thirteen years of marriage and house-hold labor, but no husband. And he with my children.

My mother's story broke down here. Her face was rumpled and red from holding the tears in, and as she talked, her hands made sharp up and down strokes through the air.

Coincidentally, ironically perhaps, the night my mother left a note on her door and never got her children back was the night on which I was conceived. Before going to California, she went to visit my father, whom she was then dating. Before she told me the whole story, I was confused about the order of events. But now I understood. She was pregnant with me when she lost the custody of the other four children. After losing the case, she returned to California to give birth to me there, in Santa Rosa, away from the scrutiny of relatives and friends, who either worried for or condemned her.

She brought me back from California when I was a baby; the other kids were surprised, because she hadn't told them she was pregnant. I pictured her meeting them: four children as I've seen them in photographs, in 1970s Technicolor. Youngest to oldest: Becki's dark brown eyes—our mother's eyes—and gap-toothed dimpled smile. Kristi's longer face, that of a more serious nine-year-old. Bobby in his wheelchair, straining for a closer look; Kirk, the oldest, at thirteen, passive faced.

And she, with me—a white bundle in her arms—handed me to Kirk like I was a new present she brought just to surprise them.

On the edges of the scene, the adults hung back and watched, smiled at her caprice, noticing the children's bewilderment. Their father and stepmother might have wondered if the event of my birth would make the kids closer to or farther from her.

I pictured this scene and then asked her about my own

father, and my conception (our conception, the conception of our life together) and how she decided to keep me. Did she keep me only because the other four were taken?

Another day, when I was fifteen, she had told me—because she was angry with me, because I was being snotty and hostile—"I could have had an abortion, you know. I considered it."

"Fuck you, Mother," I retorted, knowing she didn't mean it. My heart started to beat faster, my palms and temple got sticky with sweat, as I pictured my life cut off before it began, when I thought of this near miss.

From the scene when my siblings first met me, my mind wandered back, and I asked her again—about my conception, which she said happened the night she left the others—

"How do you know?" I asked.

"I just know," she replied. She didn't want to talk much about it. "I got in a fight with your father that night. I only saw him a couple of times after that—" And she half smiled at me, her eyes volunteering nothing.

It was difficult to get my mom to talk about this time. It was only after asking many questions that I began to piece the details together.

My mother told me this story, her eyes staring straight ahead, through the window behind me, staring out to the trees and the street outside. Her mouth became a piece of wadded-up paper, and she got ready to throw herself into the garbage like a bad piece of writing.

But—

then she smiled quiveringly, blinked her eyes twice, willing the tears down her face, and she turned to look at me, her eyes still shining under a thin layer of water. She looked at me with her deflated, spongy face, all dimpled and moist, and smiled small-ly. "But I got you (and that's worth something, isn't it?)." I stared blankly back.

I couldn't comprehend losing four children, and going on. I can't imagine the energy I would put into the one I had left, growing (barely . . . incipient, burgeoning). How would I cling to that one small baby, that small being? I would look for myself in her eyes, I would want her to say that I was worth it, too. Knowing the whole time that of course I was a good mother—of course I was. Knowing—yet wanting to show— yes I am a mother, and I will do the job right (this time).

I was meant to be proof. I was my mother's way to prove she could make up for the four that were taken away. I was the one she got to keep, and I would have to turn out more than good, I would have to add up to more than was expected.

"No," she told me, after reading this, "I just wanted you to be happy. And you were happy." Yes, I was happy.

2

WHAT DOES YOUR MOTHER DO?

I WAS BORN on November 5, 1976. It was Guy Fawkes Day in England, and the bonfires there burned bright, but in the United States only politicians' speeches were fiery on this day, a few days after presidential election day in the year that marked the close of the second century of so-called freedom. In the hospital room where I was born, there was no major celebration. My mother was happy to have a newborn daughter, but her joy was not unadulterated. She was all alone in the world, an unwed mother.

She went to California when she was pregnant because she could get a twenty-four-week abortion at an Oakland clinic, but in the end she could not go through with it.

My mother and I returned to Oregon a few months after my birth. We stayed in motels and at my aunt Jane's house until my mother got a child support settlement. She could not afford a lawyer of her own but met with my father's lawyer. She agreed to settle for $4,000, which would release my father from responsibility thereafter. She wanted the money right away in order to be able to move out of her sister's home. My aunt Jane never complained, but my mom knew that our staying there with Jane, Ron, and their six children was stressful for everyone. My mother thought that the money would allow her to get a start—to buy a car and rent a house in Portland—and that after that she would be able to make it on her own. When my mom told Jane that she had agreed to take only $4,000, Jane exclaimed, "Four thousand dollars! Why, it takes twenty-five thousand dollars to raise a child!" My mother and I can laugh about this now—now that all the child raising has been done.

My mother rented a house for us in Portland near her other children, who lived in Oregon City, a nearby suburb. She worked part-time in an office. At first, the kids visited every weekend when she had the car, but she had to sell the car after several months, because the house was expensive to rent. After she sold the car, we saw the kids less and less. It was difficult for her to bring five children back and forth on the bus, and their father wouldn't drive them to us. My mother was afraid also to walk in the streets of Oregon City because my own father worked there and she knew he didn't want to be reminded of our existence.

My mother picked me up at my sitter's one day and found a pair of scissors lying on the floor where I could reach them. She decided to quit her job and stay home with me, because she felt that she could not rely on a sitter to keep me safe. Soon, she could no longer afford the house, and for the next several years, we moved often. My mother took various live-in housekeeping and nanny positions, so that she would be able to work and stay home with me at the same time. We lived in

Portland, then Lincoln City, then in Phoenix, Arizona, and then Oregon again: first Portland, and then the towns of Sandy, Burnside, and Astoria.

The live-in jobs always ended after a short time, for one reason or another. Sometimes my mother felt that she was working an eighty-hour week and had no time for herself, or she would feel that she was getting too attached to the children she took care of. For a month, my mother took care of an elderly couple who lived in a trailer. The trailer had a wooden deck, and my mother fell through one of the loose boards. She was badly bruised and had recurring pain in her upper leg. A short time later, she sprained her back lifting the eighty-eight-year-old, 175-pound man when he fell from his walker, trying to get into the bathtub. So, another job ended after only a month.

In between the live-in positions, my mother and I stayed with relatives—Aunt Jane or one of my great-aunts. Sometimes my mother could not find work for an extended time and we would get subsidized housing and assistance from AFDC.

When I started first grade, my mother thought she would find secretarial work since I would be in school all day. I remember one interview she went to at the courthouse downtown.

"How was it?" I asked her. She had taken a typing test. My mother was a fast typist, but the electric typewriter stymied her. She had become entirely flustered by the dinging sound made by the machine at the end of each row. The sharp, high-pitched *ding!* immobilized her, paralyzed her fingers, and startled her so that it took her a few seconds to recover enough to type the next line. When she had been a secretary fifteen years earlier, there had been only manual typewriters. "At the end of each row, I kept reaching up to push the carriage over. Then I'd have to look for the return button. It threw me all off."

But my mother never did find a job.

My mother was also worried that if she weren't present with me, I too might be taken away from her. Because finding a job was so difficult for her, my mom was able to convince herself that by rights she should not have to leave her home, that she would not let poverty and single parenthood rob her of her right and duty to be an attentive mother. This helped her not to feel guilty about the checks she received from welfare each month.

My mother did the best she could for me, even when we had limited resources. I remember one Halloween, when I was in preschool. Everyone dressed up in costume, and we got to play games all day. My mother decided I would be a robot. She wrapped aluminum foil around and around me and pushed it against my clothes until I was completely silver. By midmorning I found myself playing duck duck goose, and most of the tinfoil had fallen off. As I ran around the circle of children, the foil flew off behind me, until just a few stray pieces remained.

Christmases my mother didn't have much money to buy new presents, but she was always creative. My first-grade year, she bought a Lite-Brite at a yard sale. It still had most of its pegs and black-paper picture patterns. It wasn't new or in its original box, but my mom plugged it in under the tree, put a blank piece of paper in, and spelled my name and MERRY CHRISTMAS!!! with the colorful pegs. It was the first thing I saw when I woke, and my eyes lit up as brightly as the glowing plastic pegs.

My mother did so many good things for me, but by the time I was in first or second grade, I often felt ashamed of her because she didn't have a steady job and she was different from other moms. Most of my friends in school had parents who were married, and they all lived in houses—not apartments.

At the end of the month there was often nothing left to eat except biscuits and honey. We could always make biscuits because they took only flour, water, and baking powder, no eggs or milk or anything else we had run out of. Sometimes we had no food because of a glitch in the welfare bureaucracy—the food stamp card did not arrive. My mother would then call the welfare office and find out that we had not been notified that she needed to reapply for food stamps every six months. According to my mother, there was always some reason for "them" to keep us from getting the food stamps.

We spent many hours waiting with the rows of other mothers with young children. The mothers sat lumpishly, impatiently, and the children scampered about, playing or whining at their mothers' knees. "When can we go home, Mommy?"

When my mother was called, I trailed along with her to a cubicle in the back. My mother began to speak: "We haven't gotten the food stamps this month. . . ." The man smiled condescendingly and raised his eyebrows in mock concern, while the woman shuffled some forms around in a file folder. While they berated my mother for not having reapplied for the food stamps, I thought about the old ceramic cookie jar that had a few biscuits left in it, and the jar of sticky brown government-surplus honey in the cupboard. I wondered if the welfare workers knew anything about this jar of honey and those biscuits. And about everything else, empty.

My mom was flustered and laced and unlaced her fingers nervously. She told them that she hadn't known she had to reapply for the food stamps. She started to ramble on, and they looked at her like she was a monster with two heads. I grew embarrassed and gave her a nudge with my elbow.

"Mom," I whispered, "They don't care, what you're saying. Be quiet." I didn't want them to think I had a crazy, foolish mom. I sided with the welfare workers and tried to shut her up and get her out of there as soon as possible. I was ashamed of her. I was young, but I learned whose words were valued and whose were not.

Over and over I was asked (politely, expectantly): "What does your mother do?"

My mother would look at worms with me—and things like this came to mind when I was asked this question. My mother was invisible to welfare workers, but to me she still had super-powers. She would tell me to look at a flower or a poem or a person in an upside-down, unusual way. Her superpower was in her seeing, and her teaching me to see in this way.

When I was in middle school in Astoria, Oregon, my mother and I knelt on a sidewalk on the steep hill that over-looked the Columbia River. We inspected two pieces of a worm that were separating, going two ways. My attention was diverted from these grimy, slippery bits of science by two of my school friends passing by.

"What are you doing?" the girl asked, clear-eyed.

"Looking at worms," I said, half-innocent, wary of what was coming.

"Looking at worms!" They passed, laughing and elbowing each other, looking with raised eyebrows and loud guffaws.

Reddening, I mumbled, "Don't pay attention, Ma." Of course, my mom didn't pay attention. Nothing like that ever bothered her.

*

"What does your mother do?"

Do? Do? Again, I never knew how to answer this question. She looked at worms with me, made me hand-painted birthday cards, walked for miles into town to get me a new swimsuit for camp. She opened the oven door for heat when the house was cold, and then she made me cinnamon toast and hot cocoa on Sunday mornings. She knew the names of all the flowers.

"What does your mother do?"

As a child I was ashamed and afraid to answer this question. I got good at evasive and fabricated answers. "She works as a home health aide. And she's a gardener. And she takes care of paraplegics." None of these things was entirely true. She might have worked, a few months or years ago, at one of these jobs. She might have been a gardener, in our own garden. I tried to make the intermittent, sporadic, irregular jobs into a seamless whole, a lifetime of virtuous and productive work. I tried to make my mother seem like the productive, miraculous woman everyone wanted her to be.

"What does your mother do?"

Why must we define a person by his or her productivity? Why not ask me, "Tell me about your mother. What is she like?"

Herbert Kohl describes an intellectual as "someone who knows about his or her field, has a wide breadth of knowledge about other aspects of the world, who uses experience to develop theory and questions theory on the basis of further experience . . . also someone who has the courage to question authority and who refuses to act counter to his or her own experience and judgment."

And my mother fits that description. She spent all her time learning in depth about things that interested her, and she was subversive because she did exactly what she wanted when she wanted for her own reasons. She read and learned, wrote and questioned.

My mother refused to take a job that would force her to suppress her intellectual longings and capacities. To be human is to think, question, and wonder. What is unfortunate is that our society often limits the exercise of these capacities to a small segment of the population, the academic and professional elites. My mom went to college for one semester when I was in seventh grade, but our welfare checks were discontinued because the welfare office considered her school loans to be income. We had no money to live on, so she had to stop going to school.

Many people would say that a mother supporting her family on welfare should feel it her duty to search for a job, to earn money to eat and live. The welfare workers told my mom that a job would make her more independent and self-respecting. But the jobs available to my mother, who had only a high school diploma, were service jobs that offered little. A job at McDonald's would not give her more independence and self-respect. In fact, she would earn less than the welfare stipend and have no medical benefits. Some mothers may have been able to do this and gain courage from it, but not mine.

I was aware that people judged my mother negatively because she did not have a job, she could not just find a job and dutifully work. She couldn't be satisfied with her place in life and do the honorable thing of earning money to support us. I was torn between wanting to side with those who judged my mother as lazy and irresponsible—and wanting to protect her from these judgments because I loved her and saw all the good things she did do and the intelligence inside her, the beautiful bright interesting person she is.

Only later did I come to understand and empathize with my mother's choices and perspective. When in college, I met so many people who had been privileged their entire lives. Many of these were wealthy men who had been given a great education, power and wealth and freedom to pursue their dreams. In college I also read widely about how women, poor people, and racial minorities throughout history have been denied opportunities that others took for granted.

To stay at home and read and play was the only way my mother could achieve the same privileged status that others are born into. If this was taking advantage of the welfare system, then I'm glad she did it. The "privilege" she elected was limited. She didn't work to accumulate wealth, so she never gained any power in society. She was always shackled to a zero balance in the bank account, and didn't have money for college or expensive vacations—but she took her life for what it was and traveled where she could.

Her choices were few, but she took the way with the most present freedom. While she was dependent on welfare to keep her from dollar to dollar, her time was her own. She lived inside of days, inside hours of freedom now.

Now when people ask—as they inevitably do—"What does your mother do?" I am able to tell them the truth. I don't fabricate a job or make excuses for her. I tell them about the amazing person she is.

It was a huge relief to no longer have to justify my mom's doings to the world—to no longer be worried about those who would criticize her and her choices. To be able to say: I think she's wonderful the way she is, don't you?

But I didn't think any of this until I went to college and took classes on poverty and welfare reform. As a child I knew only that my mother was incorrect—and so I was ashamed of her. Because she was my mother—I loved her.

3

THE TROUBLE WITH READING

MY MOTHER BEGAN reading to me when I was in the womb. She was an edacious reader and learner. When I was two, she read to me each night from *The Collected Works of Mother Goose*.

I also liked to play in my room with two-inch-square alphabet blocks. We had a book about birds and I learned all of their names. We had few other toys or books, but once my mother realized how much I loved reading and writing, she bought other books and even a red-leather-bound set of Britannica Junior Encyclopedias.

We lived in Lincoln City for a time, a picturesque seaside town on the North Oregon coast. It is known as the Kite Capital of the World because of its wide beaches and strong winds. The center street had wooden sidewalks and rows of tourist shops. We went to the quaint downtown to buy groceries. I walked and pushed my buggy until I got tired and then rode again while my mother pushed. Once, we stopped at a thrift store. I discovered a lacquered plaque with my name on it and pointed and said, "That's my name." My mother was amazed. I was only two years old. A few days later at home, I scrambled up onto the middle of the kitchen table, where there were paper and pencil. I said, "I write my name." My mother looked, and sure enough, there it was, written out in an awkward combination of capital and lowercase letters.

Soon after, I began printing out the shorter words from the Mother Goose book, words like *was, do, to, so, too,* and *two.* When my mother wrote letters to relatives and friends, she let me clamber up onto her lap and watch as she neatly printed words across the page. She printed instead of writing in cursive. When each letter was done, I signed my name along with hers. She signed her name Betty, so I started calling my mother by her first name because I wanted to call her what everybody else did.

My memories of Lincoln City are suffused with a blue-green light. The greenish light of sunshine filtered through my favorite baby quilt stretched over the top of a large cardboard box. I played house in this box with a neighbor girl a little older than I. We put it in the front yard of my building, a large old Victorian house converted into apartments. The cardboard box was big, because I was three years old, and small. My mother cut windows with cardboard shutters that opened and closed.

My quilt had all the letters of the alphabet, one on each quilted square. A bear accompanied each letter. Pink, green, blue, and yellow bears—bears flying kites, holding hearts, jumping rope, riding bikes. Each letter was spangled with hearts, stars, or polka dots.

Inside the cardboard box, I lay on my back, with my knees pulled up and my toes pushing into the wall of the box, and traced the letters in my mind, thinking about the words they belonged with. I told stories about each of the bears, had a name for each. I brought the quilt with me everywhere, until one day it blew out of my buggy.

The summer before I began kindergarten I read my first chapter book—*Charlotte's Web*—alone outside in the yard. When Charlotte died, I ran inside to my mother's lap. "Mommy, Mommy," I said, and the tears filled up my eyes. I showed her the book. "Mommy, why does Charlotte have to die? It's not fair."

When I began school, I had to get glasses. My mother said my vision was so bad because of all the reading. I wasn't used to wearing them, and every day at recess I forgot to take them off and had to run back inside and put them in my cubbyhole.

My kindergarten teacher was creative and kind; she played guitar for us every day in school. She met with my mother and said that I was reading third-grade material, and that I should continue reading widely at that level rather than reading more advanced books meant for older children. She recommended that my mother put me in a private school where I could get more individualized attention, but my mother told her that we didn't have the money for that.

When I came home from school each afternoon, I was supposed to nap while she watched *As the World Turns*, but I never slept. I read and played word and math games that we bought at yard sales. I peeked out the door every few minutes: "Mommy, may I come out yet?" The time seemed interminable to me.

Later, in Astoria, my mom helped me to get ready for each day of first grade. But many mornings, I was still half-asleep from staying up late reading the night before. We were disorganized, and would often rush around trying to find everything I needed. "The bus is coming in ten minutes," my mom said. But I could find only one sock. "Mom, I can't find another sock." Finally, my mom fished one out of the dirty clothes and we washed it in the sink. I wrung as much water as I could out of the wet bundle of sock, until I couldn't squeeze another drop out. My mother took the sock from me and wrung it out with her large powerful red hands, and more gray water streamed from it. I got the hair dryer and held it up to the sock. Several minutes later, I put the still damp sock on and my mom tied my shoes for me, because although I could read the same books she could, I still couldn't tie my own shoes. We rushed out the door and down the hill to the gray-planked shack where the bus picked up the neighborhood kids each morning. But there was no one waiting there; the bus had come and gone. So we trudged back up the hill.

I stretched out on my bed and opened the book I was reading—*The Voyage of the Dawn Treader* by C. S. Lewis. Immediately, I was drawn into the land of Narnia, sailing on exotic lily-covered seas with Prince Caspian, Eustace, and Jill, the bus stop forgotten. My sock was dry by now, but I did not notice.

The next morning, it might be that I had no clean underwear, and the previous morning's events were repeated. So we would go to the laundromat, and I read there as well, sitting hidden under the plastic tables in the warm air of the dryers, waiting for the clothes to dry. We folded our clothes, and walked several blocks back to our apartment, carrying the large bags full of clean clothes.

Eventually I made it to school, and I read sitting in my desk with *Heidi* in my lap. My mind was far away in the Swiss Alps, listening with Heidi to the wind's song in the tall evergreen trees, going to sleep on a bed made of a bale of hay, looking up at the stars outside, and waking to a breakfast of fresh-baked bread and a thick slab of salty goat cheese—until suddenly my teacher was standing over me. She took the book away and put it on the far windowsill for me to get at the end of the day. I looked longingly at the book—and tried to pay attention to the day's reading lesson, which was "See Spot run. See Jane play ball with Spot." I looked toward the windowsill, at my book's bright red spine, remembering the majestic mountains, the goats playing in the beautiful hilly meadows.

Books continued to get me in trouble. Many afternoons I'd miss my bus stop on the way back from school. I'd look up from my book and slowly realize that the road, trees, and houses outside the window were unfamiliar. I'd look around with a sinking feeling, noticing that there were few children left on the bus. I went up to the front and tapped the bus driver on his shoulder. This had happened more than once. I sat down in the front seat as he drove to the end of the bus line— several miles out—and then back to my stop to drop me off.

I would arrive home and find my mother frantic, having already called the police and put out a search for me. She waved her arms at me from the doorway as I approached and then gathered me in for a tight hug, her hot tears falling on my neck.

In the summertime, I was free to read books or play outside all day, without worrying about buses and school and missing socks. During the summer of my sixth year, my mom and I read *A Midsummer Night's Dream*. We lay together on the brown shag carpet. The pages of the big book of Shakespeare's plays felt silky between my fingers. I barraged my mother with questions about the fairies, about Puck, about why Lysander and Demetrius didn't realize how they had been blinded. She answered patiently in a way that I would understand. She didn't see Shakespeare's play as a text that could be understood and analyzed only by literary critics. She confidently believed that a six-year-old could be a valid critic, a voice that she wanted to hear.

I read at least one book every day. My mom would take me to the library, which was down Commercial Street, the main street of Astoria. The street ran parallel to the wide blue river, at the base of the hills that the city was built upon. Going from our apartment to the library, I ran ahead of her with my hair flying back. I loved the way the city was shaped, or the way the air moved, because at every street corner I could look down the cross street and see the blue river. But I loved most of all the strong fishy smell—rotting, warm, and good—that came in a sudden waft as soon as I passed the last building on each street corner. I loved that the buildings blocked the smell, so that it could surprise me anew at every corner, along with the flash of blue I saw out of the corner of my eye.

At the library, I got so many books that they were stacked higher than my chin.

"Will you be able to read all of these in three weeks?" the librarian asked me uncertainly.

"Sure," I said. "In one week." I toppled the books onto the counter and swung my arms when they were freed of the books' weight.

My mother and I walked through the quiet, darkening streets home, and I thought of which books I'd read first.

I loved to read in the living room, sprawled in front of the heater on the brown carpet. The heater was built into the wall. It was a floor-to-ceiling painted metal panel with a little knob and a vent. The air coming out smelled musty and hot, dusty like the carpet. It also smelled like the inside of the heater, like burning metal. The stretch of carpet directly in front of the heating vent was so warm; the air blew on my face and made me warm all around, my skin heated up. I inched closer and closer, reading or just lying flat on my stomach or in fetal position on the brown shag rug.

I sat or lay there with my palm draped over my temple, face hidden in the soft crook of my elbow, and listened to the story of the blue vein there. I imagined that the blood was pouring into my thoughts. My mom told me that the blood carried oxygen that made my thoughts work, and sugar that made me sleepy. I listened to see if I could hear a story being told by the rush of blood. In this position I would half fall asleep.

But—

"You're blocking the heat," my mother scolded me. When I sat too close, the heat always shut off after a few minutes.

"The heater can feel you," she told me, "and all it can feel is how hot your skin is. It thinks the whole room is hot, so it shuts off."

I knew this was true, but I still wanted to sit in front of the heater, enveloped and caressed by the warmth. I tried sitting diagonally from the heater, half in and half out of the warmth. Or I lay really flat, pressing my belly into the carpet fibers, hoping that the heater wouldn't know I was there. It usually found me out, though, and its hum grew softer by stages and died out, leaving me in cold and silent air.

I put my ear to the heater, listening to the echo of its motor, trying to figure out how it worked. What went on inside? The closer I got to it, inch by inch, the redder my skin grew. But the closer I got, the more it seemed to withdraw.

4

PLEASE STAY OFF THE GRASS

MY MOTHER SAT across from me in Dunkin' Donuts, in an orange mini-booth, as we sipped our coffees and nibbled on a coffee roll. It was the fall of my junior year in college and she had recently cut her hair short—out of empathy for her friend Janeth, who was undergoing chemotherapy for cancer. Janeth was from Colombia. We met her in a homeless shelter when we first moved to Massachusetts, in 1989, when I was twelve. My mother looked much older now than she did with her long girlish curls. I wanted to squeeze her and squeeze her and let nothing sad or confusing happen to her.

She lit a cigarette, tilted her head away from me to blow the smoke out of the side of her mouth. I asked about why she started smoking when she was seventeen. "Oh, I don't know, I started smoking with my friend Carol, and we dated boys who smoked. I used to smoke in the bathtub. My father said, '*Betty Jean*—if you are going to smoke, come out of the bathroom and smoke in the living room.' Terrible. My father, he should never have let me smoke in the house." She paused to take another puff, and then said, "One of the reasons I never have been very motivated to quit—look at Jimmy, he never smoked, and he got leukemia. No one's ever proven that smoking doesn't prevent some diseases." My mom's reasoning often makes sense to her alone. In high school, I used to come home from wrestling practice and fall asleep on the couch at 7:00 P.M. and wake up at eleven or midnight and do schoolwork for most of the night. When I got a stomachache, she was convinced it was from falling asleep on the couch.

I asked her, "When you think of the word *home*, what is the first thing to come to your mind?" Her eyes grew dreamy as she answered, and a smile quivered on her dry lips.

"Once—I was five—all by myself, sitting in— It must have been an old Model T, in a vacant lot next to my house. Wild roses grew into all the windows. Bright pink roses, green quiet light, I felt so at home. I felt that I had discovered a lovely secret all on my own. I marveled in the green and pinkness." I love her answer, the colors of her words. Solitude and wild nature surrounding her. This is how she lives each day in her own apartment surrounded by her three hundred plants on two porches and in every room, the avocado tree standing eight feet tall in the center of her kitchen. The lovely secrets that she keeps behind her sly smile before she scribbles stealthily into that notebook, the secrets of her mind that I know but little of.

The wild roses had reminded my mother of her own plants, and she started describing one of the mites that had taken over her forget-me-nots.

"It's like a speck of dust that crawls." She paused, significantly, to let the image of crawling dust settle in my mind.

"Unless . . . you look at it closely.

"They were a bunch of babies, growing up. I yanked them

all out, and drowned them." Taken out of context, he.
might have made an eavesdropper think, as I did .
moment, that my mother was a murderer without mercy.

"You'd think there wouldn't be one left. But there they are,
crawling specks. The ornery little buggers!"

"What's that, Mom?" I said.

"Here I sit, chasing red spider mites, whiteflies, and
gnats," she said, "but what do I do to help the world?"

My mom's earliest memories of being at home are of her
childhood in Oregon—mine are too. The best part of living in
Oregon was its natural beauty. Portland—with almost half a
million people—is the only large city in Oregon. The rest is
sparsely populated, a land of tall evergreen forests, dark winding piney roads, and swirls of fog and white water crashing
into stark coastal cliffs.

Burnside and Astoria are near Fort Clatsop, a favorite picnic spot for Aunt Jane and Uncle Ron to take us to. I loved the
story of Meriwether Lewis and William Clark, who traveled a
year and a half from St. Louis before arriving at the Pacific in
November 1805. They built and lived in Fort Clatsop that first
winter. I loved climbing in the old stone fort, clambering over
barrels of giant cannons and peering through peepholes,
imagining I was a famous explorer surveying the land. From
my earliest years, I sensed that Oregon was the incarnation of
freedom, pioneering, and exploration.

The land itself was beautiful. In Burnside, where my
mother had a live-in job taking care of an elderly woman, I
had a friend, a boy my age who lived a quarter mile down the
road. It was never very hot or very cold near the coast of Oregon. It didn't snow, and temperatures in the winter were well
above freezing. In the summer it was seldom warmer than

seventy degrees. His property was full of good hiking trails. We played cowboys and Indians. We ran down to the creek and sat fishing in the shady trees with sticks tied with string, paper-clip hooks, bread crumbs for bait. We built a plank bridge over the bubbling water and crossed over it to our fort. The fort was made from two fallen trees. We made a green roof by winding freshly picked feathery green ferns through the fallen trees' branches. We made soft mattresses of piled-up moss. I dug a kitchen sink in the ground and lined it with rocks so that the water would stay. We lost hours in this make-believe land, lying on the moss and listening to the cows' low mooing, smelling the happy aroma of cowpatties baking in the sun.

In Burnside, we also knew a couple who had a peacock farm. "Did you know?" my mother asked me. "There is a story about how the peacocks got eyes in their tail feathers." She told me about a hundred-eyed Greek god named Argus. "The goddess Hera got angry and turned him into a peacock, and all his eyes went into the peacock's tail," she said. Then I picked up many iridescent gold and green peacock feathers with their shimmery blue eye-shaped markings. Back at home, I put them in the tall vase in the living room's corner.

The house we lived in at Burnside had a hallway door that was supposed to open onto a porch, but the porch had never been built. Instead, the door opened into air and the earth several feet beneath. Sometimes I opened this door to look at the side yard, of which every square inch was covered with bright yellow daffodils. Butter-and-eggs daffodils, my mother called them. The daffodils reminded me of a Wordsworth poem that she had recited to me so often that I had it mostly memorized myself—*I wandered lonely as a cloud/that floats on high o'er vales and hills,/when all at once I saw a crowd,/a host, of golden daffodils.* My mother taped poetry and famous texts—the Gettysburg Address or the Preamble to the Constitution—over the kitchen sink to memorize them while she washed and dried the dishes. She recited them while she vacuumed, dusted, and cleaned the house.

When I was six, after the elderly woman my mother took care of in Burnside died and we moved to Astoria, my mother had no job so she had more time for gardening. She grew corn, tomatoes, and all kinds of flowers in the tiny patch of yard outside of our apartment. She dug in deep with the shovel, and when she hit a rock—the shovel went clank. She dug the dirt out all around the rock and I reached in to help her pull it out. We unearthed many centipedes and earthworms. I was squeamish at first, but then she told me about how the earthworms helped plants by creating oxygen in the soil and that the centipedes were harmless as long as we left them alone and let them go back under the earth. She grew crisp and sweet green snow peas that the other neighbor children and I picked off of their stalks and ate while we played.

My mother made a beanstalk tepee near the center of our apartment's little yard. She planted a circle of tall sticks in the ground and tied them together with a string at their tops. She planted the beans all around the circle. The beans grew thicker every day. Within several weeks, the beans were tall and green and climbed all the way to the top of the tepee. I sat inside bathed in the emerald light and pretended I was a young Native American, remembering that my mother told me that one of my great-great-grandmothers was from the Iroquois people. I sat still for a long time and tried to see the stalks growing, but I never saw them move. Like the beanstalks, I too was growing in ways unnoticeable to me then.

Our apartment was on the corner of a row of apartments and had a tiny patch of lawn. Every day, groups of our neighbors would cut across our grass to the Mini Mart behind our apartment. There was a brown path worn through it, and the grass was almost gone where so many people had tread. My mother couldn't stand the thought of all those bright blades being trampled and broken. She watered the grass every day to try to get it growing again. I was upstairs and heard laughing people crossing our lawn. My mother shouted down from our window, "Walk on the sidewalk please." The people would look up, laugh more, and not listen. No one in our neighborhood cared about the grass. My mother put up a sign: PLEASE STAY OFF THE GRASS. She was known as the crazy woman who lived on the corner.

One night at dusk, I heard laughing and loud swearing. I looked down from my bedroom window. A woman known around the neighborhood as a motorcycle mama, a youngish woman who wore a black leather jacket and long black hair, had my mother sprawled against the side of the building and was breaking her nose because my mother had told her not to walk across our lawn. The sight of blood on my mother's face scared me, as did the crowd of shouting and swearing onlookers. My mom's boyfriend Bill came up to tell me that my mom was going to be okay. An ambulance came soon, and I saw my mom later that night with stitches and big bruises on her face. I thought my mom was crazy too, for caring so much about a few blades of grass.

My mother dated Bill on and off for several years when I was in elementary school. I was jealous of her occasional boyfriends. But he was quiet and easygoing and was around for so long that I got used to him. I still felt uncomfortable when he was around, because I didn't want to think of my mom being sexual in any way. I felt threatened, perhaps because I thought that men could not be trusted because my father had never been there for us.

At some apartments, my mother and I had to share one bedroom. Sometimes my mom was in there with Bill and they locked the bedroom door. She would put sheets on the old couch for me, out in the living room. Pink flowered sheets, faded with big pink flowers that had yellow centers, covering over the gold tapestry of the couch. But I felt that I could not—absolutely could not—sleep out there. For hours I would lie near the doorway to the bedroom, screaming and crying for my mother, trying to look underneath the door to see if there was any light inside. Wordless screams hurt the back of my throat and left me exhausted and shuddering at each hiccup. When I had spent all my energies and was certain no one would ever come to let me in, I crawled back to the couch, which seemed to me harder, narrower, and colder than anything I had ever slept in. Lying down flat on my back, staring at the moonlight shapes of the windows stretched above me, light on the dark ceiling, I began to feel remorse. I thought about Bill, my mother's boyfriend, whom I liked well enough during the daytime, when he wasn't locked in the bedroom with my mother. I thought he must hate me and find me despicable and spoiled. The thought of what an awful child I was, and how I seemed to be placed in this position of awfulness without knowing how to get out, made me cry more and more until my limbs began to relax into the hard couch. My swollen eyes and face warm and wet sank finally into the couch's pillow and into sleep.

In the morning, opening my eyes to squares of sunlight on the ceiling where there had been moonlight before, I rose out of the couch and walked tentatively to the door of the bed-room, which was now open. Walking in, I saw the pile of bed-clothes on the floor, because our bed either had just been sold or was not yet bought, and my mother's nightgown in a pile, too, on the floor.

"Mom, you didn't change in front of Bill, did you?" A pause while she looked at me, trying to think of a correct answer.

"Did you?" She still wouldn't answer me.

"Mom, that's not nice! You're not supposed to do that unless you're married! You can't do that!" I was ever vigilant that my mother keep her chastity. I felt that I was the closest person to her, and felt threatened by her doing anything with someone else that she wouldn't do with me.

Bill was a logger and he used to take me and my mom, and his niece Pooter (her real name was Angela), up into the moun-tains in Oregon, in the back of his pickup, up and up the wind-ing gravel and dirt roads to the top of the world. The steep and uneven road made Pooter and me hang on to the metal cab of the truck, feeling like we might fall out and tumble down the hillside at any moment if we didn't hang on tight. Higher and higher we would go, around and up, far from any houses, to the ends to the world, he'd take us, and stop the truck on the edge of a small canyon.

We saw the tall cliffs half-shorn, covered with the carnage of burnt and cut tree stumps, scattered tall and majestic trees standing among them. Pooter and I would look for Bigfoot's footprints. We'd wait and maybe see a very old eagle, the one Bill had told us about, high in the highest tree. The eagle had been here ever since he could remember, as long as he'd been a logger, for over twenty years. The old eagle sat like a lonesome king, on the highest branch of the tallest tree just across the canyon, twenty yards away from us. He filled the world with his aloneness. I felt that this aloneness was so powerful that it could fill the canyon and stretch toward me like the orange light of the sun dropping swiftly toward the earth's horizon. So powerful I felt that eagle was, to be so solitary and far away, above the whole world that I knew.

The eagle matched with a feeling I had about my mother and myself, a feeling that there was power in being alone even though it was overwhelming and frightening at times.

5

THE KIDS

A few times, standing, holding you to keep you from cry-
ing—gazing at the four photos on the wall, and then I
would be the one crying, you now content upon my shoul-
der, while I was missing so much the other children, worry-
ing about them, especially Becki, who missed me the most.
You were born into such a volatile mixture of emotions:
love, sorrow, anger, moral confusion, innocence, happiness
at your birth, but ultimately the contentment of maternity.

—From my mother's journal

MY MOM ALWAYS called my half brothers and sisters the
kids. The kids are coming, she used to say, and I would think
of them in capital letters, The Kids. They would call, and I'd
say, Mom, it's The Kids!

Sometimes they came to visit us at our apartment at the
Hillside Apartments in Astoria, where I lived during first, second, and third grades. I stared out of my second-floor bedroom window, pacing back and forth between the windows

and my bed with the pink checkered ruffled cover (it should have had a ruffled canopy on top, I always thought, as I looked at the white ceiling instead). I kneeled on the brown shag carpet near the windows, my chin resting on the windowsill, staring out and down for any sign of Kirk, Becki, and Kristi: The Kids.

"A watched pot never boils," said my mother to me as I kneeled there. This was a new concept. I thought about the scene outside the window as a pot on a hot stove, and that when The Kids came it would be boiling. My brother and sisters would come like bubbles roiling down the sidewalk, boiling up to meet me, but only when I wasn't looking for them.

I slid down the brown shag stairs on my bum, down the smooth worn parts of carpet at the stairs' edges, and through the brown beaded curtain at the foot of the stairs. *Rustle-clickety-clack*, I announced my arrival downstairs. I wandered around looking for something to do.

I looked through my books, hoping to find one I had read several times but was now perhaps in the right mood to read again, and poked through the cupboards and refrigerator. Eventually, I could no longer keep my eyes off that pot. I wanted to peek to see if maybe more steam was rising from it now. Maybe they were almost here.

Kirk was driving down, in their dad's old station wagon, because he was now nineteen and old enough to drive. Kristi and Becki were fifteen and thirteen.

I ran out to the front of the apartment complex, where I could sit and see the highway down below. I sat and waited and waited. My friends Tiffany and Jenny came by, and I told them (proudly, excitedly) I was waiting for The Kids, The Kids were coming! My mom came out and told me that Kirk had called—they would be late. Finally they would come and I would be happy and only a little worn from waiting. It was sunny and The Kids were here.

I was marvelous to them. I was six years old, and I sat on the bed with my mother and my two sisters, while they made me do math problems in my head. I was all little, propped against the wall with pillows, my legs spread straight in front of me, toes pointing to the ceiling. The three of them focused their eyes on me.

"Mom, watch this," they would say, getting her attention.

"What's two hundred seventy-four plus four hundred seventy-nine?" they asked me. I wrinkled my forehead and the numbers popped into my head: 200 plus 400: 600. 70 plus 70: 140. 740. 9 plus 4: 13. (In school, I tried to explain to the math teacher how I got my answers and she said it was all backwards. "Why don't you carry your numbers?" she asked. I didn't know. "They just carry *me* along with *them*," I tried to explain to her.)

753.

"Seven hundred and fifty-three," I answered after a moment of thought. They played this game again and again with me. I was a human calculator. I loved it because it brought me love. Again and again they picked three-digit numbers randomly out of their heads, and I added or subtracted, as they asked. I was their little doll, mechanical and to be played with. And I was strange to them, a little wonder.

Later on, years later, this strangeness remained and grew, even after being marvelous no longer brought me love but only an expanding space of not understanding.

I loved The Kids because they were something I didn't know enough about, but they belonged to me. My sisters and brother. It was only later that the word *half* (*half* sister, *half* brother) became important and placed a separation between us. This halfness . . . this thing of them being all-of-one and me something half different. Half out, half not them while they were all of each other.

My mom talked about either Becki or Kristi coming to stay for a summer, but they never did. "Oh! I hope it's Becki!" I said, but then felt bad and hoped Kristi didn't hear. I didn't want to hurt her feelings. Becki was my favorite, the closest to me in age. She had our mother's dark brown eyes and brown hair. Everyone said that Becki and I looked alike in our school pictures. I put Becki's first-, second-, and third-grade pictures next to my own first-, second-, and third-grade pictures in my photo album, hoping people would mistake her for me, so that I could say proudly, "That's my sister. Don't we look alike?" I also felt closer to Becki because she had my mom's same open-eyed innocence and wonderment, and was not as practical as Kirk and Kristi.

Kristi was two years older than Becki, and they both had their father's long face and nose—Kristi more so than Becki—with our mother's eye shape and smile. The girls wore their hair in braided pigtails. But Kristi had lighter, sandy brown hair and turquoise eyes, and was taller, skinnier, and more sarcastic and cynical. Kirk was a gawky adolescent, a little bit shy, with a cowlick and pure blue eyes.

My eyes are called hazel on my driver's license—they change from light brown to orange to green—cat's eyes. They show up in photographs as a see-through olive green. But growing up I thought that I had brown eyes, a lighter brown than my mother's. Young children sometimes stare at my eyes and ask after a few moments' curious contemplation—"Why are your eyes yellow?" Or they say—"You have orange eyes."

They are a mix of my mother's dark eyes and my father's bright blue eyes.

Through The Kids I tried to understand the mystery of being related by blood. In their faces and movements, I saw glimpses of kinship through forests of separation.

I don't have as many memories of my mother's younger son, Bobby, because he died of muscular dystrophy when I was five and he fifteen. He was born on Valentine's Day, and my mother appropriately describes him as her "little sweetheart" with "long dark swooping lashes, cupid's bow lips, a dimple in his chin and in both cheeks."

One of my earliest memories is of him. My mother and I were visiting The Kids at their house for a large family event. I was very small, clinging to my mother's pants and holding on to her knees. Craning my neck up, I saw Bobby's wide smile as he sat in his huge (to me) wheelchair, his hands beckoning me to sit on his lap. Someone, probably our mother, put me there. I got comfortable, snuggling into his warm body. He asked me if I wanted a cookie. I nibbled on the cookie shyly, looking all around at the unfamiliar people, whom I could see better now, from my new vantage point.

This memory sits in my mind like a photograph that I need to touch and look at again and again, to remind me that Bobby is my brother and belongs with me somehow. It is my way of claiming, to myself and others, that he was my brother too.

One Christmas when I was three The Kids came to visit for ten days. We didn't have a tree, but my mother found an evergreen bough that had blown off a tree and hung it in the window. Kirk pushed Bobby in his wheelchair around the empty lot next to our apartment, both of them laughing as Kirk spun Bobby in circles.

My mother clutched my hand. "Kirk! Be careful, don't hurt him!" They just kept laughing and spinning until Kirk wheeled Bobby over to my mother and me. It was strange having them with us. On the day they left, Kristi and Becki were sad. Bobby asked, "Mama, when can I come back to live with you?"

"Not now, honey. Your dad needs you." My mother tried to keep a smile on her face and stop the tears from welling up in her eyes.

"But, Mom, I want to go back to the blue house in Portland where we lived before. We had so much fun there."

"We can't go back, honey" was all my mom could say. It broke her heart to hear him ask what she also wished for—a chance to go back and make things right. "But you can visit here again."

But this was not to be. We moved to Phoenix, Arizona, the next year. In Phoenix, my mother got a live-in job taking care of two blond-haired children.

One month after she started this job, a phone call from Oregon came on a sun-bright morning in April. She was in her bathing suit when the call came.

Her ex-husband said, "I have bad news." The moment she heard him say this, she knew something had happened to Bobby.

"No . . . no . . . ," she said.

"You better sit down," he said. He didn't have to say any more.

"No. . . . When?" she asked.

"Last night, some time between ten thirty, when Becki checked on him and midnight, when Reitha [the kids' stepmother] did."

"Why?" my mother asked.

"He was sick with a cold and didn't want to go to the hospital . . ."

Just the week before she had talked to him on the phone and asked him if he was taking his vitamins.

"No, Mother."

"It's important, you know, you need them. . . ."

"No, Mother, you don't understand—I *can't* swallow them. I can't *swallow.*" The muscular dystrophy had advanced so that it affected his throat muscles and he could no longer swallow vitamins or food. My mother looked at photos of Bobby and cried when she thought of this, and cried when she thought of how she wasn't the one there for him when he died.

She called her mother, sister, and father, and they sent money for tickets so that we could attend the funeral. My mother got through the day somehow, gave me a bath, and packed our bags.

Kristi and Becki and their father met us at the airport. The girls had happy smiles to see us. They were twelve and ten at the time. My mother's ex-husband drove us to their house, where they lived with his new wife. My mother and I slept in the top bunk in the girls' bedroom.

The next day we went to the funeral home. My mother touched Bobby's arm and forehead in the casket. Although I was four, I wanted to be carried everywhere and held faster to my mother than a ship to its mooring. My mother thought I was tired because we had done too much walking in Phoenix while looking for a job. It wasn't that my feet were tired. But the ground was a shifting sea of strange people and sights that might pull me out in an undertow if I was let go. Maybe I sensed also that my mother needed to hold tight to me.

The funeral was held outdoors in the April sunshine. It was a beautiful Oregon day and the rhododendrons were blooming everywhere. We didn't know many people there. I slept through the entire service while my aunt Jane held me.

*   *   *

Kirk was almost thirteen when our mother took her vacation to California. He seemed to build stronger ties with his step-family than did his sisters. He is the only one to call his step-mother Mom. I think I understand his longing for a normal family, wanting it to be all of one piece.

Kirk now installs air-conditioning and heating systems for a living. He has a warm and welcoming wife and four children. The two oldest are girls, the two youngest, boys. They own a property that has horses and cows and other livestock but is just at the edge of Oregon City and less than a half-hour drive to Portland.

Although Kirk tries to live a responsible and quiet family life, in a way the antithesis to his mother's example, he cannot help but be like her in some ways. If an unusual word comes up in conversation, he runs to the big Oxford unabridged dictionary that he keeps on the coffee table in his living room. My mother and Kirk get the same twinkle in their eyes as they flip through the dictionary's pages and triumphantly pause upon a word. It is strange to see Mom, her gentleness, in his male form.

My mother's children are her pride and joy. To her, each of them is brilliant and delicate, perfect and unique. She shared a poem with me that she wrote about Kirk: "*Kirk: Yesterday I saw a beautiful locust tree/As I walked west on Lincoln Street/And it reminded me of you./As things so often do:/*

/*A handsome movie star—/This tree was tall and covered with blossoms,/like a lovely ivory wedding dress./On the right side of the street as I walked on the left,//It stood, as you do, mature./Each cluster of bloom,/another of your fine qualities.*"

Becki is married and has three sons—the oldest, Gunnar, and his two younger brothers, Garrett and Griffin. A few summers ago, she told me, "I still feel hurt that Mom left us. I never understood why she would do that." She tilts her head slightly to one side and looks at me. "I remember, I was only six, and it hurt so much. I didn't want her to leave."

We were picking blackberries on her property near the southern Oregon coast. Gunnar and Becki's dog, a big black Lab, were running around at our heels. Garrett was snuggled into the stroller. Becki could never imagine leaving them. I looked back at her through the tangled vines, putting a handful of juicy berries into our bucket, and I didn't know what to say, or how to explain the different perspective I have on our mother, having lived with her my whole life. (An image before me of our mother, her face all rumpled from holding the tears in, telling me, *"Becki was the only one who wanted to go with me. But he pulled her back, he took her other arm there in the street, and I had to let go. . . ."*)

I can't explain any of it to Becki, other than to say: "I think she meant to come back. She didn't know what would happen, that she wouldn't be allowed."

That same summer I also stayed with Kirk and his family for a weekend. We were all in the car, riding to church. My mother's oldest grandchild, Sarah, was six. She didn't quite know what divorce was, although she'd heard it talked about. "Daddy," Sarah asked Kirk, "is Grandma Elizabeth your mommy?" He answered that she was—but that he had two mommies, because Grandma Reitha (his stepmother) was also his mommy, and Sarah paused, thought hard, wrinkled her forehead in the same way my mother does. "Then . . . then, is Grandma Elizabeth di-*vorced* from Grandpa?" she asked, pronouncing the word carefully, enunciating both syllables. She already knew the answers to these questions, but the world behind the word was a mystery. She asked the same questions over again, hoping someone would volunteer some information. But no one did.

I watched her as she grew increasingly impatient with this car ride and adults who never explained what they talked about. She swung her legs and banged them against her car seat. "I am not having any fun in this car," she said, pouting and shaking her wispy sand-colored curls around her head, making an angry V with her tiny eyebrows. "I am not having any fun—in this car. I am divorced in this car." Maybe she got the meaning exactly right: divorce is like a long car ride of miscommunication and separation.

Last spring, my mother let me read parts of her journal, about how she cried while looking at the kids' pictures on the wall and holding me. I too dissolved in tears, looking through my windows at all that was visible above the neighboring brick building: the brilliant green outline of the half-clothed tree limbs and burning blue canvas of sky behind.

I know my half brothers and sisters a little, in the way you might know longtime acquaintances, or your best friend's boyfriend. I think maybe I've given up some time ago on ever really knowing them or ever feeling that they belong to me in any way. There's so much in them that's not in me; so much in me, not in them.

I first met my father when I was nineteen, which multiplied by two the number of half siblings I had a chance to get to know. You'd think with seven half siblings, you'd at least get three good full ones by adding them all up. But it isn't as simple as adding numbers in my head was when I was six. It just doesn't work that way.

6

DISCIPLINE, PART I

discipline 1 a a branch of knowledge or learning **b** a closed box, a horse wearing blinders, sunglasses worn at night, a straight line of rules, a telescope through which objects scrutinized are distant and distorted **2 a** training that develops self-control, character, or orderliness and efficiency **b** My mother's attempts at discipline failed utterly, for I ran every time she got out the belt to whup me. **3 a** result of such training or control, specifically self-control and orderly conduct **b** If my mom had more discipline, she would go out and get a job, work for a living, like every orderly citizen does. **4** I would have learned to fit my education into a discipline, if I had been better disciplined.

OUR APARTMENT WAS a mess, and my friend Josh told my mother so when he came in and saw the piles of stuff all over. "Geez, your house is mes-*sy*."

Our apartments were usually a mess, although I never thought much about it. They were clean but chaotic, cluttered, and haphazardly layered with clothes, papers, and books. Dishes dried on rumpled paper towels on the kitchen table, the paper shrinking under circles of water. At one time, a bed stood in the corner of the kitchen. My mother took naps, curled up there.

My mother saved every newspaper she read. When she had spare time she'd cut out all the articles and file them in folders by topic so that she could have a ready library for easy reference. When I grew older, I told her that the library had rolls of film called microfilm, each compact roll an entire half year of newspapers. She could look up any subject and find the articles by putting the microfilm into a viewing machine. But she was stubborn and insisted that she wanted to have all the information right at hand, organized in a way she—and perhaps only she—would understand.

Of course, whenever we moved, we had to leave such things behind, but she would then start anew.

This was the only kind of home I had known, and I liked it very much, although sometimes the tall piles of newspapers made me nervous, lurking, waiting to topple on me when I dug in the closet behind them. When I was in high school, one closet door hadn't been shut since we moved in— it was too full. Each spring my mom would begin to clean the closet out. For a few weeks I would have to climb over the contents of the closet into my small back bedroom because the closet's innards overflowed into the hall. Eventually everything was shoved back in, as messy as ever, filling floor to ceiling. What good was this cleaning process? I wondered.

Once I looked for a broom in that closet. It's in here somewhere, I thought, but couldn't get it out because it was stuck to the floor in a pool of dried pink paint. Oh well. I let the broom be, and soon it was covered with clothes, hangers, and a sagging cardboard box.

Some of the mess was dirty laundry—scattered around or in plastic garbage bags. My mom washed clothes in the bathtub and sink, and hung them to dry on windowsills, over chairs, draped near the heater, or over the couch. The clothes dried stiff and wrinkled, molded into the shape of the chair or couch or window they were laid on.

"Geez, your house is mes-*sy*," is what Josh, my third-grade playmate, said, and that made my mother mad. Josh wasn't allowed in anymore, so when we played we played outside.

We had to do everything for ourselves. We didn't have money for a car, or for a washer and dryer. We made frequent trips to the store because we never had enough money to buy much. I went everywhere with my mother, because she needed me to carry things. We drank powdered milk because we got it free from the food bank, but we also bought it because it was easier to carry. The muscles in my back and arms grew strong from carrying the groceries and bags of laundry.

We walked all day because there was no other way to get there. There was always someplace far to go, like the welfare office, which was always several miles away, on top of a hill. I was small, and had short legs and little patience, so everything seemed far to me.

We lived by ourselves. There was no father to discipline me and my mother was softhearted, so I was seldom punished. Once I wanted a new pair of jeans with flower patches on the pockets, like the ones Becki and Kristi wore. When they came to visit, they encouraged our mother to wear their blue jeans. She had to lie down and suck in her stomach in order to zip the pants up. The three of them then went for a walk, my mom giggling like a young woman, and happy to be with all her daughters. I practiced walking like they did, making my butt wiggle on purpose, but all I had were polyester pink and blue hand-me-down pants with white stripes down the sides that my friend Jody's mother gave me. I needed the jeans, to make the walking right, but her answer was firmly no. We could seldom afford new clothes.

Instead of punishment, my mother Reasoned with me. Even when I was a little child, three or four years old, my mom talked to me as if I was grown up. Aunt Jane remembers going to the grocery store with us: "You were a tiny little thing, and your mother would kneel down there in the aisle and explain to you why you couldn't have what you wanted." If I misbehaved, my mother gave me the Reasons why my behavior was unacceptable, and what problems such behavior would cause me in the future. I could Reason back fairly well. I learned early in childhood that I could get by with almost anything by Reasoning with my mother. She was too easygoing to spank or discipline me. I would get to do whatever I wanted, and my punishment would be Natural Consequences. My mom was a firm believer in them.

My neighborhood friends asked me, "Doesn't your mom ground you? Does she spank you? Don't you get in trouble if you stay home from school?"

"No," I would reply regally. "She believes in Natural Consequences." With an air of superiority I implied that grounding and spanking were unnatural, illogical processes.

"Mom, I'm not going to school today. I just don't feel like it."

After trying for a bit to convince me that I should go, she would say, "All right, dear, that's up to you. You know the Consequences."

But as far as I was concerned, there were few bad consequences when I missed school for a long time. At home, I read books and felt that I learned more than I did in school with Mrs. German and her cursive letters. The *m* had three humps, and *n* only two. I knew this already. I was bored by most of the lessons that were taught in school. The books I read at home took me to new and exciting worlds; I learned along with the characters and their many adventures.

Natural Consequences were beautiful and simple, and I loved them. My mom explained them to me using Newton's third law: For every action there is an equal and opposite reaction. It seemed perfectly simple. It meant that if I did not go to school, there was a mysterious reaction that would someday happen to me, and whether bad or good, it would match the act of not going to school. If I didn't eat all my peas at dinner, I would not grow up to be big and strong and play basketball and baseball as my cousins—Tim and Jeff, Aunt Jane's two youngest sons—did. Such were the Natural Consequences. My cousins had me make a muscle with my arm and then teased me by pushing it down and saying, "Aw, there's nothing in there. It's just jelly, all marshmallow." So I ate all my peas because I wanted to have big muscles like them.

I sucked my thumb up through my sixth-grade year, hooking my index finger up over my nose as I did, which would cause my cousins to ask me if it tasted better that way, which question I pondered a moment and then replied, "Yeth," with my thumb still in my mouth. They tried to scare me by telling me my thumb would fall off, but this didn't stop me. I didn't stop until sixth grade. My mom told me that as long as I sucked my thumb, I was not grown up enough to be able to wear makeup. She said that a reasonable consequence of giving up my habit would be having my own makeup case. When I quit, she would buy me the big deluxe $6.99 makeup kit from Newbury's Five and Dime. So we went to the Owl Drugstore, which my friend Maggie's father owned, in Astoria, Oregon, and bought a little vial of spicy vegetable potion called Bite No More, which was intended for chronic nail biters and thumb suckers. By the time I was in sixth grade, I sucked my thumb only at night. I put the potion on my thumbnail, and it burnt my mouth something awful. I quit sucking my thumb forever, after only one night of treatment.

My face looked like a paint-by-number painting the next day in school. I slathered on the dark blue and green eye shadow from the base of my lids to my eyebrows—added bright stripes of red blush on my cheeks and a lipstick smile. I looked more ridiculous than I would have had I sucked my thumb. Two ratty-haired smart-aleck boys in my class called me a painted whore. I didn't know what the word meant (I guess it wasn't in any of the books I read), so I couldn't care. But I did feel older.

Once—I was in second grade—my mom got so mad that she lost her Reason and sense of Nature's justice. She decided I must need a spanking. She got a belt with a big buckle and chased me. I ran through the rooms, sprinted up the stairs on hands and knees, dodged the doorframe, and catapulted onto my mother's bed. I bounced up and down, jumping from one side of the bed to the other, and she whipped at me with the belt. It left sudden stinging slaps on my bare shins and thighs, but I kicked and laughed. And laughed. "Ha ha, you can't get me!" I giggled. I moved around too much, and my mom became red-faced, sweaty, and out of breath. Her laughter at this ridiculousness brought her down on the bed doubled over and reaching out to hug me. We collapsed together with our bellies aching from laughter, and Natural Consequences reigned again.

*

There was a long list of things my mom Believed in, Natural Consequences being the first on the list, followed by Making It Yourself, Walking, Eating Yogurt, Sprouts, and Cranberry Juice, Whole Wheat Bread and Licorice (but only one piece a day—to prevent cold sores, stay healthy, and to benefit the kidneys), and that Children Are People Who Should Be Listened To. There were many things she did not Believe in: Candy, Soda Crackers (no nutritive value), Water Guns (or any kind of gun), and Forcing You to Go to School. Her system of Beliefs guided my cognitive development.

My mom did not Believe in Candy or in Having Too Much Sugar, but every chance I got—when not at home—I fit in as much sugar as I could. When I stayed over at my best friend Lorraine's apartment, her father bought us an entire tub of neon gummy worms, complete with little plastic tongs. We put the tub by her bedside and stayed up most of the night, giddy from the sugar. By morning we had eaten all of the 320 gummy worms, and we were two tired girls, happy except for our stomachaches.

Another opportunity for me to shun my mother's discipline by eating sugar came when I was with my baby-sitter. She made peanut butter sandwiches with a thick oozy layer of grape jelly. I greedily licked the sweet jelly off of the sides of the sandwiches. My mother's sandwiches were mostly peanut butter, so that I could hardly taste the jelly.

My baby-sitter and her boyfriend also took me to see my first movie, *Superman III*, when I was seven. I stared wide-eyed at the screen that was so big, larger than life. Even though the screen was so huge and colorful, the movie didn't come to life for me the way the characters in my books did. I had read the Lord of the Rings trilogy by J. R. R. Tolkien five times, and it grew more exciting to me each time. I still jumped up and shouted and ran in glee around and around the rooms of our apartment after the biggest battle in the War of the Ring, when the faithful allies, the Riders of Rohan, came to save the day and defeat the dark wraith, the Nazgûl. When their line of horses appeared on the horizon with the first rays of sunlight, my heart beat faster and I shouted to myself, "The Riders of Rohan are coming! The Rohan are coming!" My mom did not usually have money for movies. I saw only three movies before I started high school.

At the start of each day of school, my classmates huddled around the aisles between the desks and dissected the movies or TV shows they had seen recently. "Remember that movie . . . the part when the bad guys chased them . . ."

I sat silently and listened in, trying to pick up clues. I never had anything to say. It was a universal language that I didn't speak, a mysterious world of pop culture from which I was excluded.

The only time my mother broke her own rule forbidding me to have candy was the summer after I was in sixth grade. I had to leave for camp the next day after church, and I didn't have a swimsuit. We had had to wait for the welfare "payday" before we could buy one. We lived in Swenson with my aunt Jane and uncle Ron at the time. They were away; we had no way to get to the nearest store in Astoria, ten miles away. I had to have the swimsuit. My mother decided we would walk. "We'll be there in a couple of hours," she said.

My mother loved to walk. After a day of walking, she got out the map and traced the streets and highways, counting up the miles. Before she did this, though, she guessed how far she had walked by how sore her feet were. "Feels like seven miles," she said. She was satisfied if she was about right. If she had walked more than she guessed, she felt proud. I was slightly bored by these calculations and by walking. I just trailed along after her. Walking again.

So we walked the first mile and a half down the road past all the houses and fields and livestock and stopped at Swenson's one grocery store, where my mother bought a bag of candy bars. We needed them for quick energy, she said. Normally she didn't Believe in Sugar, but this was an exception. Perhaps she wanted to distract me from how far we were to walk. We headed for the winding, evergreen-lined highway. Our discipline was to eat only half a candy bar each at every mile marker. We walked on and on. I looked eagerly for the white numbered posts. I savored the sweet chocolate for as long as I could, paying attention as it slowly melted inside of my mouth without help from tongue or teeth. It was a game I played to relieve the tedium of walking. By the eighth mile, my feet ached and I was tired of eating candy. We were a few miles out of downtown Astoria. My mother said that from here we could catch the city bus. I sat down on a stump and waited by the roadside, the pine trees engulfing the concrete on either side. I questioned whether I really needed a swimsuit this badly.

After I had picked it out—an aqua blue one-piece with pink and lavender flowers—my mother called her boyfriend Bill from a pay phone and asked him if he could give us a ride back to Aunt Jane's in Swenson. It was the only time I had known my mother to ask Bill for a ride. I knew my mother must love me a lot to be breaking so many of her usual rules. Bill came in his old red pickup truck. I sat in the middle of the front seat between the two of them and we drove back. My feet had blisters like little balloons that slid against my socks as the truck wound back and forth down the highway.

*

All the activity I got as a child gave me a love for walking and an awareness of my body. I now prefer walking to taking the subway or riding in a car. I grow impatient waiting for a bus. In the city, I love to walk and see the tall dark buildings on either side. The neon lights make me feel warmer than hot chocolate. The cold air sweeps the day's dust from my throat. I wonder why my mind feels as sharp and clear as the lights. It is because my toes are cold and connected to me. I walk for miles and miles.

7

THERE AND BACK AGAIN

THE YEAR I was to enter fourth grade, my mother decided that we should move. She hoped to find a job in the Industrial Belt of Southern California, and she preferred the warm weather there to the cold rains of Northern Oregon. I didn't realize what moving would mean. I don't remember being especially sad about moving. We had to move out of our apartment anyway. We had been evicted because the landlord didn't make repairs necessary for the building to pass the housing authority's inspection.

We held the rummage sale inside our apartment of the past three years. We displayed our possessions around the edges of the rooms and stuck price tags made of bits of masking tape to them. Piles of things were stacked on the edges of the brown shag carpet where I had built forts out of blankets and couch pillows and chairs. This was the rug that I had fallen asleep on every winter afternoon, reading books in front of the wall heater, the warm air making me languorous and dreamy. My bike and my Lite-Brite and my giant stuffed raccoon sat outside on the porch for passersby to speculate on. My mom had stacked her plants high on a multitiered plant stand. The layers of sunny green were among the few things we had that sold for more than their original price, since most of my mom's seeds and seedlings were free, transplanted from people's overflowing gardens or from friends. All of my books—the Ramona books by Beverly Cleary, The Chronicles of Narnia by C. S. Lewis, *Harriet the Spy, The Borrowers,* Nancy Drew mysteries, the Great Brain books, *Charlotte's Web, The Hobbit,* a whole collection of Golden Books whose spines made a long golden rectangle on my shelf, *Lady and the Tramp* and *The Aristocats,* which had records with them, Lloyd Alexander books (fantasy adventures), and many others—were sold. We made fifty dollars from selling my books and toys. My mother told me that she'd put the money in the bank for me to save for a bicycle.

The next morning we boarded the bus to California. I didn't get to say good-bye to any of my friends. That is always the way on journeys and leave-takings. You think there will be time or occasion for one final good-bye, but there never is. There is only time for countless unofficial good-byes. *I'm sure I'll see you again so I won't say good-bye now.*

Things did not go as expected when we arrived in California. The rents were high, we had little money, and finding a job without recent training and experience was harder than my mother had anticipated. For a month we lived in a shelter in San Jose, located off of the edges of town in a large institutional building. The inside was made up of cinder-block cubicles. In the basement was a cafeteria and lounge. The rooms had no windows. They were coded by color and number; each had two sets of bunk beds with bare mattresses. My mom and I lived for a month in Yellow Number 3. I remember one day clearly—being sick, puking and hanging over the edge of the bottom bunk and looking at the doorway, the yellow paint and stenciled number. Two children at the shelter gave me a get-well note. On the outside of the card a childish script scrawls: To Yellow Number 3.

The shelter had its own schoolroom for the children who were too mobile, too much in transition to go to the public school. The kids in the classroom ranged from age six to sixteen. The teacher was a tired man with a light brown beard. He gave us each a big packet of reading and math sheets and walked around through the rows checking our work. He was surprised that, though I was among the youngest in the class, he had to give me the most advanced packets. We stayed in that room all day except for a short recess. The playground had lots of bright orange wood chips and many plastic tubes to crawl through. One day on this playground, I said something naïve, and one of the older girls flipped her honey brown hair at me and said, "No shit, Sherlock." I burst out crying inexplicably. All I could think of was Sherlock Holmes.

One windy day in San Jose, my mother sat on a park bench, waiting for the bus. She felt cold, even though it was August. So she thought, Forget about this, we're moving farther south. So we moved on to Santa Barbara.

In Santa Barbara we lived in the Wings of Love shelter for a few weeks. It was a small religious shelter that looked like someone's home. I became friends with a fifteen-year-old girl named Star. Tall, thin, and muscular, Star had deep brown sparkling eyes and dark brown skin and braided hair. She and her mother and brother Chris and my mom and I all stayed in one carpeted room. Star and her mom were in the bunks across from us. Her brother Chris—who was in eighth grade—was in the bunk above me. My mom and I were stuck sharing a bunk because I was small for my age.

The first night we were there, Chris repeatedly sang the "Revenge of the Nerds" song, face upside down from where he was sprawled in his upper bunk, teasing me because I was so nerdy with my glasses and my shyness. I hunched in a corner of the bunk, my nose in a book. It was one of the last times I read in a long while.

When I think about our brief stay at the Wings of Love, I see bright-colored walls and blankets, and thick carpets everywhere. The colors of Star's and Chris's faces blend in with the dark brown wood and flashy colors of the room. The woman running the place wore a cloth headdress like a nun, and she made us go to church all the time. She cooked grits and other food I wasn't used to, but I was hungry so I ate it. After a few weeks, we moved to the Salvation Army shelter. I didn't give Chris and Star much thought because by now I was used to leaving people behind. I expected the faces around me to change every few weeks. At the Salvation Army, I saw the crazy woman who ran the Wings of Love on the news. It turned out she had been keeping all the money she was given for the shelter for herself instead of using it to help the people who lived there.

We stayed at the Salvation Army for a few months, maybe half a year. In stark contrast to the Wings of Love shelter, it was big, institutional, and bleak, with rows and rows of cots in a large room lit brightly by white fluorescent lights. The room had linoleum floors like a schoolroom, and white cinder-block walls with high windows along one side.

There was no place to be alone, no place to be by myself. I woke up at six each morning to bright lights, a long cement room, strange people scurrying, rows of cots. I felt myself dispersing into the wide whiteness of the shelter's walls and the noise of strangers' words.

Each night before bed, I put clean clothes and a small towel at the bed's foot. When I woke, I would jump up before I could begin to lose myself in the confusion. I grabbed my bundle of clothes and scooted to the showers. There were only a few for many women.

Inside the shower, I rested my knee, shoulder, and face against the warm yellow tiles. It was the only place I felt alone and undisturbed. I folded myself into the corner, standing on one leg like a stork, the other knee pushing into the corner. The warm water wrung itself over me, and I would begin to feel at home, no cold spots. The door to this yellow cubicle was shut tight, and the glass grew cloudy with steam.

I wanted to stay in that warm womb forever. I couldn't, it wasn't my own home. But before I left for the day I could daydream and imagine. My imaginings resonated around me, reverberating off the yellow tiles and enveloping me. I shut my eyes, pressed my forehead into the corner. I thought of a rectangle shape cut into a door. This was the mail slot in the door of my new house. *Swoosh-plop*, a magazine fell through onto the floor inside.

I wanted an address so badly, just to have a spot where I could get mail and magazines. Sometimes at newsstands in California I looked at the subscription cards in kids' and teen magazines—"only $10 a year—six issues." How easy life would be if only I could fill out that little card. I could fill in the address and have a home as well as a year's subscription sent back to me. A year to sleep in the same place.

My mother told me that we had to spend the money from the sale of my books and toys. I felt betrayed because she'd told me we would buy a new bicycle with it, but I accepted her decision because I knew we had no other money.

Books had been a solace for me throughout my early childhood. But the year we moved to California and became homeless, I no longer had any desire for books. My eyes were opened instead to the new worlds around me.

During that year I went to four schools, but I cannot say that I attended often. The schools I went to are a blur of strange playgrounds, blacktops, children jumping rope while chanting unfamiliar melodies. The lessons did not interest me when compared to life outside the school and inside my head. I did not understand why we had ended up in this place. We wandered aimlessly all afternoon after school until the shelter opened at 6:00 P.M., and our nights were filled with a strange uncertainty and people I didn't know. I was nine; I missed my friends; my feet ached from walking; my throat was parched from not eating or drinking (many stores did not take food stamps). Most of all, I did not understand why we couldn't just go home—to Oregon, or anywhere—to sit and rest.

All of this wandering, tiredness, and newness wore me out and made me grumpy. I threw tantrums. I wanted to be sure that everyone knew I was not happy.

My mother, in her mid-forties, had a boyfriend in his twenties, whom she met at the shelter. I despised George intensely, because he was so young and clung pathetically to my mother. To me, he was ugly and awkward. His eyes blinked too slowly behind his thick brown-framed glasses. I was jealous of George. I wanted to say to him: "This is my mother, the only mother I have, and you will have no piece of her." Too young to articulate my feelings, instead I became hard to handle when he was around.

One day, in the dim light and concrete box shape of the Salvation Army lobby, while people were lingering around and waiting for family members, George picked me up onto his lap. He talked and laughed while I squirmed. He began to tickle me, and I squirmed and squiggled more, screaming at him to stop. "I have to pee, I'm going to pee my pants!" He didn't listen until the lukewarm urine soaked through the front of his jeans. It just kept coming, a fast and hot stream hissing at him.

"Shit!" he said, standing up and dumping me on the dirty concrete floor. He retreated with a bowlegged swagger for the men's part of the shelter. I picked my shameful self up, sobbing, and looked around in bewilderment at all the people watching me. My breath caught sharply between each hiccup. The heat of the urine on my skin, and its pungent salty odor made me scream all the more hysterically. I was left with only my embarrassment, the hot sweet smell of urine, and the unforeseen satisfaction that I had shown George how much I hated him.

The next day, George bought me a Cabbage Patch doll watch. The top of the watch was the head of a doll, and it opened to reveal a digital display of the time. I loved Cabbage Patch dolls, although I myself had a Flower Kid, a cheaper imitation at $14.99 compared to the price of a real one—$30 to $40—a fortune it seemed to me at that time. I wanted the watch but not from him. I made him take it back. I loathed myself for my open cruelties to George, for the insults I screamed at him and at my mother. But I hated George more than even myself for his futile attempts to win my affection. I wanted the watch but not from him. It hurt me to think that he would be kind to someone as mean to him as I was.

After the scene with George, a willfulness opened within

me, and there was no turning back. I was like Macbeth, whom my mother and I had read about, in his murderous rampage, who said he was "in blood stept in so far that, should I wade no more, returning were as tedious as go o'er." With every tantrum, I murdered another connection to sanity and calm, drowning myself in anger as if it were warm blood.

I began to refuse to go to school. One day at 8:00 A.M., as I walked away from the shelter with my mother, something grabbed me from inside and I lay down on the sidewalk. My mother leaned over me, talking to me in a calm, kind voice. "You need to get up, you can't stay here." But I refused to go anywhere other than that spot of cold morning concrete. I looked over at my hands and feet pounding, flailing, and I felt detached from my own limbs. I felt detached from my own screams as well. From here, facedown, the pavement didn't look as smooth as it did when I was standing up. The gray pebbles looked larger, more real, and felt cooler, sharper. I stared stubbornly at these pebbles and not at the line of the tall dark policeman stretching above. This was the only way I knew to talk to adults: I tried to make a dent in the concrete with my body parts so that they would know how angry I was, how much I wanted to go home. But could not.

The policeman—I don't know if he just happened to be in the area, or if someone had called him because I was creating a scene—called me little girl and said, "Do you know how much trouble you are to your mother? You need to be in school. There is nowhere else for you."

I wanted to tell him there was nothing in school I could have learned. I was bored with the packets of papers, the rows of neat handwriting. The teacher was distant and unreal, and she dissolved behind my veil of tears. The tears wouldn't dry, or roll back up my cheeks, or shrink back into the bloody vein-red corners of my eyes. The tears were born far inside of me, inside the pain and exhaustion of trembling flesh. I couldn't make them stop; I couldn't take them back.

That year the world appeared to me more often than not through wavy lines of salt water that kept coming, forming wet curtains and glints of out-of-focus rainbows. One night at the Salvation Army I imagined that I saw my older half brother, Kirk, standing in the doorway of the shelter. I screamed and screamed and was inconsolable. I caused such a ruckus in the women's dorm that no one could sleep, not even the flea-ridden bundled old woman who was crazy and usually slept through everything, including the wake-up calls, harsh lights, and noise of morning. I had to be taken to a hospital, where finally I calmed down. Soothing, nurturing nurses fluffed my pillows. They brought water and hot chocolate with marshmallows, and crayons and a pad of paper, on which I drew hobbit houses and square box houses with chimneys and straight stone walkways lined with red flowers almost as large as the house itself. A gray picket fence marched around the house that I drew, enclosing it and separating the home from the world of blank page that lay beyond. My mother sat at my bedside, an anxious frown wrinkling her forehead. Her eyes were full of worry.

At the shelter there was a woman named Violet, who was very nice to me. One evening as we sat on our beds, she pulled out a cream-colored envelope and carefully opened it at the seams and laid it out flat. On the outside of the envelope were the handwritten address and postmark, but on the inside there was a clean space, framed at the edges by the glue from the envelope, and the frail tendrils of paper were rough where she had pulled the glue apart. She began to sketch my face in pencil quickly, and then she gave the portrait to me. I was proud and happy.

My childhood photos were lost in one of our moves. I remember one picture taken when I was three years old. I had a short pageboy haircut and wore a white '70s print shirt with large orange flowers with black pistils. I sat on a sunlit swing, holding on to its chain links and twisting them as I leaned into the camera, green leafy trees in the background. In another photo, a four-year-old me stood with a boy my age on a wooden deck on a cloudy day, the beach behind. My soft shoulder-length hair was in two ponytails at the base of my neck, and a faded royal blue one-piece bathing suit clung to my thin body, slender legs with knees unbent. The boy wore swim trunks and held a red rose. But those photos exist only in my memory now.

Although most of my photos were lost, I managed to hold on to Violet's drawing. On the cream-colored surface is a small pale girl face with clear and steady eyes that seem to look not at but beyond the person she faces. In the sketch, I look sad and challenging: a person who will not be comforted but dares you to try. My hair looks so thin and straight that it would melt away if I tried to touch it.

After a month, Star and her family moved into the Salvation Army, too. I was happy to see her again. We resumed our friendship. My mother allowed me to go anywhere for any length of time with Star, trusting the older girl to watch out for me.

Star was in high school, although she usually didn't go. For months, we played hooky almost every day. Star made up stories to tell people we met on the street or walking near the beach. Her dark eyes flashed in seeming sincerity, a sly smile played on her lips as she talked.

We took long walks on the bicycle path next to the sand beach, pausing to watch a glamorous woman in leopard-skin pants and roller skates. She did fantastic tricks near the fountain of leaping stone dolphins, skating backwards in graceful circles within the circle of palm trees, her black hair flowing like a mane.

On our walks, I saw homeless people living and eating around a giant mangrove tree. The tree was huger than any I had seen, each root large enough to shelter one sleeping person. At night, the tree's roots gained living inhabitants. During the day the tree's vast shade covered cookouts and conversations. My mind opened to new definitions of home.

Star and I made a good pair. I admired how she could swing her hips from side to side as she walked. She loved having a little sisterlike friend to tag along and follow where she led.

Once when she and I were sitting in a doorway of a building on State Street in Santa Barbara, a comfortably dressed man, hands in the pockets of his khakis, came by and said, "Don't you girls have anywhere to go to? Why don't you go home to your mothers?"

Star's eyes widened, and she went into storytelling mode. "We don't have mothers and we don't have homes neither."

I watched as Star convinced the skeptical man that we had no parents to care for us, and that we traveled around to different cities, surviving on our own. The man was so overcome with pity that he pulled a five-dollar bill out of his pocket and gave it to Star. I laughed with her over the trick we had played on him. "It's not really a lie," she said. "We don't have homes really."

Star also taught me how to steal. I don't remember when I

started. I knew it was wrong, but I liked the pretty clothes. I wandered through the aisles of Kmart, my eye caught by packages of glinting metal bracelets. My fourth-grade classmates treasured these inexpensive baubles. They wore dreamy armfuls of them. I glanced surreptitiously up and down the aisle, and seeing no one, picked up the pretty bracelets, dropping them swiftly into my bag. I continued down the aisle, carefully nonchalant. I shifted my eyes subtly upward, glancing to be certain there was no camera watching me.

Star got me a warm coat by walking out of the dressing room wearing it under her own fluffy coat, which she had stolen the week before. We then exited the store, the employees suspecting nothing. The coat had brightly colored buttons. I looked up to Star even more from then on.

My mother never questioned where we got things. Star would tell her lies. "My friend got this cheap and she doesn't want it anymore." My mother trusted us completely; it was her nature. We told her we had a job working for a woman, keeping her house. We told her that the woman gave us money and clothes that her daughter didn't want.

Shoplifting made me feel powerful. I could get watches and clothes and bracelets and food anytime I wanted, with little effort. It was a game with valuable rewards; it brought a thrill of fear culminating in euphoria. It was a way to get nice things for myself and other people, especially for my mother.

We became shoplifting experts at the supermarket, stuffing a quart of orange juice into the sleeve of a coat, filling large brown bags with food for our mothers and Star's younger brother. She ordered fried chicken from the Safeway deli—I wondered why they didn't arrest her on the spot, because she walked away so calmly, not paying. Only after many days did I figure out that the deli didn't care, it was the checkout stands in front that took money. Each time she got the chicken, I panicked. I thought this would be the time we would be chased and found out. The quart of orange juice made my coat sleeve very square. I wondered if the lady moving the carts would notice this odd shape, but she did not. We would slip past, bags of groceries full as if we'd paid.

We shoplifted thousands of dollars' worth of merchandise. Star explained that the stores were ripping people off anyway, that they had lots and lots of money and they would never miss the things that we took. It was fun to outsmart the stores, with their two-way mirrors and hostile yet unsuspecting clerks. I had two stretchy knit outfits in leopard prints, one turquoise, and the other shocking pink. I had jeans, and Cabbage Patch Kid shoes, and over a hundred metal and plastic jelly bracelets. When I took them out of their shoe box to admire them, I put them on and they stretched up both arms above my elbows.

I had Christmas presents for my mother—a black sweater, soft black silk gloves, and a handbag to match—all from a small women's store with expensive prices. The smallest stores were the most challenging, required the most subtlety and daring. My mother had never had such elegant clothes before. I was proud to be able to give them to her. The stolen goods should have made me feel guilty, but I felt only a vague nervousness that I dismissed.

One day Star and I were at the Thrifty drugstore on State Street, picking up a few things like relaxer for her hair and batteries for her Walkman. The store had an ice cream counter in front. You could get ice cream cones for only twenty-five cents there. A double scoop was fifty cents. My mom would sometimes take me there, and the scoop of ice cream was always precariously stuck to the top of the cake cone, ready to fall off into my hand at the slightest jostle. Worried, I used my tongue to shove the ice cream down into the cone, making tongue imprints on the ice cream and tiring my tongue out with the effort. My mom told me that she and Aunt Jane also used to do this to their ice cream cones when they were children.

On this day at the Thrifty drugstore, I wasn't with my mother.

I surveyed the rows of socks hanging on pegs, as if trying to choose between one pair and another. Star stood slightly behind me, covering for me as I put two pairs of red socks inside her jacket. We left the store, and as we were walking through the parking lot, we heard a rough voice addressing us: "Hey!" The voice came from a guard in a dark blue security uniform with official insignias on its shoulders. He had a stern and implacable manner, and his eyes didn't move from us. We held out our hands as he instructed us to.

"Unzip your jackets, please."

"What?" Star asked. "We only bought a few things."

"Show me what's inside your jackets and empty your pockets."

Star tried to hide as many stolen items as possible and acted like she couldn't believe that this was happening. The cop said, "I know you've done this hundreds of times and never thought you would get caught. You'll probably steal a hundred more and not get caught again. But it happens."

The handcuffs snapped around our wrists, chaining us to one another, as we were led back across the lot to the store. I stared nervously at the ground, watching as Star dropped items from her coat with her free hand: batteries, a candy bar, hair gel. I was mortified. My life couldn't be over this soon, I thought, not when I was only nine. We climbed the stairs to an upper office, and I sat down on the black vinyl couch in front of the security guard's desk. I curled my knees to my chest, wrapping my locked arms tensely around my calves. Huddled far back into the couch, I imagined a photograph of Star and me on the front of a newspaper. I pictured my mother seeing this photograph, rustling the page closer to get a clearer look, and reading the caption underneath. My mother's face crumpled with shock and disappointment, her bottom lip dropping and starting to shiver as it did when she was upset.

My fearful reverie was interrupted by the sound of Star reporting her name to the guard. "Stacey Brown," she said sullenly. That wasn't her real name! I imagined an even worse scenario, my mother reading about our crime and then seeing the false name. She would know that I was a liar as well as a thief. The thought of my mother's sadness engendered a rush of fear and nausea in me. I sniffled defeatedly from the corner, the tears pouring down my face. "That's not your name. We have to tell them our real names." Now was not the time for one of Star's stories.

The guard told us we were banned from all Thrifty drugstores forever. All I could think of was that now I could never get a twenty-five-cent ice cream cone again. I would never again hurt my tongue pushing the cold ice cream into the fragile cone.

A Santa Barbara policeman soon arrived at the store, and we went downstairs to the police car waiting to transport us to the police station.

Star's mother screamed angry curses at us when she arrived at the station, but my mother was crying. She held me in a tight hug and held me out in front of her to look at me, her eyes red and wet. I looked down after a moment, frightened and ashamed. I thought she was horribly disappointed, but she told me later that she was only sad about the situation and didn't place the blame on me. It was at this moment that my mother decided we had to return to Oregon.

We lived with Aunt Jane back in Oregon after a year in California. The tantrums and the arrest were more than my mother could bear. In addition, she'd been unable to find a job after many months.

My fourth-grade classmates' innocently secure voices and eyes unclouded by worries startled me. In fourth grade I felt anything but innocent. When I saw my new classmates sitting in rows at their desks, I kept thinking back to the parking lot where I was arrested, or to the white walls of the shelter, or to standing on a street corner ringing a Salvation Army Christmas bell with my mom. There was so much they didn't know—all that was inside me. My isolation from my classmates hit me oddly, like an invisible wall that I tried to reach through but knew I couldn't. School life no longer felt the same as it had before, when I had accepted it as the only realm I knew. I felt small and all alone. But if I was small, then I was a small rock and had a knowledge hard and unchippable.

In the months after our return, the stark and bright events of Santa Barbara faded in my mind and became unreal pictures. My mom was back with her old boyfriend, Bill. And I was going to school every day.

I began to feel like Santa Barbara was only a vague confusing dream, but the clothes that I wore still reminded me of that dream, and the leopard-spotted outfits gnawed at my conscience. I still was not sure if my mother knew that all of these clothes were also stolen. One evening I lay in the double bed I shared with my mother, determinedly waiting out the night until she returned from her date. The room was dark, but my eyes stayed open, focused on the long slender triangle of light that reached into the room from the hallway. The small bright crack of light seemed to call out a promise of a future that was clear and honest. Finally, my mother returned and sat on the bed's edge, holding my hand as I told her about the clothes.

"They must be taken away—completely away," I said solemnly.

"Okay, dear, then we'll give them to the thrift shop," she said, squeezing my hand.

Several weeks later I was at Astoria's only library (finally I was reading again) and something funny happened. I looked over at a girl about my age and noticed that her mint green pants looked familiar, and that I recognized the pink lightning streaks and purple squiggles. "Look, Mom," I whispered, pointing. "Those are my pants." I laughed, holding tight to my books, almost feeling innocent again—but with new knowledge, feeling freer than ever before.

8

1509 FRANKLIN

AFTER SPENDING THE summer at Aunt Jane's, my mother found us an apartment in Astoria.

I knew when I walked in the front door of the building at 1509 Franklin that it wasn't a nice place to live. The depressing dank hallways smelled of sour rotting carpet and stagnant air. In the doorway across from our apartment stood a corpulent and unkempt woman in a yellowed nightgown. She swore and bellowed at an unseen man in the apartment behind her. All the drapes were drawn, and the only light came from the flickering TV screen, whose noise competed with the woman's shouts.

The apartment was made of two studios, and it never felt quite right. We had two bathrooms, one with a decrepit, rusty, freestanding metal shower. We never used it because it shook with a terrible noise when the water was turned on. The other bathroom had a white painted bathtub with yellow claw feet. It reminded me of a hollow animal that you might take a ride in. I took baths instead of showers.

There were also two kitchens. One came with a old oval-shaped refrigerator swarming with small orange flat bugs. Hundreds of them were caught in the cracks of the rubber edging. My mom cleaned it out with Lysol and a rag, wringing the dead bugs out into the sink.

The other kitchen could have been a bedroom for me, but we had only one bed. Instead my mother filled it with plants. They covered the sinks and counters. Plant food, green plastic and ceramic pots, gardening tools, and soil stocked the cupboards underneath and above.

I liked sleeping in the big bed with my mom though, covered by an old cozy patchwork quilt Aunt Jane gave us. I sprawled on this bed and read by lamplight on dark and rainy winter afternoons—the Oz books, the Lord of the Rings trilogy, and all of the Anne of Green Gables books. In the mornings I excitedly dressed while it was still dark, and walked by myself up the big hill to the middle school, carrying the school-loaned violin that I had just learned to play that year. The hill was so steep that many of the sidewalks had concrete outcroppings like little speed bumps. My mother called them pigeon steps. On field trips, riding down the hill, I and the other students in the back of the bus were lifted out of our seats at the dip of each street. I had never been to an amusement park, but imagined I was on a roller coaster.

Astoria was the rainiest place on earth. On Halloween, we went trick-or-treating in soggy costumes and ate candy from waterlogged candy wrappers. Christmas was never white, but rain was always likely. Fourth of July went without fireworks because of the damp weather. Easter "sunrise" services were held under covered porches watching the rain pour in sheets outside. We prayed for the moment when we could go inside, out of the wet, to eat an early breakfast of ham, pancakes, and scrambled eggs with pepper.

When it rained and rained and would not stop, I went outside in my bare feet and watched the rainwater pouring in rivers down the curbs of the big hill. The gutters were unable to keep up with the flow of water; it pooled at street corners and rushed past, up to my waist. Above the metal grates, I sat down and let the cool water stream around me.

I sometimes borrowed my mother's gardening tools and played with Isaiah, a younger boy who lived downstairs. Days after the rain were good for mud pies. We took our shoes off, rolled up our pants legs, and covered ourselves with mud while filling tin after tin, any container we could find, with mud. Mud with strands of grass and worms, mud that was gooey and thick and rocky. The mud made delicious mud pies that tasted, in my imagination, just like the chocolate pudding pies my Grandma Harman made on Sundays. Grandma put her pies in Tupperware pie keepers with plastic handles. She brought several of them each week to Aunt Jane and Uncle Ron's house ten miles outside of town for Sunday dinner. When Isaiah and I had assembled row upon row of tins filled with mud, we threw our pies at each other, running and shrieking all over the yard.

My mother and I were alone together. The tension between being ashamed and angry and still loving her caused me to pick terrible fights. I challenged her on everything and there was no mediator or peacemaker. I called her horrible names and accused her of being a bad mother. I wanted her to defend herself but she never did. She just stared at me tight-lipped, her eyes flashing and eyelashes quivering with each word, but she never would say anything. If I tried to push her, she just held out one arm, fist clenched, and moved it wherever I tried to push her so that I couldn't touch her but she wasn't hurting me. I would end up sobbing curled up on the floor.

Sometimes I felt the tension so physically, I thought I would explode. I lay on the floor making myself convulse and vibrate, tensing and clenching each part of my body one at a time, until I felt peace and exhaustion come over me like a calming wave of cleansing water.

I was playing in the yard with Isaiah one morning after fighting with my mother. His mother, Nancy, came out and asked me, "What was all that noise in your apartment last night?" Ashamed, I looked away and said in a breathy voice, "My mother and I had a fight . . ."

My hateful words ricocheted back to me filtered through Nancy's ears. How horrible she must think we were. This judgment was worse than the actual fight.

"Next time you're going to fight with your mother, do it more quietly, okay?" she condescended.

"Okay," I whispered, looking down.

That day at dusk, I ran inside and smelled the Hamburger Helper that Nancy was cooking for dinner. I felt suddenly lonely. The salty, spicy warm smell of the meat was drawn into my nostrils, as I wanted to be drawn into the picture the smell aroused in me. I wanted to sit at a dinner table at a regular time, with the certain and solid sustenance of a meaty dish set before me. I began to step slowly up the stairs, thinking about my mother's blank face when I asked insistently, angrily, "What's for dinner? Aren't we having dinner?" Her figure framed by yellowish light and bare walls, standing in front of a couch that floated, unanchored, in the center of the room, covered by a sheet that wrinkled and shifted, chaotically askew, bare patches of old couch peeking out all over.

With only two of us, we had no regular mealtime. My mother would often make a can of soup and a sandwich and call me to eat when I was reading. Eventually I would go and eat, when I finished my paragraph, or page, or chapter. My mother gave up on a regular mealtime because I was never hungry at the right time, and wanted to keep reading. Also, we often did not have enough money to afford the ingredients for complex dishes or full meals. But the smell of someone else's hot supper made me long for a dinner table set for a family that I did not have. A father and a mother, a brother or a sister. Anything would be better than just the two of us, sometimes.

Children need to trust in their parents' ability to provide for them, but many poor children cannot. They see their parents' weakness, see them as slaves to the welfare dole. I knew that the welfare system was strong and powerful, and not my mother. This knowledge produced an inner conflict, a trauma, a yearning, a shame and anger and fear that battled with my desire to love and trust in my mother. I was angry with my mother because she could not give me what I yearned for. I wanted to lash out at her, accuse her of being weak. I wanted to agree with the welfare workers and say that my mother was lazy and unworthy. I was afraid of being tainted by my mother's shame and weakness. I was full of self-hate both because I came from my mother, and therefore must be shamefully similar, and because I showed my weakness by so easily disowning her.

As a child I sensed that if my mother was unable to provide for me, then I must bear responsibility to care for myself. I longed to relinquish this responsibility, to place it in the lap of some imaginary all-powerful, all-capable, ample, and strong adult. It was a sigh I longed to release. I wanted my needs and burdens to melt into the smell of someone else's hot dinner. And I wanted a home, a house, where the thin walls of the shaky old apartment building would not betray me.

The fights continued when I was older, and the emotions were the same.

One day I came home after wrestling practice in high school. I had spent three hours on a wrestling mat being pounded into what felt like one big pulpy bruise. I was exhausted and tender to the touch. I dropped my bag filled with schoolbooks and heavy sweat-soaked clothes. Seeing her just sitting there was too much. I didn't understand.

My mother was sunk back in the armchair, leaning to one side. She wore her coat and winter knit hat indoors, as she did almost year-round. It was covered with fuzzy pellets. She looked like a bear in a cave or an Eskimo in an igloo, huddled there hibernating. She was never warm enough in the winter.

"You're just going to be more cold when you go outside," I told her. "It's not cold in here."

She rolled her eyes, half smiled, and shrugged as if I was an insect buzzing and tickling her ear.

She pulled her hat down over her ears. Bits of gray and black hair frizzed out of the cap; from time to time she'd push them back in. Her book and notebook sat with her in the chair, the stenographer's notebook filled with Gregg short-hand that she learned when she was a secretary before she got married, mysterious indecipherable loops and lines that hid her most mundane and philosophical thoughts. When I was younger, I wanted to learn this shorthand too. I got my own stenographer's notebook. She translated some of her notes, and showed me how to make the tiny markings that signified letters, parts of words, or whole words. I didn't have the drive or attention span, however, to learn the notations, so they remained enigmatic to me. An empty coffee cup and plate of toast crumbs sat on the TV tray next to her.

"Why do you eat toast?" I chastised her. I'd been learning about nutrition and I followed a stringent wrestling diet. "You don't eat because you're hungry. You eat because you're bored. And that will just make you fat."

It was like philosophizing with a statue. She looked the other way. Maybe she thought if she ignored my pestering, I might go away.

She muttered, "I know, I know," hoping this response would be enough to make me go out like a rushing tide, receding back into my room so that she could be alone with her thoughts. Sometimes in the midst of an argument she'd suddenly agree with me. This tactic was as transparent to me as the skin of the jellyfish I had seen at the aquarium in Boston. I could see her contracting inward on herself, like the jellyfish with its tiny waving hairs. She'd just agree with me to shut me up, and then withdraw again.

Her withdrawal and stillness offended my youth and busyness. She clashed with me like pink clashes with red, like sky blue with burnt orange.

I came back out of my room, after dropping my book bag and gazing at the chipping paint of the mint green walls that I had covered with inspirational sayings, Bible quotes, and colorful fabrics.

"Why don't you just get a job?" I screamed at her, slamming my fist into the kitchen table. "You will never get a job because you can't get along with anyone. You push everyone away!" She didn't speak back, and her quiet smiles made me angrier.

"Why don't you answer me?" I asked her, as I hurled a loaf of white bread into a corner. "You are infuriating! Everybody hates you! You are a bad mother!"

"If this is how you are going to treat me," she said, finally speaking, "I will do nothing nice for you. You'll see. You'll have nothing that you want," in a calm voice.

"What?" I asked mockingly. "You won't buy me things? All the money you have comes from welfare, and if you keep it all for yourself, I will call them and tell them!" I kept on throwing everything on the kitchen table into the corner of the room. The bread, cups, napkins, silverware, oranges and apples, and finally a ceramic dish. I banged the Corning Ware only when I got angry enough to really break things. Only when I needed to throw something fragile enough to shock me out of fury and back into sadness.

When my anger had subsided, my cheeks turned red and hot with tears. I picked up all I had thrown. I placed the items back on the round kitchen table and began to sweep up the jagged white shards.

But it was the orange that made me most sad. The oranges and apples had been part of my mother's Thanksgiving decorations. She bought them especially for me because I hardly ate anything else. Fruit was expensive but so good and health restoring.

When I picked the orange up from among the broken pottery, a tiny sharp noise began inside me. The pieces of Corning Ware had sliced clean rounded curves—pretty lacy patterns—through its leathery skin. I did not want to look at it. I cupped its veined flesh in my hand, but if I opened my fingers, the gouged skin wouldn't hold the fragrant feathered pulp inside. I stood and looked at it through my tears, my hand and body trembling. The orange's round shape wouldn't cohere. It fell out of itself. The neat wedges were opened and spurting juice that stung the small cuts on my fingers. I had wanted to break the dish but not the orange.

The orange was connected to every other mistakenly broken thing in my life.

9

SCHOOLTEACHER

IN SIX MONTHS we moved again. My mom wanted to move because our neighbors across the hallway were loud and dealt drugs. Also, we couldn't get a housing subsidy there, so we paid almost our entire welfare check in rent. Once the housing authority approved our application for subsidized housing, we moved to the Blue Ridge apartments, a few miles outside of downtown Astoria.

However, at the new apartment we still didn't escape loud drunken fights at three in the morning, punctuated by the sound of shattering glass. And there were still plenty of drugs. I smelled marijuana every day at my friends' apartment, although I didn't know what the smell was. Among my fifth-grade classmates, Blue Ridge was known as the Village, a sobriquet that conjured up images of simple, uneducated people living in hovels.

Living in the Village may have held a stigma, but it was better than our old apartment. We had more space and two real bedrooms that weren't kitchens. The bathroom had a real bathtub with a shower, no claw-foot bathtub or shaky shower. And there was countryside and more room to play and run around.

Clusters of oxalis—green wood sorrel—grew in the forest behind our apartment. They looked like three-leafed clovers. "You can eat them," my mother said, "but not the ones that grow close to the highway—the cars' exhaust contaminates them." To me the leaves tasted like green apple skins. The stems were crunchy and watery. There were also large green ferns, whose fronds I turned over to find dusty brown spores that marched in rows like good schoolchildren.

The neighborhood children and I rolled with abandon down the steep hillside amidst thick bracken and vines, gathering momentum and glee, crashing down until the vines caught and held us in a tight net. We scrambled back up, pulling the vines to keep balanced. Then we'd lie down and do it again, until we were brown and muddy as frogs.

When the sun began to set, it was time to play school in my room. "Please, please, can we have school?" my friends Cathy and Jenny asked me each evening.

I had been playing the game of schoolteacher since I was four years old in Burnside—when I put a sign in the dewy grass of the front yard one early summer morning, advertising the Apple Summer School. The white sign was made of a cardboard panty-hose insert—decorated with a red crayon apple and uneven black lettering. Even though at that time we lived out in the country, a quarter mile from our nearest neighbor, I was convinced I would have students.

I didn't have students then, after all, but in later years I did.

At Blue Ridge, my mom was going to buy me a bed, but I asked for a sleeping bag instead. My room was a classroom, and a bed would only be a distraction and a waste of learning space.

My mom was an Avon lady for a couple of months, but quit because she was worried I'd have no way to reach her when she sold door to door. But I did get to keep the large cardboard boxes that the cosmetics came in. The boxes had flat removable lids and made great desks. I taped a paper name tag on each "desktop," put supplies inside, and lined the boxes up in rows in my room. I made packets of papers for each neighborhood child, different for each one, depending on their ages: work sheets I made myself, pages torn from outdated math workbooks bought at yard sales, and the purple-inked mimeographs that my teachers cast off into their recycling bins. I hole-punched the packets and tied them together with yarn from my mom's crocheting supplies.

My room was also decorated like a schoolroom, the walls ringed with brightly colored construction paper numbers and letters. They marched around and around—Aa, big A, little a, Bb, big B, little b, Cc, and so on.

We played school for hours. My students were remarkably diligent. Cathy and Jenny, who attended most frequently, were sisters and my friends. Cathy was nine and Jenny seven, both special needs students. Every evening in the spring and summer when it began to get darker and we tired of playing outside, they eagerly requested that we "have school." We spent hours going over the work sheets. While Jenny was doing cursive letters, I did arithmetic problems with Cathy. "What's 7 + 0? 3 + 4?" I asked her, using the colorful pictures on the math work sheets to explain the problems to her in a simple, logical way.

Cathy had thick glasses, thicker than mine, and was the slower of the two though she was older. They both had sweet gap-toothed smiles. Their faces lit up over all the attention.

It may be that I re-created the "schoolroom" in all of my various homes because school in my mind was a place of harmony and progression and it appealed to a sense of order that I yearned for. When my life was stable at home, I did well in school, and perhaps I wanted to pass on to others the achievement and joy I found in learning. Also, teachers who taught from the books but could not answer my many questions of "why?" frustrated me. I wanted to be a teacher who could answer "why" and make learning easier for my students. I loved making lesson plans, the challenge of finding ways to bring them to understanding. I enjoyed being able to creatively and patiently guide them, as my mother had with me.

Each night I pushed the cardboard desks against the wall and slept in a sleeping bag in the middle of the floor. I was a lone island in a sea of brown carpet. Falling asleep at night, I saw dimly the faded green, pink, yellow, and blue construction-paper squares forming a ring about my wall. They glowed faintly in the moonlight and I glowed back with joy and pride in another day's success at "school." In the morning I stuffed the sleeping bag back into the closet, my room transformed once again into a beloved schoolroom.

10

NAMING

Words . . . have the power to move us emotionally. . . . As
replicas capable of disassembling the "beings" they
replicate, they make possible the breaking and destruc-
tion of those beings, and hence also their reconstruction
in different forms.

—Henri Lefebvre, *The Production of Space*

AT AGE TEN, I was fascinated by names. I had a name collection in a cardboard shoe box. I had covered the box with
gift wrap and cut a slot in the top to drop names into. A string
with a pen was attached to the box with masking tape. I cut
wrapping paper into piles of little squares, kept close by. On
these squares, I wrote characters' names from my favorite
books. I made up names to put into the box, and got others
from name dictionaries.

It was about this time that I wanted to know my father's
name. I didn't want to know anything else about him, and my
mother wouldn't have told me more anyway—he was not a
subject she talked about. "He doesn't want you to know," she

told me, looking away. "He doesn't consider himself to be your father." She had written to him when I was four, but he had not responded.

I stared at my mother, waiting for her to tell me. I followed her around the house, my eyes focused on the centers of her brown eyes. We went to the store and I stared at her in the grocery aisles, so that she fumbled with the cans of green peas, dropping them with a bang on the linoleum floor. At home, I stood over her bed and stared at her, until her eyes opened white in the dark. She looked up at me, said the words. And shut her eyes.

I went to bed with his Name scrolling across my mind in all kinds of handwritings: white, black, big, small, fancy, plain. The words scrolled across my closed eyes like cloud letters up in the sky, like glowing letters on a movie screen.

Knowing it was like knowing a secret about myself. Saying the words aloud made me more real. There was power in a name. I wanted to know just enough information to box him up in a corner of my mind, label him, make him smaller somehow.

Years later, though, when I sat in the half-dark on our apartment's front porch with my mother and thought of my father and the four things I did know about him, I felt as scattered as soil by earthworms, as loose as a loose-leaf notebook. The space between me and myself expanded, opened. I felt like an open universe. Vast pockets of space seemed to become vaster, to fill with particles and antiparticles, mesons and mu-mesons that met and annihilated.

It was around the time that I learned my father's name that I learned about another name that applied to myself. I sprawled on the floor of my room reading a romance novel with sex scenes, a book my mom would not have thought appropriate. I came across a strange word and called her into the room to ask about it, hiding the book under a pile of clothes.

"Mom, what does *bastard* mean?" She gave me a curious look, then told me, reluctantly. I thought about it and knew that I was one. *Bastard* ripped through my mind like a metal ball hung from a chain, breaking through mental walls. I said aloud: *bastard,* and felt its power. I was illegitimate, unlike my sisters and brother. I was free-floating, unseen. Born into a void, unpredicted life; I hadn't entered this world in the proper way.

I began to think of myself in relation to the larger world. It was my first glimpse of myself from the outside. The words *illegitimate* and *bastard* were meant to condemn mothers and the children they bear out of wedlock. Yet I took this rejection as a form of freedom. These words meant that I was not bound by those traditions and proprieties that collared existence that governed respectable people.

For me at age ten, this freedom was scary. But "illegitimacy" was my birthright and could strengthen me at the same time that it made me vulnerable.

Words have power to label or to free. Words could be labels that limit and confine—or they could free me if I chose to shape the words to my own ends. I could reconstruct the labels to wear them proudly.

I was intrigued by names and their power to transform or to conjure up mental images of a person. I bugged my mom to tell me the history of our names. This history was more complex than I had imagined.

My mother was born Betty Jean Harman and later became Elizabeth (she always wanted a "real" name, a name with weight and respect). She was born Betty Jean, but she did not have to stay a Betty all her life. She did not have to become what the name Betty entailed. My mother believes that we can change our names to better fit our own lives and situations—that naming is a way of becoming even more oneself, more whole. When I was born, my mother didn't want me to have her maiden name, because she "wasn't a maiden." She didn't want to keep her ex-husband's name. And she didn't want me to have my father's last name, since he didn't want to be my father. So she decided we both needed a new last name. She found our name in a song, "A Summer Place" by Andy Williams, popular in the year of my birth. The chorus goes: "There's a summer place/Where it may rain and storm/yet I'm safe and warm/in your arms . . ." Our name became Summer.

When I was born, my mother named me Lauralee, after a friend who rubbed her back in the delivery room. Several months later, after my mother lost touch with her friend, she decided I needed a new name. She chose Amelia, naming me after Amelia Earhart, the first woman pilot to cross the Atlantic—a pioneering name. But later, when she found out about Earhart's tragic death, that name was a bad omen and wouldn't do. She then named me after Amy Carter, the president's daughter, because I was born when Jimmy Carter was elected president in 1976.

In middle school, there were seven Amys in my class of eighty people.

"Amy's such a boring name, Mom. Why'd you name me that? What would you have named me if it hadn't been Amy or Amelia?"

"Oh, I thought about Jenny, and Katie."

"Those are boring, too. Everyone has those names. Couldn't you be more original?"

After several times of thinking I'd been called to in the hallway at school, only to find out that the caller wanted "the other Amy, *not* you," I began to think about changing my name. I knew that my mother had changed our last name when I was born, so I didn't see why I couldn't change my first name as well. When I was twelve, I changed my name back to Lauralee. I liked the way Lauralee sounded when I said it, and it was much less likely that I would run into anyone else with my name. I thought that if I changed my name to Lauralee, my whole persona would change, too. I would become glamorous, self-assured, beautiful.

Later, in high school, I started to worry that I had given up Amy (beloved) and Amelia (industrious) for a name without an inspiring meaning. A laurel was just a kind of tree, and *lee* was a word for *bay*.

A tree growing by some water. What good was that?

But I started thinking, and realized that a (laurel) tree is a symbol of new life and growth. And a bay (lee) is made of water, which is purifying, cleansing, and needed by trees(!) in order to grow. My name began to make sense. I was a tree: growing, shooting out in new directions, and sending roots down to drink water. Add my last name, and I was a tree growing by water in the summer.

11

COSTUME MAKING

AFTER A FEW MONTHS at Blue Ridge we moved again. We didn't leave Astoria but moved three more times within the same town. It was always the same, the subsidy ran out, the building we lived in was sold, or we were evicted because the landlord had not made repairs. I began seventh grade in the fourth apartment we had lived in in the past two years.

For back-to-school shopping, my mother liked to "work her way up," which meant that we started off shopping at the thrift store, getting as much as possible there, then filling in the gaps at consignment stores, then JJ Newberry's, which my mother called the "five-and-dime," and finally—top of the line—JCPenney's.

I hated the thrift store because I had to buy clothes there that were radically unlike any that my friends wore or that I saw in the windows of JCPenney's. I raked through the racks of musty-smelling clothes, looking at every item, picking out what I thought were "halfway normal" clothes and rejecting the racks of pill-covered stirrup pants that were years out of date. I tried hard not to ask my mom for new-new clothes (as opposed to the "new to me" kind). But she usually bought me one or two new items after I pleaded with her that this was what I really wanted and I wouldn't ask for anything else. That year I asked for and got a twenty-dollar shirt from Penney's. It was a black and white striped tunic with a royal blue zip-down collar. I also got royal blue spandex jeans to go with it. I liked this outfit but felt guilty. Twenty dollars was the most we had ever paid for any clothing item and would have bought four or five outfits at the thrift shop. My mother never bought new clothes for herself. She seemed to like clothes from the thrift store just as well, but she didn't have classrooms full of fashion-critical seventh-graders to face every day. I often feared that I would end up with my classmates' cast-off clothes without knowing it.

(This was years before shopping at "thrifts" became fashionable. Years before one of my classmates in college wrote an article in *The Harvard Crimson* about the coolness of "kitsch." She could supplement her thrift store outfits with expensive accessories. She wrote that she felt akin to the welfare mothers that she combed through the racks with, but she didn't recognize that the difference between privilege and necessity made such kinship meaningless.)

My mother spent hours looking over the unmatched dishes and broken lamps. While I waited for her, I found a yellowy-paged paperback—a Harlequin romance—and in the half-dark underneath a rack of thick wool skirts pulled my knees up to my chin. I read, getting the mildew of the book all over my hands. I loved my secret place, the different perspective I got from watching feet going by in the well-lit world and listening to the voices that went with them.

*

So I began seventh grade in the JCPenney outfit, with my limp brown hair curled into long awkward spirals and my bangs teased up with the "skinny-mini" curling iron that my friend Maggie had given me for my birthday the year before. I finished it all off with a dose of wet, chemical-smelling hair spray, grabbed my book bag and violin, and left the apartment.

I was concerned with "cool," that bug that infects middle-schoolers everywhere, a universal virus and rite of passage. I knew that it was desperately important to be accepted by one's peers, and by the right group of peers. Unspoken laws and standards placed all students in their respective social groups and rankings. The social groups were most apparent in the lunchroom, in which the long row tables with round attached seats were like coin counters that the students slid into, filling up the slots. The popular crowd was the Preps. The girls in this group were the tallest and prettiest, cool and untouchable, with a different-colored pair of brand-name sneakers to match each outfit. The boys were of course the ones with the cutest smiles and the most confidence, well dressed every day in fresh polo shirts. Some of the Preps were quiet and aloof, as if they lived behind a wall of glass, with smiles as cold and beautiful as winter. Others were naïvely cruel, as only adolescents can be. They would catch you unawares with a comment as blinding as bright sunshine flashing off a car's silver hub-cap on a sweltering day. The painful swatch of white striking your eyes so that you immediately turned your head down and away as if ashamed.

The Carps were another group with high social status, a group of handsome, tough, pot-smoking youths. The girls wore tighter clothes and brighter lipstick and were louder than the Preps. The boys wore thick flannel plaid shirts in blues and reds. During recesses they would disappear into the woods on the edge of the track and the playground, hanging out and smoking until the bell rang for us to return.

In the lunchroom, most of the tables were filled by the worthless currency of nerds, dorks, and dweebs—girls and boys whose faults were that they could not dress right, were too shy or too smart or too awkward. They were the faceless metal slugs that the social vending machine of seventh grade spat out into the return change slot with a clank.

The girls I had been friends with in elementary school were in the second tier of popularity. They could talk to the Preps without trepidation and did not get made fun of. They compassionately strove to salvage me from complete nerd-dom by teaching me how to curl my hair and how to wear my pants "pegged" (folded in at the bottom to create a taper and then rolled up).

My mother had often admonished me to be independent and not care what others thought, so she didn't understand why I tried so hard to wear the right clothes and be accepted. She would have told me to design my own costumes, not to dress in an outfit tailored for me by someone else. She thought that the clothing designers that made the outfits in Penney's were getting rich off of other people's wasted money. The world was filled with an accumulation of products that people discarded every year as the fashions changed. The bins at the thrift store were full of perfectly good clothes.

Make your own wings, she would have told me, and fly above what other people think of you. At first you are the only person who sees the wings. Let them think what they want. Do not plod the dusty road. Sew your own costume, your wings and cape, and fly. If you make mistakes, you can pull out the seams and begin again. But you will fly.

I was lucky that my mother gave me the fabric of confidence to sew wings with and a comfortable space of understanding in which to don my wings. I was lucky too to have the material things I did have. There are many children living in poverty who do not have the emotional resources or even the limited physical resources that I did. How can they fly?

My first book report for seventh-grade reading was on *Watership Down*. It was one of the few books in the school library that I hadn't read, and it looked promising. I read the 450-page book—hardly stopping for food, water, or sleep—in a day and a half. I read lying on my side, my glasses off, the book propped on my face a few inches from my eyes because I was so nearsighted. When book reports were corrected and returned two weeks later, everyone got theirs back except for me. The teacher called me up and asked me in front of the class if my mother had written the report for me or helped me with it. No, I told her. My mother had only typed the report, but wouldn't change even a comma. The teacher looked at me suspiciously. She flipped through its pages, picked out a phrase. I had written that *Watership Down* was not formula fiction as were the Nancy Drew and Bobbsey Twins books.

"This phrase," she said. "How could you know to write about formula fiction? No seventh-grader could have written this." She said she would keep my report for now.

I told my mother what had happened. I lay awake late into the night picturing what I would say to the teacher the next day in class. The next day my mother told the school principal and counselor that I did not need to be in reading. I already knew how to read at an adult level.

I was a failure in school, an outsider. I was a girl who read books under her desk while the teacher was teaching penmanship. I was always slightly out of line—too contrary or absentminded. One reason I failed to fully adapt to the hierarchical structure of the schools was that I had already received too much education outside of school.

In school I should have learned to value hierarchical social organization. Yet the social organization I knew best was the family that consisted of my mom and me. My mom rarely imposed her law or authority based on her position above me in a hierarchy. She never said, "Because I said so, that's why" or "Because I'm the parent and you're the child."

I hated school, so I often dragged my feet in the mornings and missed the school bus. Once I had missed the school bus, I didn't want to face the embarrassment of taking the city bus and coming into school late. I felt that the city bus driver scrutinized me. "Late again." So I would miss the city bus and then I just wouldn't go.

The next day I wouldn't want to go and have everybody ask me if I was sick when I hadn't been. So it would go on this way for five school days and finally I would know I had to go back and would brace myself for everybody's questions that I would have no explanations or answers for.

Then came the day in early March when I decided I wouldn't go back, just couldn't go back. The school year had gone to seed for me like a dandelion's white crown. Each day I missed was another of the white tufts severing its fragile connection with the stem. The feathery seeds were there, almost transparent, just waiting for a bit of wind—an adolescent's ruthless laughter, friction with a teacher—to disperse them into the wide blue air, until at last there was no connection left and the stem stood naked and green. It was easy after I crossed a threshold to not go back. I had missed half a year of school before, in fourth grade, and nothing happened.

My mother supported my decision to stay out of school. She thought many of the teachers were incompetent.

We talked about getting books for homeschooling but never got around to it. We probably couldn't have afforded textbooks anyway. My mother mined newspapers for education articles. She read that Boston had good schools and was rich with cultural history. It had some of the finest universities in the world. She told me that she thought we should move to Boston so I could have better schooling. We would take the Greyhound bus.

This time I was ready, unlike when we moved to California. I was ready to shed my old sad, nervous self and fly. I would sew my costume from the transparent white fabric of a dandelion seed. I would be borne aloft to alight in a faraway place and flower again.

My mother had described Boston as an educational center, at the heart of comings and goings, the "hub of the universe." So I pictured it in the middle of the country, maybe just below Kansas, which was where my grandmother had grown up. I was surprised when I looked at the map with my mother, and Boston was a little black dot all the way in the far northeast corner of the country, on the opposite side of the continent.

"It's kind of out of the way, isn't it?" I asked my mother.

12

VIEW FROM A BUS WINDOW

WE LEFT FOR BOSTON at dusk on an early October day in 1989. I took only clothes, toothbrush, the book I was reading, my journal, and my pillow. We left behind boxes of photos, my new running shoes, my Flower Kid doll, all my books— with a friend, to be sent for later. We could have only one suit-case each and a carry-on on the bus, so we brought only the essentials.

My mom and I stood there at the small bus station—it was only a door with a small Greyhound sign above it and a small concrete lot for the bus to pull into. Once we were on the bus it was exciting, as if this odd assortment of people were leaving on some long-awaited school field trip.

The bus was the only mode of travel for poor people who didn't have money to fly. While some rode the bus for only a few hours' trip, as would seem logical, many made the bus their home for several days' journey—say from Portland, Maine, to San Diego, California. When each dawn broke, the sleepers would rise to another day on the bus. It was like being at camp, waking up with friends you had made just the day before—disheveled, wiping sleep from their eyes in the seat next to you. They had names you had never heard of before (Fernando and Miércoles, and a boy named Cody from Cody, Wyoming). We exchanged small talk or our life stories, nothing in between.

A bus contains many cultures. There were three distinct strata. The front was occupied by old people, women with canes who couldn't get around well on the bus and old couples who liked to chat with the bus driver and see the open road, the land parting in front of them. The middle of the bus was mostly families, seats crowded with diaper bags, snacks, and small children. The back seats were the smelliest because of the bathroom, and the wildest people sat there. Pot-smoking, booze-smelling cowboys and gangster kids sat near the back, as far from the driver as possible, so that their illicit activities wouldn't be noticed. People who just met made out there, or discussed making out. I sat quietly and read, only occasionally talking to a friendly person who struck up conversation.

On the bus I was only the girl in the striped shirt or the girl with dyed-red hair or the girl who slept with her hood up and her stuffed bunny rabbit in her arms.

People packed up their lives into a Greyhound bus as if it were a modern-day version of a covered wagon. They packed up their lives in bags stored beneath each seat, and the bus ventured into the unknown, into each passenger's manifest destiny, into multiple visions of the American Dream. Whether the bus was headed west or east, south or north, it always headed down the concrete road to opportunity, to an expanded new life.

The bus pushed through Montana's huge width. One small overhead light shone steady with the engine's hum, and I sat under it, writing. A lone fugitive from sleep, surrounded by the sprawled bodies with heads leaning far back against the seat cushions, mouths gaping open. Other people propped themselves against windows, pillows or clothes wedged between their faces and the cold glass.

It was hard to get comfortable, and difficult to sleep when my thoughts kept me awake. There was so much time to do nothing but think. The bus became emptier, not as many people traveling through the remote areas of this huge state. My mother slept fetuslike on two seats, her head on her purse.

Being passengers on a bus took away the responsibility we had to carry ourselves through life facing each frighteningly untraversed moment. In real life, we had to have responsibility and courage to move beyond our habits and flaws. But on the bus, we could sit back and let the vehicle carry us forward into goodness without having to do a thing. There was nothing to do but sit calmly, dreamily watching ourselves move forward into our futures, our new lives. I was in a liminal space between here and there, the east and the west, the sun and its setting, the past and what was coming. Being on the bus was a suspension of real life, a time hung on four wheels in a rectangle built of borderlines, between here and nowhere.

Each mile vanished outside the window of my consciousness. Each fugacious moment produced a strange landscape—landscapes that were gone as soon as I arrived. The pine-armored cliffs of the Oregon shore were swallowed up by the thirsty Snake River in Idaho, which disappeared inside the vast Montana sky. A sky that stretched blue and round every place I turned until it was eaten by the teeth of unwieldy North Dakotan rocks. Rocks that vanished and gave way to endless

Iowa cornfields, and brought me finally to Pennsylvania farmhouses and red-silo barns.

I was wide awake, thinking that the day after tomorrow we would arrive. I looked out at the fullness of elephant-sized rocks and rivers that contrasted with the empty sky and its one bored cloud. The cloud had no one to play with. So he played games with me, racing along, keeping up with the bus, looking for other cloud play-friends. He found some, and forgot about me. The highway carried on below the bus's wheels, overwhelmed from thinking about how far it still had to run, to the sea, to the ocean. I fell asleep exhausted by the thought of the distance the highway had come, how far I had come with it.

Our bus was rerouted, and we were now going to pass through New York City on our way to Boston. It was already the early hours of the morning as we approached the city. I noticed that the people on the bus had changed since we left Oregon. These people seemed more sophisticated, more self-contained. There were fewer families and more single people.

The road widened into an eight-lane highway. The red taillights ahead looked like measles dotting the highway's face. The green signs above pointed white arrows at the measles, naming them, names like West Portal, Bloomsbury, Pluckemin, and Irvington. I amused myself with these hideous metaphors.

Although most of the trip is a blur of moments that seemed to slip away as soon as I noticed they were there, one moment stays with me clearly. My most important memory of the four-day trip is of night shadows flitting over the bus's interior, of my head on my mother's lap somewhere in North Dakota, and of realizing that home was not a place. The castlelike home of my dreams, each of its four walls toppled outwards, the roof became a cloud and drifted away. I looked up at my mother and thought to myself that home could, perhaps, be a person.

*　　*　　*

The pillow was an embarrassment to me when we arrived on that warm orange-lit October evening. I had to carry it in the streets of downtown Boston. In my memory this then strange place appeared on a larger scale than it does now. To my eyes still dazed after disembarking from the bus's spell-like reality—leaving the lulling motor behind—Boston seemed dry, dusty, golden, and bustling with fast-moving silent blurry-faced people. I walked a block behind my mother while she carried our two pillows. Her indignation at my self-consciousness showed in her brusque walk. It meant nothing to her to be seen with a pillow. But I was twelve and wanted to die of shame for being seen walking around with my pillow. I felt like I was wearing my underwear on the outside of my clothes. I felt displaced, dragging this remnant of home around with me. I gave the pillow to my mother, dropping the responsibility of finding a place for us to stay on her, too.

13

HE IS BLUE AND I GRAY,
FRAGMENTED

DUSK GATHERED as I set down the heavy suitcases while my mother called the YWCA from a pay phone. "How old is your daughter?" came the voice through the receiver. My mother had called the Y from Oregon to check room prices. They did not mention then as they did now—"We don't take children under age eighteen."

My mother and I dragged our luggage to the nearest hotel—the Westin at Copley Place.

"We need a small room," said my mother.

"There is one room available, two hundred and fifty-nine dollars plus tax." My mother shook her head. She had only three hundred and something dollars with her. We took our bags and got on a subway to Downtown Crossing. I sat down inside the station. I was upset and tired. My hair and skin felt scummy—like things might be crawling on them from not bathing during the four-night bus ride. I leaned over and rested my head on our luggage, and started crying. My mother couldn't get me to move. A policeman came by, asking, "What's wrong?"

"We just got here—and need a place to stay but can't afford a hotel," my mother explained. The policeman went into an office and made a phone call.

"The family shelters are full," he told us. "An adult shelter—Long Island—takes families on an emergency basis. The intake is at Boston City Hospital on Massachusetts Avenue. You get on the subway here. Get off at Mass Ave and then take a bus to the hospital."

The bus wheezed and bumped along to Boston City Hospital, a many-storied cement building. Even from far away, we saw its covered bridge crossing over Massachusetts Avenue. As we drew closer, we saw the panoply of people, a line of mostly men, some young, some old, some drunk, some not, some black, and some white. People were searched, then let into the waiting room inside the big glass walls. In the waiting room were rows of chairs and also cots for the overflow that would not make it into the shelter.

My mother and I waited in line with our suitcases, my mother holding the pillow. A middle-aged man walked by us, talking loudly to an invisible audience, ". . . so pathetic. I can't believe that God even likes human beings, they're such assholes." A lady next to us was dreadfully deformed, her face half sickly white and half covered by a splotchy dark purple birthmark, her throat with large bulges protruding from it in the wrong places. She looked at me and said, "It's the right time of year for it!" with a horrible cackling laugh. Another man shuffled toward us in a soiled orange quilted coat. He stood for a moment and said "Hello," then shuffled away again. The tall, thin man in front of us with a majestic blond mane looked like a cross between a lion and a frizzy Barbie doll. He elegantly held a tattered paperback, flipping the pages. He stopped to carefully underline a few sentences. "How are you today, madam?" he said to my mother, pulling out a stenographer's notebook. He told us he was writing a film and a novel.

A woman searched us quickly for weapons. I put my arms up and out like a bird ready to burst into flight. The woman slid her hands along my upper and lower arms, my torso, and then the inside and outside of my pants legs before motioning me onward. My mother and I signed a list of names. We were told to see the nurse—across the street in the hospital's other wing. She would help us begin paperwork to be admitted to a family shelter and given assistance. I began crying again, big gasps for breath. These were birthing tears. I was twelve and this was happening again. I couldn't have explained how I felt then—overwhelmed, young, torn apart, without anything to latch on to, like a lone molecule in space.

One of the centers in my life is that first evening in Boston, a twelve-year-old girl standing under Boston City Hospital's bridge. Thoreau wrote in *Walden*, "This is the only way, we say; but there are as many ways as there can be drawn radii from one centre." All the events of my life in Boston in the following years are lines radiating from this center. The lines of hundreds of possible and actual events, an infinity of possible radii, trace a large circle around this girl, protecting her. She has become almost invisible. I can hardly see her, but I am never far from her either. I run circles around that girl, who still stands there, blank, unknowing.

When I see her I want to reach out and stay, stay among

those who didn't have their own homes to live in. Stay with those who used the old rusty doorless toilets in the long cement women's bathroom at the Long Island Shelter, where we stayed those first weeks. The showers with yellowed curtains, the mildewed pipes and faucets, industrial sinks down the middle. I want to hold her, hold on to her. These feelings and images flash upon my mind, and I squint my eyes at the shadowy memories, the senescent memory of pain.

Eventually we boarded one of the buses of people leaving for the shelter. It took us to Long Island, one of thirty small islands in the Boston Harbor, part of a National Guard base. On our way there we stopped and the bus driver talked to a guard. A blockade was lifted for the bus to pass. We crossed a bridge and arrived at the island.

At the shelter, there was another sign-in desk in the hallway. The shelter nurse gave us a tour and showed us where to get sheets in the basement. She told us that this was a shelter for five hundred adult men, one hundred adult women, and only a few families. She guessed that over three-quarters of the shelter guests were infected with HIV.

The shelter was a rat's maze of cubicles whose walls rose only to eye level: full of corners with cots and hundreds of flimsy metal bunk beds. Coughs of tuberculosis echoed through the black cubicles at night. The family room was down the hall, near the stairwell, away from the other beds. Next to it was the "lounge"—a bleak linoleum-floored classroom-sized room with just one bright orange couch in the middle of it. The TV was hooked to the ceiling with hinges like those in hospital waiting rooms, so that no one could change the channel. A few other chairs with clipboardlike desks were scattered around the room.

*

The family room was the same size as the lounge and had several cots in it. Roaches crawled leisurely across the floors. Only one other family was with us while we were there. The mother, Virginia, spoke mostly Spanish but was friendly. She talked to her eight-year-old son, Jimmy, and then he—slightly impatiently—translated for us.

We slept in the little cots in the empty, windowless room. At 5:00 A.M., fluorescent lights were turned on so that Jimmy could get ready for school. His school was far away in Jamaica Plain, where he had lived before becoming homeless. He took three buses and arrived at school by 7:45. I hadn't started school yet, and I thought that Jimmy's early departures must be one of the more disagreeable parts of becoming homeless. I turned my head into the white pillowcase and squeezed my eyes shut.

I woke up groggy and worn-out. My mother wanted to let me sleep, but we had to get up. We had already missed breakfast and had to rush. The last bus left at 8:30, and everyone had to be out.

We got off the bus in Chinatown and walked down Washington Street to the ABCD housing office, where we were to spend much of almost every day for the next few weeks. On our way there, we passed theaters with marquees proclaiming XX ADULTS ONLY, NUDE GIRLS, and signs that read ADULT BOOKSTORE.

Late in the afternoon we returned to Boston City Hospital, to stand in line and be searched again. The first bus was too full, so we waited for the next.

When we got back to the shelter, a box that I had left in the family room had been taken. In the box were a book, a hair crimper I got for Christmas the year before, and a few souvenirs from the bus ride. I learned that anything could disappear at any time. I was a little sad because the things were lost, but mostly I felt let down to think that someone thought it okay to steal. "Maybe whoever has it needs it more than you do," my mom said. What she said helped me to feel more peaceful and forgiving.

This time we made it to the shelter in time for dinner. The dining room was full of circular tables. As I made my way through the Twister game of tables, I was aware that I was the only person in the large crowded room who was not an adult. My mother and I sat at a table with two young black men.

One of the young men introduced himself as Benjamin. He was tall, thin, and handsome, with a big white smile and a gold tooth that shone in his dark brown face. He had kind dark eyes and joked with me like a big brother. He was only nineteen. I developed a crush on him during the three weeks we stayed at the shelter. He would have been my second pick for a future husband, after the New Kids on the Block's Donnie Wahlberg. One morning when we got off the bus, he gave me a pack of Paradise Punch gum that was squashed flat from being in his back pocket. I carried that gum around all week. It smelled like Benjamin, a combination of Paradise Punch and a musky masculine smell. Now when I pick up a pack of this gum in a convenience store, I remember being twelve almost thirteen, standing underneath the concrete bridge of the Boston City, looking up into Benjamin's grinning face and being completely infatuated with him.

James was the other young man at the table. He was black or Latino with light skin, a big nose and mouth, long eyelashes, and tight curly hair. He was an artist and constantly drew in his sketch pad. All his sketches were of robotic, metallically muscular women holding machine guns. He offered to draw a picture of me, but I was a little alarmed by the idea of being drawn with large pointy, triangular breasts that looked more like weapons than body parts.

Most of the adults at the shelter loved to talk to my mother and me because they didn't have children in their lives. If they did have children, they were separated from them and did not often see them.

That night I saw a man in a big white turban sitting at a nearby table. I had never seen anyone like him. I wondered why he wore it. There were adults of all ages, races, and religions at the shelter. In spite of this diversity, I didn't witness any conflicts. At dinnertime everyone was worn out from being outside all day. We were just thankful to be inside for the night, sitting down, eating food. I imagine it was like a less severe version of a concentration camp. The people here were so weary and numbed that they did not have energy to waste on prejudice or ill will.

After dinner we went down to the basement. A man in a small room passed us our thin white sheets from behind a half door with a shallow ledge. In the morning we would return them to the big-wheeled laundry bins to be washed.

In the basement, I saw the turbaned man again. He knelt on a mat on the floor, his arms stretched out in front of him, head bowed, facing diagonally into one of the concrete cinder-block walls. His white robe draped around him and matched his turban. He lowered his torso to the floor again and again. I was very curious.

I sat near him the next night at dinner. He was friendly and smiled, so I did not feel nervous. His name was Ibrahim. I asked him why he wore the turban, and he said he was Muslim. Even from the rough cement floor of the shelter basement, he knew the direction of the shining minarets of

Mecca's most sacred shrine, the Kaaba. He bowed and prayed this way three times a day—at dawn, sunset, and night (and twice more in the day while he was out). Before he prayed, he washed his hands and feet, face and mouth, he told me, so he would be cleansed when he said the prayer. His simple turban and seamless white robe symbolized that all Muslims were equal before God, called Allah. His prayers gave him faith to achieve his goals. "I am a recovering alcoholic," he told me. "I've applied to a halfway house. I hope that I can move there soon." I was impressed that he kept up his faith and religious practices despite the disorienting and chaotic poverty of the shelter.

"Do you like to play checkers?" he asked me next.

We didn't have a checkerboard, but Ibrahim thought we might be able to make one. That evening he stopped by the family room with a square of cardboard and a permanent marker. With the marker, he made a grid on the cardboard, coloring every other square in black. I found an old puzzle in the lounge. Many of its pieces were missing, but I picked out pieces of gray clouds and others of blue sky to use as checkers. We each sat on a plastic milk crate in the hallway and put the checkerboard on another between us. He was blue and I gray, fragmented pieces of sky and cloud.

We played checkers each evening outside the family room. Some of the men stopped by to watch, giving advice on moves and telling jokes. There was little to do or see in the shelter, so our checkers games attracted much interest. Many of the men who came by knew Ibrahim. Most of them were respectful of the fact that I was a twelve-year-old girl. They didn't use foul language in my presence and were gentlemanly and polite. Children were scarce in the shelter, and were treated with awe and indulgence. I didn't feel vulnerable, because my mother and Virginia were nearby in the family room or lounge, and the shelter staff was there to keep the guests under control. Eight-year-old Jimmy lingered around, wanting me to play with him. But I liked the checker games with Ibrahim. They took my mind off the future's uncertainty, and all I had to focus on was the next move to make with the puzzle pieces.

One evening I went into the lounge to read. A skinny black woman in tight white pants and an orange shirt sat on the bright hospital waiting-room couch with one knee up, craning her neck up to stare vacantly at the TV. Helene, as she introduced herself, began to talk without stopping, telling me all about her family, her boyfriend who had a Mercedes and her father, that she was thirty-two and her favorite color was blue, that there was this one time and . . . She was so friendly and really liked to talk. I mentioned that to a couple of women in the bathroom the next day. They laughed and said, "Oh, honey, don't mind her. She's always all coked up." I was puzzled because the only drugs I knew of were alcohol and marijuana, which had distinct smells. I thought that all drugs had smells so that you could tell when someone was on one. People were supposed to look sleepy or act more strangely when they were on drugs. It was new to me that anyone could be on a drug at any time and I wouldn't know the difference. I knew little, less than I had thought.

One day in the shelter's back stairwell, a toothless man came up behind me. He put his arm around my waist and stumbled. "'lo little girl. Do you have a boyfriend?" He pushed me into the landing's corner, mumbling, "I'd jump your bones myself." He left his arm there for a few moments before I said, "No." I tried to slip away and continue down the stairs.

A large strong-looking black woman came down the stairs behind us. She directed a few curses at the stumbling man and walked with me down the stairs.

"I'm Hilda," she said. "Anybody mess wit' you, you let me know."

Hilda became my friend. We would talk and hang out in the women's bathroom. She was a recovering coke addict. She was cheerful and welcoming and made everyone feel comfortable. I felt better when she was near because she was so powerful and self-assured. She would say, "Here, now, I need a big old hug, so that I won't be wanting to go out on those streets lookin' for a fix." She was struggling hard to overcome her addiction, because she had a daughter my age from whom she was separated and whom she missed very much.

I felt proud and like I belonged when she offered to braid my hair in cornrows. I pictured my hair stuck to my head in lines and patterns, tiny braids like little ropes swinging out from my head. But we moved out of the shelter before she braided my hair.

14

THE QUARTERDECK INN

WE STAYED AT the Long Island Shelter for three weeks. The family shelters in Boston were overly full. To create more affordable housing, the government provides housing vouchers—Section 8's—that can be applied to any housing which meets government guidelines, provided the landlord agrees to participate in the program. However, there were long waiting lists for Section 8's, so the welfare agency paid for homeless families to live in "welfare motels." The Boston motels were full, so we were placed at the Quarterdeck Inn in the town of Hull, about ten miles south of Boston.

Hull was a long skinny town built along a narrow peninsula. It was a blue-collar community and a winter ghost town with scarcely ten thousand people. In the summer its population swelled to almost fifty thousand when people visited its five miles of beaches.

The Quarterdeck Inn was two stories of weathered gray wood, ringed by a large upper deck. The manager, Agatha, was Polish American and wore her hair in a bun. Stern and quiet, she did not socialize with the guests. Patty, the cleaning woman, was plump and motherly and had a bleached yellow-white mane of hair. She had kind squinty blue eyes and talked in a slow southern drawl. She called everyone baby. "Hi, baby! How's your mama?" she called down the hall whenever she saw me coming.

Everyone on the floor shared the bathroom, which was also a kitchen, because dishes were washed in the sinks, and a laundry room—we washed clothes and wrung them out in the showers.

The residents were mostly black and Latina single mothers. My mother and I were the only white residents at the hotel.

We had one small room with a double bed. Patty wheeled in a cot for me, but when folded out, it took up all the floor space. After a while I gave up and slept in the bed with my mom.

We had a small refrigerator in our room. Many of the welfare motels didn't. In another hotel, a woman we knew kept her two-year-old daughter's milk cold by putting it outside the window ledge. She had to stop when the motel management said it was against the rules. "It's so hard—we eat junk food all the time because we can't cook or keep anything cool," she complained. Food stamps can't buy restaurant meals either, so people in the welfare hotels often have no way to eat regular, balanced meals. At least at the shelter we ate two hot meals a day. But at the Quarterdeck Inn we were lucky in another way. Agatha put a microwave in the lobby for us. Each evening a long line of mothers waited to use the microwave.

I turned thirteen a few days after we moved to the Quarterdeck. It was a special day, my mother said, because I was going to be a teenager. She told me I was lucky my birthday was at the beginning of the month because she still had money then and could afford to get the boom box I'd been longing for. It was a big, awkwardly rectangular contraption with a red power light and little green lights that danced up and down with the music. It cost one hundred dollars, almost one-third of our monthly welfare check. At first, I propped the radio against the wall at the foot of my cot because there was no room on the floor. The first tape I got was Ziggy Marley and the Melody Makers' *One Bright Day*. The first nights there I sometimes felt sad or nervous. As I went to sleep I watched the little green lights dancing up and down and felt comforted.

Hull was a difficult place to live, especially in winter. There were few stores—no places to buy clothes or other daily needs. There was only one small expensive grocery store. The penny arcades, a carousel, and many of the restaurants closed during the winter. One rickety old bus went between Hull and the neighboring town of Hingham. It came only once every two hours. It had high-backed green seats like a school bus. Once a week my mother took this bus to Hingham, and then another bus into Quincy, and from Quincy she took the subway into Boston to go to the welfare office for a voucher for the hotel.

The hotel cost $250 a week for one room. We had lived in subsidized apartments before, with vouchers that the government paid to the landlords. I had a good understanding of housing policy, housing subsidies. I didn't understand why the government wouldn't create more housing subsidies rather than pay almost $1,000 a month for each hotel room. My mother's trip to get the hotel voucher would take an entire day. They wouldn't send the money to the hotel. Paperwork and bureaucratic procedures are designed to ensure that homeless and poor people "work" for what they are given.

Ironically, the bureaucratic hurdles also ensure that poor people are left with less time to actually look for jobs or advance themselves—little time to do anything other than get by; like hamsters on a wheel, they are left continually dependent on the system. When she came back it was time to get in line for the microwave.

Once in a while a local bakery would donate its leftovers. The dozens of stale donuts were dumped into a big cardboard box in the hotel lobby. Everyone at the hotel took some, but there were still so many left—crumbled up donut pieces, the cinnamon with the powdered, the jelly and chocolate frosting smeared around the edges of the box, coconut and butternut. People didn't seem to like the plain ones and the cinnamon ones. They were left for last. After school I would be hungry and pick out a few pieces and eat them as I went up the stairs. The donuts dwindled into masses of crumbs. Finally, someone threw the box out.

Val and Gabi Lopez were my best friends at the Quarterdeck. A few days after we moved in they invited me to watch TV in their room. Val was fifteen, in the ninth grade at Hull Junior-Senior High School. She was tall and slender with curly black hair that she wore in bangs and two little tufts at the top of her head. Her sister Gabi was fourteen and shorter, with a rounder face, paler skin, and a thick mane of perfectly spiraled curls.

They lived in a small upstairs apartment, separate from the other rooms, with its own weathered gray staircase and a small deck. It had a living room, one small bedroom, a tiny kitchenette and bathroom. It seemed luxuriously big compared to my mother's and my room, but eight people lived there. Val and Gabi had a younger brother, Marcos—called

Macho because he was the only boy. The youngest, Elena, was nine. Their parents—Nestor and Gloria—and an uncle and a cousin often slept there as well.

The Hull school wouldn't let me start until they had my records from Astoria, and those were several weeks in coming. This delay keeps many homeless children out of school. If a child moves several times a year, he or she may hardly attend at all.

Hull was my first experience with tracked classrooms. The eighth grade was divided into five levels: 8-1 through 8-5. I started off in the lowest track, 8-5, maybe because they placed all new students there, or because that was usually the level in which students from the welfare hotels were placed.

I was soon moved up to 8-1, and then the only class Gabi was in with me was Spanish. We sat in the back and passed notes back and forth every day. Spanish was useful because many of my friends and people I met in the shelters spoke Spanish. When grades came in, I got an A, but Gabi got a C, because she never paid attention to where she put the accent marks or exact grammar and spelling. "No fair!" Gabi said but didn't really care—she thought it funny. But I felt that something was not right. The grades didn't show who was more fluent in Spanish. School was not reflective of real life.

Doing homework was hard because there was no place to spread out the textbooks and papers. I sat on the bed's edge, balancing my textbook on my lap. I often spent afternoons at Val and Gabi's apartment, sitting on a couch cushion doing homework while watching cartoons with them.

Val loved to pretend she was a singer in a pop band. She wrote a song, "Boy, You Play Me for a Fool." I was impressed that she wrote a tune as well as lyrics. She performed using a hairbrush for a microphone. Someday we might be famous singers, if we could just get instruments, maybe a keyboard, and a microphone.

I often slept over at Val and Gabi's apartment, and we would go to sleep while the adults were still dancing, listening to Spanish-language radio. One night Nestor asked the DJ to dedicate a song to all of us. "*Escucha! Escucha!* Listen!" he said. As the song began, the DJ said a string of Spanish syllables, and then I recognized our names. "*Y esta canción está dedicada a* Nestor, Gloria, Val, Gabrielle, Lauralee, Marcos, *y* Elena . . . *en* Hull . . ." How strange and wonderful it was to hear my name—embraced by a foreign language and the names of my new friends.

They let us four girls sleep in the bedroom. We piled over each other in the double bed like matchsticks in a matchbox. The best thing was falling asleep in the middle and waking up surrounded by the comfort of warm bodies, one of Gabi's thick legs flung across my knees and her arm over my stomach, Val's face inches from mine on the pillow.

I was lulled to sleep by the rhythmic percussion of the waves outside the window, crashing and resounding, singing a nighttime lullaby. My eyes closed, I pictured the dark blue-brown waves rolling up into solid peaks glistening in the moonlight, then the foam—white as snowdrifts. I felt the waves' undertow pulling me down, away from the sandy shore of alertness. I imagined we were adrift in a boat, tight in a cabin's bunk, on our way to the lily-covered edge of the world like Prince Caspian in *The Voyage of the Dawn Treader.*

One night at the motel, while I was sleeping in my own room, my mother and I were awakened by screams. A woman who had two children was arguing loudly with her boyfriend in the hallway. He had a knife and said he would use it on her. She had a gun and said she'd shoot if he did. I was awake now and had to use the bathroom but didn't dare to. I peeked out through the door's chain latch. The women from neighboring rooms were in the hallway whispering among themselves. They glanced at me as they talked. It was 2:00 A.M. Through my window, I saw flashing lights and heard sirens of police cars arriving outside. The policemen came up and pulled apart the fighting couple.

The next day my bloodshot eyes burned with tiredness. A girl in the row across from me in English said, "I heard there was police at the Quarterdeck last night."

"Yeah," said another girl, "I heard about that." Everyone was interested.

When I got home, I turned on my radio and lay down and didn't wake up until the next morning. I realized I hadn't done any of my homework. But my teachers understood. They'd heard about the fight from the kids in school.

The day after the knife fight, my mother went to a regional real estate office to look for a room or apartment we might afford.

The real estate agent knew a woman in a town farther down the shore who had a room for rent and also needed a part-time caretaker for her son, who was paralyzed in an accident when he was fifteen. My mother called this woman and made arrangements with her. My mother would take care of the son for five dollars an hour. His mother, Hope, said that our rent would be $105 a week. This amount was far less than what the government paid for our room at the Quarterdeck— but it would be harder for us to get by now, because we had to pay this amount without help from a government subsidy. It was expensive for one room, but we could use the kitchen and laundry room, too. The money my mother made taking care of the son would help pay the rent.

We called a taxi and gave the Lopez family good-bye hugs. The taxi arrived, and we moved our belongings to our new residence.

15

SEASHORE DRIVE

THE SMALL ROOM had two twin beds and was unheated. My mom had an outdoor thermometer that we used indoors. The red streak of mercury often rose only to fifty degrees when the temperature dropped below freezing outside, every day and night during that long winter. The house on the beach was unprotected from freezing winds that cut through clothing and flesh like sharp knives. I was used to the temperate climate of Oregon, and had never known such cold before. I did homework on the floor, leaning against one of the beds, wearing layers of sweaters and tights under my jeans. The rest of the house was warm.

Eric, my mom's part-time charge, was handsome and good-natured. But he was almost completely paralyzed from the neck down. My mother enjoyed taking care of him. He had many friends and interests and often called up radio talk shows to give his opinion. He was reconciled to his handicap, and never let it stop him from doing what he wanted. Though he couldn't feel his own hands, he could feed himself with metal devices that held a spoon or a fork attached to his wrists.

After we lived there a few weeks, Hope revealed another side of herself: screaming fits, directed toward me, sometimes toward my mother. She yelled at my mother for removing her clothes from the washer and putting them in the dryer so that she could do her own laundry. My mother did no harm by moving Hope's clothes. She only meant to help. But Hope wanted to be in control and was unforgiving and irrational about even small things. To her, my mother and I were sub-human. Although we were allowed to use the laundry room, we should have to wait while Hope's clothes sat in the washer. She was the ruler, the queen. We were her unworthy subjects. We could pay our rent to her, so that she could go shopping at Talbots for expensive clothes, but we were not to make our-selves seen, felt, or heard in any way. If we did, we were sub-ject to Hope's tirades.

One day I came out of our room and was about to go down-stairs when I overheard Hope talking to friends, saying, "They're two homeless people I took in off of the street," and laughing. She portrayed herself as kind and generous, when in truth my mother paid around $450 a month—almost all the money we had—for the small freezing room. I walked down the stairs past Hope, saying nothing. I went out to the beach, and ran and ran, past the jagged blocks of frozen surf that were as big as people, to the end of the shoreline. I took my ponytail holder out and let my hair blow behind, exhaling all the tension and sadness I felt, inhaling forgiving sea air. I headed back. I felt better, enough for that day at least.

*

One day at dusk, I was cooking macaroni and cheese at the stove when the lights went out, leaving me in murky darkness.

"You don't need the light," Hope said as she walked past, with a steely gaze, challenging me. She did this kind of thing often, handing me a broom when I walked across the kitchen. "You've made the floor dirty, you can sweep it."

It was my fault if anything was out of place and needed cleaning. I was personally responsible for all the dust in the house. I was a diabolical dust producer. I had the superpower of creating chaos and filth wherever I walked.

And I didn't need light; I didn't deserve light.

I turned the light back on. "You little bitch," she said. "I ought to smack you right now." She leaned in and waved her hand at my face, poked me in the chest, turned the light back off.

"I thought you were bright," she said to me another time, flinging a toilet paper roll at my face. "Don't you even know how to put the toilet paper on the holder?" She wanted the paper to roll out from the side near the wall so that it would be harder to pull off.

Another time, she couldn't find a package of food she had bought. I was in the room upstairs and she yelled up, "You ate it! I ought to throw you and your mother out of here!"

I couldn't hold back. "I didn't eat it. I've never taken anything of yours!"

She ran up the staircase toward me, but I escaped into the room and shut the door. Later that evening, my mother and I were arguing. The door was half-open. Hope bounded toward me. She shook me by the shoulders, her long fingers and nails like metallic claws digging into my skin. She pointed her finger in my face and pushed me back against the wall, yelling at the top of her lungs and shouting to my mother as well. I didn't even know what she was screaming about. I didn't say a word back.

"Thank goodness you didn't say anything back to her," my mother said. "That was good of you."

I started crying and screaming at my mother. "I hate it here! I can't live here!" I grew hysterical. I felt so miserable and hopeless. No one cared, no one was looking out for me. Not even my mother, who was just glad that I hadn't talked back to Hope. I kept crying and put my leg over the upstairs railing, threatening to throw myself over. My mother tried to pull me off. The entire time, Hope rasped out threats at me from downstairs.

"I wish I had pills!" I screamed at my mother. "Where are some? I wish I could take them so I could die!" I tried to dash for the bathroom medicine cabinet, but my mom blocked me. Hope kept screeching obscenities.

"She wants me to die," I said. "Why don't I just get it over with?"

I don't think I really wanted to kill myself. I wanted someone to notice that my basic human needs weren't being met. The next day my mother called the Department of Social Services (DSS) and told them that she didn't know what to do with me. She said that I needed to be placed in a foster home because she was unable to provide adequate shelter for me. Most children placed in DSS are taken from their parents because of neglect, abandonment, or abuse. Parents can also voluntarily place their children in DSS care if they feel unable to adequately care for them, which is what my mother did. This decision was difficult for my mother; it tore her heart out to be separated from me.

It might have seemed that my mother was abandoning me, but I felt that she was finally making the best decision to take care of me.

My mother stayed on at Hope's for a short time after I left. She liked Eric and wanted somehow to continue to take care of him without having to live there. One night Hope locked her out in the cold. My mom hadn't been given a key because someone was always home. My mother walked to a pay phone and called the police. They came and told Hope that she had to let my mother in.

The next day, my mom moved to Father Bill's, an adult shelter in Quincy.

16

REFUGE

THE CAR PULLED into the driveway of a big brown house with leaves of green trees arching down overhead. The wind rustled the branches outside my new foster home in Braintree.

I wondered what it would be like living in a house without my mother, a house full of strangers. I got out of the car with my social worker and my mother. Four frantic dogs barked and ran around me. My new foster mother's name was Mrs. Sargent, a name that sounded like she didn't stand for any nonsense. We entered the kitchen, and the fading sunlight hit the equally faded plastic tablecloth as we all sat down. A tall girl about my age with long brown braids hung around the kitchen doorway to see who the new girl was. I sat shyly and properly and let the adults talk. The social worker talked about how Mrs. Sargent was one of the best foster parents in DSS. She'd cared for foster children—hundreds of them, in and out—for the past thirty years. My mother was anxious to know I would be in a good place and looked reassured.

My mom gave me a big hug. I knew our separation would be temporary.

So then I was left all alone, immersed in this strange new world, but I rather liked it—living in a bouncing house with seven children and Mrs. Sargent, who really *wouldn't* stand for any nonsense. Her home was exactly what I needed then, in eighth grade: orderly life with a stable sense of community.

Mrs. Sargent was tiny, with intent blue eyes and short dark brown hair. She was a school crossing guard and had been for thirty years. Each morning when we went downstairs she was sitting at the head of the kitchen table, in her blue uniform with shiny brass buttons and matching cap, the fluorescent orange sash across her torso. She didn't eat the hot breakfasts she cooked for us; instead she ate handfuls of dry cereal from the box that lay on its side on the table in front of her. She was a widow; her husband, Mr. Sargent, had died the year before.

Nicole was the girl with long braids and almond-shaped brown eyes I'd seen the first day. She was a year younger than I was, and we became good friends. She was tall, slim and pretty, excitable and wistful. She had a diagonal scar just below her nose through her upper lip, from being hit by a piece of broken pottery. And one of her ears was ripped where an earring had been yanked out. She had repierced her ear just above the rip and always wore earrings so that the tear wouldn't show.

Nicole had moved into Mrs. Sargent's because her older sister, Melissa, was already living there. Melissa, who was seventeen, was always up before the rest of us. She drank only black coffee for breakfast, and her boyfriend, Mike, picked her up while the rest of us were still eating. She was a senior at Braintree High and often stayed up late doing schoolwork or going out with Mike. Nicole and I often fell asleep to the sounds of her big manual typewriter—*clickety clack clack.*

Melissa was almost an adult. She could have been adopted by Mrs. Sargent but wasn't—out of loyalty to her parents, or perhaps because she was independent enough to take care of herself. She was very organized, strong, and self-sufficient.

Nicole, however, was torn up inside—rebellious and sweet by turns. Melissa and Nicole's mother had abandoned them when Nicole was three and gone back to her hometown in Texas. She occasionally sent cards with pictures of herself and their four-year-old half sister, Penelope. Their father was in and out of jail for drugs. Nicole tested everyone by acting aggressive and angry to see if we would leave, if we wouldn't love her anymore. She was searching for an identity, a perfect family, just as I was.

Between ages five and seven, Nicole lived with a foster family who wanted to adopt her, but her father wouldn't allow it. Massachusetts law mandated that a child under age fourteen must have permission from her biological parents to be adopted. Nicole would sometimes to live with her father for a short time, before returning to DSS care when he went back to jail or neglected her once again. From ages seven to nine, Nicole had been shuttled through a few more foster homes before going to Mrs. Sargent's. The family who had wanted to adopt her still sent presents on her birthdays and Christmas, and she saw them occasionally. She hoped to be adopted by them when she was fourteen, and this hope prevented her from feeling too at home with Mrs. Sargent, although she loved Mrs. Sargent very much.

The youngest children were Carl, Sissy, and Danny, ages eight, seven, and six, respectively. They were biological brothers and sister and had been living with Mrs. Sargent for almost three years.

Carl was pale and serious for his age. Sissy and Danny were ruddy cheeked, with big unsmiling eyes, long eyelashes, and Cupid's bow mouths. They were small boned and had limbs that looked easily breakable. Sissy was strikingly pretty, with round blue eyes the color of the ocean at midnight, and charcoal black straight hair cut in a short bob. They were quiet, though when they spoke it was with adultlike cynicism.

At one point they went back to live with their family in a town several miles away. One early afternoon shortly thereafter, Sissy showed up at Mrs. Sargent's doorstep, dressed in a thin T-shirt and shorts on a chilly spring day. She had walked the long distance from her parents' house to visit Mrs. Sargent. Her parents had left her and Danny and Carl at home by themselves for the weekend. Mrs. Sargent called DSS, and then Sissy and her brothers came back to stay with us.

The house was bustling with children and dogs, and two of Mrs. Sargent's grown children also lived there.

Jan, Mrs. Sargent's youngest daughter, was in her early twenties and lived in a room down the hall from ours. She was the owner of the four big dogs and a big aquarium full of fish.

Mrs. Sargent's older son, Keith, lived in his own apartment in the basement. Mrs. Sargent's was a home that no one liked to leave. Keith's son, Keithie, lived with his mother, but he visited often. He was thirteen, a gawky, lanky teenager with glasses.

Phillip, an eleven-year-old Korean boy with a chunky round face and belly, moved in soon after I did. He was sullen and slouched, his dark hair flopping over his eyes. He dressed in jeans and a collection of T-shirts with rock band logos or cartoon characters and sarcastic sayings. Although he was Korean, he had spent most of his life in a Chinese foster home. He was unfriendly at first, and would speak only to add a negative comment to the conversation. Soon we all got along, though, and he became only as annoying as any brother would be. He brought with him a little jar of bright orange-flecked hot sauce that he put on everything, even peanut butter and jelly sandwiches. I tried one of these sandwiches, but it was so spicy that my face puckered up like a shoelace being pulled tight.

Phillip often ran away. Jan and Keith would go out with flashlights to look for him, and usually found him in a nearby park. He wouldn't want to come back. They would talk to him and convince him to return. From our upstairs window, I watched Jan and Keith drive away and then pull up again a while later with Phillip in the backseat.

While he was at Mrs. Sargent's, Phillip grew taller and thinner and began to smile more. When I went back to visit my old foster home after several months' absence, I scarcely recognized Phillip because he looked like a different person, with a neat short haircut and all the plumpness gone out of his face and body. He looked more like any other healthy, active twelve-year-old boy.

And then there was Toby, a nine-year-old with buckteeth, eyes that looked ready to pop out of his head, and a huge smile. He came to us covered with bruises and welts all over his arms and back. He wouldn't talk about it and was very loyal to his family. His younger brother was still living with their parents. I winced when I thought of Toby's damaged back, imagining how scared and guilty he must feel, and wondering how his little brother was faring.

Toby was the foil to Phillip's sullenness. He was one of the most lovable and exasperating children I'd ever met. He told long, outrageous stories. They were so obviously exaggerated that Mrs. Sargent would have to hide her smile behind her hand while the rest of us rolled our eyes and looked at each other, trying to keep straight faces. He was hyperactive and bothered even the younger children with his need for attention.

The boys slept in bunk beds in a downstairs bedroom. Toby wet the bed almost every night. He wouldn't tell Mrs. Sargent, but Carl, Danny, or Phillip complained that their room smelled. Mrs. Sargent made Toby take the sheets down to the basement and put them in the washer. Soon he got used to doing this task and would emerge from the boys' bedroom each morning, his buckteeth hidden behind tightened lips, carrying the bundled sheets and rushing right past us, down the stairs, as if he had an urgent errand to run. At night, he'd want to drink lots of water and we would remind him not to.

He bit his nails into jagged stubs, making it difficult to peel an orange without the juice stinging his raw fingertips. He jabbed and scratched away at the top skin of the orange, and then bit into it just as if it were an apple. He made Nicole and me watch as strings of sticky orange pulp slid down his chin and his face filled with delight. He explained to us how we too could eat an orange in such a way, as if it were an exciting new discovery, before finally throwing the ravaged remains in the trash and wiping his sticky fingers on his jeans. Nicole and I shook our heads in amazement and disgust.

The day before Toby's first supervised visit with his family, he was so nervous that his body quivered with excess energy and tension.

"Mrs. Sargent, can I clean? Mrs. Sargent, I'm going to clean." He looked at her anxiously, rocking from toes to heels and eagerly reaching for the bottle of Fantastik and sponge she handed him. He ricocheted around the house, squirting and wiping down every surface. Doorframes, door handles, counters, all the kitchen appliances, behind the toaster, the cupboards, inside the cupboards, the table legs, chair legs and backs, the windowsills.

His desire to clean was touching, just like a kid to believe that if he works hard enough to clean everything up around him, he can clean up his own life and make all the people in it gleaming and perfect, too.

I remembered myself at age nine, how I, like Toby, had been uprooted to a strange place, how I couldn't express my feelings and instead acted out in other ways. He must have remembered the bad times when his parents had hit him, and how ashamed he might have felt when his bruises were discovered. But he must have remembered the good times, too. He had showed us a picture of his family, the four of them sitting close together and smiling happily. Did he feel guilty that in some way he had betrayed his parents?

"Lauralee, look how clean I made this! See—how smooth!" He stroked his hand over the white counter and shiny cookie canister with a big toothy smile of pride, his eyes looking as if they would pop out of his head like two twenty-five-cent Super Balls.

My foster siblings were strong. Like myself, they didn't think they'd had hard lives. They accepted their lives as normal. They didn't know better than to find joy in each day in any way they could. There were hard times, clouds of confusion, darkness, and little joy, but why dwell on those? In order to survive, they believed their lives were good enough as they were. When I thought of all that they had been through, I was amazed. My life was incomparably easy.

I had never lived with an abusive or neglectful parent. My

mother had never been in jail or done drugs. She had always sacrificed her own desires to give me time and attention. She took care of my physical and emotional needs and education, though not in a traditional way. My life seemed enormously rich in some ways, compared to those of the other children.

During the first weeks at Mrs. Sargent's, I slept in a queen-sized bed in a room off the upstairs hallway, and Nicole and Sissy slept in twin beds in the spacious sunny room at the hallway's end. Nicole and I yelled between rooms so loudly that Mrs. Sargent soon moved Sissy into the hallway room and me in with Nicole.

Nicole and I pushed our twin beds together and pretended they were one big bed. We giggled incorrigibly well past our bedtimes. She was the sister I'd always wanted.

Each school morning after Nicole and I awoke and dressed, we went in to wake Sissy. We pulled her clothes from the drawers—a small pink shirt and matching stretch pants. She was sleeping diagonally across the huge bed, her limbs unconcernedly askew. We laughed at her, a little princess with a huge room all her own and a queen-sized bed when none of the other children except Melissa had their own rooms.

We pulled her covers off and poked her until her blue eyes opened wide. She was still dazed and pink from sleep, her dark pixielike hair uncombed. We dressed her and then hurtled downstairs. Every school morning we had eggs and toast, or pancakes, or French toast (four pieces for each of us), or hot cereal. I appreciated the set things Mrs. Sargent did to take care of us, like cooking a hot breakfast each day. I loved her reliability and order.

After school, we had a small snack—two or three cookies and milk, or a banana. Then I would go upstairs and sit at my little desk doing homework until Mrs. Sargent yelled up the stairs at dinnertime. The younger kids took turns setting the table.

Mrs. Sargent often made a tuna casserole that I loved. But her ham, cheese, and potato casserole soon became my favorite meal. It was so thick, savory, and nourishing. It made me feel so good.

After dinner, Nicole, Phillip, and I washed the dishes and put the food away. We divided these tasks among us, alternating who would do what on each night. Even Phillip liked the New Kids, so we often sang "I'll Be Loving You (Forever)" as we cleaned up. Phillip had a better falsetto than Nicole or I did.

All my life I had lived with my mom in crowded rooms of shelters or small apartments. I lived with piles of newspapers, clothes, and junk that seemed to close in on me, tall piles that lurked in corners, threatening to topple. I felt claustrophobic and disorganized, but I was so used to it that I assumed chaos was part of my being.

When I lived with my mother, I would forget why I had to go to school. I spent many days wandering back to the apartment after missing the bus, with my head in a book, my mind far away, thoughts sailing in the deep blue waters of Ursula K. Le Guin's Earthsea or some other fantasyland.

Mrs. Sargent's home was to me a refuge of order. We did our homework after school. It seemed there was always plenty of time to do it *and* have time to wander around the house, read in a quiet corner, go in the swimming pool, or walk to the store with Nicole and Phillip to buy candy, and still be in bed by ten. Each day had its own order: a getting-up time and a going-to-school time, snack time and homework time, dinnertime and chore time. All eight of us children went to school every morning. On time. No matter what. Nicole had three gold-sealed certificates, earned for three years of perfect attendance. She proudly hung them on the wall with the New Kids magazine cutouts. When I had conjunctivitis, Mrs. Sargent sent me anyway and waited for the school nurse to confirm the illness. I came back home only when Mrs. Sargent was sure that the school didn't want me there. Aside from that day, I had perfect attendance.

Mrs. Sargent's house was not a place of make-believe, wandering, or missed buses.

Neither were there ominous piles of clutter lurking. Each child had a daily chore. I spent many Saturday mornings dusting Mrs. Sargent's collection of animal figurines, kept neatly in rows inside a glass case. Other Saturdays, I vacuumed the carpeted crannies of the living room floor, cajoling each speck of lint into the loud vacuum. The order I helped keep in Mrs. Sargent's home restored order and balance to my own life, to my perceptions.

Nicole and I were obsessed with the New Kid Donnie Wahlberg. We had 109 New Kids on the Block pictures on the walls of our room. Donnie had just bought a house a few blocks away.

On the night of the Boston Music Awards, we guessed that Donnie would be at home getting ready. Nicole and I waited with the group outside his house. We knew we should go home for dinner but were sure he would come out soon.

He came out wearing a tuxedo, smiling and waving, asking how we were doing. All the girls screamed and held on to each other, hyperventilating. Nicole yelled, "We love you, Donnie!" She put on her sexiest look and come-get-me eyes, flipped her long brown hair around her face.

"I love you, too!" he said, and with another wave and an air kiss, he got into the car and drove off. We strained to catch a last glimpse of his face through the car window.

We got home and were in big trouble. We had missed dinner entirely, and Phillip was almost finished cleaning up.

"You guys are going to get it!" he told us with a pursed-lip smirk. Mrs. Sargent was angry and shook her head. "You were expected home," she reprimanded.

"You just don't want us to have fun!" Nicole yelled back. "It's not fair!" I felt awful inside and didn't say anything. Mrs. Sargent left plates of food warmed up for us in the oven. We ate and were sent directly to bed—grounded for a week.

"I hate her! She's so mean!" said Nicole to Melissa and me upstairs in our room. "All we did was miss dinner! It's not fair. Why do we have to be here every night?"

"She'll get over it," said Melissa knowingly. "She used to get mad at me, too. Just give her a couple days to cool off." Melissa was taking psychology at high school. She told us that we had let our ids overtake our superegos.

"What?" We looked at her blankly, distracted for a moment from our tribulations.

"Your id is the pleasure-seeking center of your brain. Your superego is what you know you should do, your conscience. You just let your desire for pleasure overrule your superego, that's all. It's natural." Melissa knew everything. She had us all figured out. But what she said didn't help us much with Mrs. Sargent's being mad. She had done many good things for us. I didn't want her to be angry and disappointed.

But Melissa was right, and we were soon back in Mrs. Sargent's good graces.

Even though this was the first time I was on my own, I had

very few problems. I had never realized that I needed set discipline and tasks. Nicole chafed against Mrs. Sargent's discipline—whereas I craved it. Nicole complained that Mrs. Sargent never let us do anything or that we were allowed only two or three cookies and milk for an after-school snack. But I loved the limits, the guidelines. They made me feel safe, cared for, contained. The huge responsibility I carried around lifted—I could just be a kid. My middle school teachers marveled that I adapted so well to a new school.

My mother was in Father Bill's shelter in Quincy for most of the time I lived in the foster home. I felt independent, visiting her on Saturdays, taking the bus to Quincy by myself, seeing her waiting smile when I arrived. We would eat lunch and talk and go shopping for little things I needed or wanted.

I stayed at the foster home five months, until the middle of July. My mom then decided we would take the bus to Oregon for a few weeks to visit relatives whom we hadn't seen in almost a year. It had been a long year, full of many changes.

Mrs. Sargent found a big tapestry-patterned suitcase in her attic for me to use. She and Nicole drove me to the Greyhound station to meet my mother. My mother wasn't sure exactly what we would do when we returned from Oregon, but she planned for me to stay with her. We hoped we would find an apartment. I waved good-bye to Mrs. Sargent and Nicole, sad to think that I wouldn't be living with them when I came back.

Recently, Mrs. Sargent sent me a Christmas card and a couple of photos of us children. We are at her house on the deck next to the pool. I am sitting in a deck chair, wearing lime green shorts and an oversized neon orange T-shirt that says YALE in big fluorescent green letters with ornate white trim. Nicole stands behind me with her arms slung around my neck. I look so scrawny, hunched over, plastic-framed glasses and thin brown hair in a wispy ponytail high on my head. Sissy is curled in a ball on a chair next to us, unsmiling, her cheeks billowing out with the big lollipop she has in her mouth, her dark blue eyes in a solemn stare that makes her look as if she were one hundred years old. Danny stands with his hand on the arm of Sissy's chair, looking scared and defiant, his mouth a straight flat line. Phillip is in the background, away from the rest of the group, his hair drooping over his face, in his favorite T-shirt with a cartoon cat on it. Toby is the only one smiling. Shyly he gleams from the corner of the picture, perched nervously on the edge of a flower box, his knees together and hands folded in his lap. It is odd to me that we all look so undernourished, gaunt, sad, and timid, because I remember it as a happy time.

Clearest in my memory are Nicole's braids, walking to school in spring sunshine, being safe in bed each night before ten.

17

QUINCY HIGH SCHOOL

WHEN WE RETURNED from Oregon, we did find an apartment, a two-bedroom we would share with a woman from our church and her daughter. Our housemate and her daughter, who had epilepsy and was handicapped, shared one room, and my mother and I were to share the other. In our room, the light was dim. Two rusted metal cots with dark maroon sheets clashed with the mint green chipping walls, making me feel plain and disconnected. One bare lightbulb glared at me from a small bracket on the right wall. I can't stay here, Mom. We're not staying here. There's no way. Tell her we're only staying the night, that we're leaving tomorrow. Mom, please? I can't live in a place like this. And we ended up staying until I finished high school. My mom gave me my own room so that I could have privacy and room to do homework, and she slept on the couch for the next four years. Eventually I covered the plain walls with decorations and filled the room with objects, made it my home. It was a small place for four people, but we all got along well.

I began high school a few weeks after we moved in. The first day, I wore my plain brown hair held back in a ponytail. I was determined to wear it back and off my face, a symbol of the openness I felt. I would not hide my face behind my hair. I could taste autumn in the crisp, rank air, and it spoke to me of fresh starts. No one knew me. I had no past, only the desire to do well. I was determined to do all that I could to mark up a perfect school record, an astounding résumé. When I graduated, I could go to college, as my mother had never been able to, so that I could support myself and be independent. I was also eager to meet people and make new friends.

Most Quincyites were Irish and Italian working-class people. The wealthiest students' parents were schoolteachers, and these were the kids in the advanced—college bound—classes. One-third of Quincy's population was Chinese American, mostly Cantonese. Quincy was on the Red Line of Boston's subway system.

Quincy was the biggest school I'd ever attended. It had thirteen hundred students, half of whom were in the vocational-technical program. It was a square stone building several stories tall, with blue-sashed windows and a U.S. flag on the pole in the small front lawn. I clutched tightly to the book bag that held my new notebooks and walked up the wide steps and in through heavy glass doors covered by iron latticework.

The classes at Quincy were tracked: advanced, honors, standard, and basic. Advanced and honors were college prep, standard and basic were not. I signed up for mostly advanced classes. I received top grades in each class. I liked my classes, but I was extrinsically motivated. The learning did not matter in itself. I realized now that what mattered most was to have a good record for college.

The classes I was in were small, varying among the same

ten and twenty students. The advanced kids had been in a "lab" gifted program at Central Middle School and were bright, studious, high-achieving students.

I joined band and learned the flute, since QHS had no funding for an orchestra, so I couldn't play violin. The conductor, Mr. Coviello—a short Italian man—proclaimed "Angina! Angina!" and clutched at his chest whenever we were not in sync. I loved the challenge of the flute, learning to shape my mouth so that a resonant sound emerged from the long thin metal instrument. It was so different from playing the violin, but it was still satisfying to feel that I was inside the music. We played concerts and at every football game and city parade. Our hideous band uniforms—royal blue polyester with black and white trim and tall hats with blue feathers— had been in the musty closets of the band room since the 1970s. The pants never fit right; they were too big around the waist and awkward fitting at the bottom, requiring much adjustment with safety pins. For football games, we wore only the jackets, so it was not quite so uncomfortable. I remember many dark autumn evenings, sitting on the concrete steps of the band section of the stadium, warming the cold air with renditions of "Hawaii Five-O" and "Proud Mary."

In addition, I did three seasons of track: cross-country, winter, and spring track. I joined Amnesty International and any after-school club I could fit into my schedule. I worked hard doing homework after track practice, sleeping only three to five hours a night.

At the end of the year I was ranked number one in the class—to my classmates' astonishment.

I began my sophomore year intending to stay at the top of my class, but my grades went down. Sophomore classes were more difficult, and I was taking two math classes in order to catch up with my advanced classmates, who had taken more math than I in junior high school. I had no free periods. I was late to school almost every day. Whereas the previous year I had been able to get up in the mornings after little sleep, this year I could not do it.

Chemistry, one of my hardest classes, took up the first two periods. I usually missed most of it. The teacher gave pop quizzes, on which students rarely scored above 70 percent. I missed lab periods and had trouble doing the lab reports. The Science Department head called me into her office and asked what was happening to me. She understood that I was behind, but why couldn't I come in early to get extra help, as the other students did? Didn't she know that I had a hard enough time getting to class? I would never be able to come in early. She told me I was going down the drain. As I left her office I had tears in my eyes. I was angry. I didn't want to go down the drain. I didn't want to become part of her sewage system.

I was not doing well in my other classes, either. I had Geometry right after Chemistry. The work was not hard, but the teacher irritated me by stating that my friend's proofs were "unlogical." I thought the correct word was *illogical* but didn't say so. I looked it up in the dictionary to prove myself right. We also did not get along because I took notes using a system called brain mapping. My notes radiated out from a central point in circles and trees all over the page. I could organize my thoughts better this way, but to her it was just messy. She gave me all F's for notebook grades.

Another hard class was Algebra II. I had it just after lunch and fell asleep every day. My friend Ashley and I kicked each other under our seats and wrote notes back and forth to stay awake. The teacher wore polyester slacks and brightly colored

159

Hanes sweatshirts that she appliquéd with autumn leaves out-lined in glitter paint, and Christmas sweatshirts bedangled with glued-on faux jewels and sequins. She had glasses that made her eyes so huge that when she blinked, if I was awake, I jumped back in my seat.

On my first report card, I received low B's and C's. Instead being inspired to do better, I lost all motivation. I missed more and more classes, and fell back into the pattern of previous years: in California when I skipped school with Star, and in Oregon when I never seemed to make the bus and stopped going to school. Every third or fourth year, I seemed to crash and be unable to deal with school and life anymore, in spite of all my good intentions.

It was at about this time that I met Mr. Charles Maclaughlin.

18

MR. MAC

WHEN I ENTERED the heavy black door that said HER-
ITAGE, it was like entering a different world. It was a large carpeted room with big windows. Students sprawled in armchairs
around two tables, chatting about many things at once. Here
and there, they sat on the floor helping each other with schoolwork. Wooden cubbyholes—built by Mr. Maclaughlin, the
Heritage program director—lined one wall. I envied Heritage
students, who didn't have to scramble to remember—in the
five minutes between classes—combinations to the gray metal
lockers in the school's main hallway. A small refrigerator and
microwave stood in one corner, near a "store" where students
bought microwave popcorn, sodas, and other snacks. A sign
read: PROCEEDS GO TO THE HERITAGE SCHOLARSHIP FUND.
Student-made collages and bulletin boards with announcements and newspaper articles covered the walls. A cabinet in
the center of the room was cluttered with mechanical gadgets
and a big upright log wearing a vest, a stocking cap, and funny
glasses.

Mr. Mac's desk was slung diagonally across the back left corner of the room. I made my way over and sat perched on the edge of a flower-patterned armchair.

"Hello, wise guy," he greeted me. He was in his late fifties—his brown hair graying and thinning in parts. But it wasn't his hair I noticed first, rather his smile and kind eyes amplified by his glasses. He was wearing paint-splattered jeans and a short-sleeved dress shirt because he was working on Drama Club sets in the back room. His hands were rough, and there were bits of paint stuck under his fingernails. I was surprised, because other times I had seen him in the school hallway, he had been wearing a white button-down shirt with trousers and a tie.

Mr. Mac explained the program. Heritage was a smaller school within the school—a place where students received more individual attention. It was a "homeroom" that was a real home for students. There were fifty students in the home-room. They began their day in Heritage and had all their study halls there. Any student could spend time in Heritage even if not part of the homeroom. These students—called Heritage Rats—often ate lunch and spent free time after school here. Many "fringe" students felt more comfortable here than in the main school.

The Heritage motto was *Veritas et fides*, Truth and trust. The program's motto meant that Mr. Mac thought students should have room to make mistakes and learn from them. Students should be respected and have a voice in their school schedule and courses. Mr. Mac took risks with his kids in trusting them, but he believed that the risk usually yielded good results.

Heritage was different from many alternative programs in that it was not only for gifted students. Students of all ability levels could meet and learn from each other there. It included advanced students as well as low achievers and other students with emotional, family, or medical issues that meant they benefited from a program that gave them more flexibility and support.

Heritage had two functions. One was to be a nurturing environment where students had a friend and counselor-advocate in Mr. Mac. Mr. Mac did not work in isolation. He kept up relationships with teachers as well as sports coaches. If the other teachers were amenable, he liked to work with them to help the students.

Heritage's other function was to allow students to be creative with their schedules. A typical Heritage student might take fewer high school classes and more courses at Harvard Extension School and Quincy College. Many students did apprenticeships in the community for part of the school day.

One student took classes at Harvard Extension and Harvard Summer School. During the school year she worked every afternoon at a cancer research lab in Boston with Mr. Mac's brother. She was a very driven student who graduated at the end of her junior year and went into a premed program at Cornell University.

Mr. Mac also told me about Lisa, a gifted advanced-track student who had been frustrated with school. She loved Drama Club and wanted more acting experiences. Mr. Mac helped her design a reduced school day with afternoon acting at the John Adams estates, where she played the part of Abigail Adams. In the evening, she took college classes. Lisa went on to major in acting at Sarah Lawrence College and spent a year in London through the program there.

Mr. Mac described one of his most memorable students as a nightmare. She was angry and uncooperative and an alcoholic.

After she'd returned from several rehabs, it seemed unlikely that she would succeed in school. Mr. Mac put together a program of high school and college courses that would allow her to graduate. She responded to his trust and confidence in her—she went to AA meetings every day at noon and managed to graduate.

Mr. Mac asked me if I could bring something in to help him learn more about me. I had a "journal"—it was a bunch of lined paper stuffed into a pink school folder. During the next few days, Mr. Mac opened the journal and read:

> *I could disappear in a puff of smoke and the only thing anyone would notice is the puff!*

> *I have so many thoughts flying around in my head I can't grab hold of one without dropping another. It's like all those ping-pong balls that bounce off each other. . . . What's it called, Brownian (random) motion. Just like that. I feel like I'll burst . . . and so I am like the ping-pong balls constantly moving and flying in all directions at once . . .*

> *A horse gallops thru my stomach wildly.*
> *If I wanted to sit serenely still he would not allow it.*
> *12-12-91*

A few days later, Mr. Mac saw me at lunch and called me over to his desk. "I was amazed by what I read," he told me, handing the journal back. "I mean, whew! You go a million miles an hour all the time, don't you?"

"I guess," I said.

"You need to slow down," he told me. But I didn't want to, yet. I was worried about class rankings.

He told me I could join the Heritage program.

I was so grade-conscious that I even graded myself on the previous year's New Year's resolutions. I received an A in "Become More Confident of Calling People" and "Help Mary AMAP (As Much As Possible) with Schoolwork." I earned an A— in "Send X-mas Cards Early" (although I got an F in "Send Rest of This Year's Cards").

I had a B average for "Take Care of Skin," "Read a Book Always," "Have a Plan for Everything (term, month, week, day)," and "Student Council (Tues. morns.)." I scraped by with a B— in "Be In School Every Day (unless deathly ill)."

I received a C in "Run six times a week (five miles a day at least)."

Resolution Number 11, "Be a Better Person" was subdivided into "a. Less Gossip (say something good instead of bad)"—B—, "b. less yelling w/ Mom"—C, and "c. improve relationships with friends"—C.

Unfortunately, I failed at several resolutions, my grades for which were as follows:

D in "Violin Practice (maybe lessons)"
D— in "Cross-stitch While on Phone"
F in "Get all A+'s 3rd and 4th quarters"
and "Clean My Room at least Once a Week."

Mr. Mac helped me to see my education as a personal process. He told me, "Some things you have to do to get by, you know, jump through the hoops. *Then* you do what you want the rest of the time. You live your life."

In tenth grade, my first year in Heritage, on the counsel of Mr. Mac and other Heritage students, I dropped two classes: World Cultures and Chemistry. Since I dropped Chemistry, which took up the first two periods of the day, I didn't have to come into school until nine or ten in the morning. I was able to sleep later, and being well rested helped my other classes. Heritage was unique in that students could come in whenever their first classes started, instead of at 8:00 A.M. as the rest of the school did.

I dyed my hair turquoise-green, pierced my nose, and wore outrageous clothes, and teachers saw these as signs of defiance toward authority: Danger! Danger! We are losing this student—she is going down the drain with her sewer green hair. What Mr. Mac saw was that I was not just an intellect and a machine. He saw that my eyes were tired and bloodshot. He saw that I was making an attempt to express myself as an individual—to figure something out. "I like it," he would say, "when kids dye their hair—red, blue. To me it means they have something going on up here"—he'd point to his head— "they are expressing themselves." To Mr. Mac, expressing oneself was one of the chief goals of education.

What Mr. Mac was telling me was different from what other teachers had to say. They made me feel that I was doing something wrong if I didn't take all the hardest classes, do anything to get an A. Mr. Mac was the first adult in public schools who told me that what I dreamt of, what made me happy, my own questions and dreams were the most important, even more important than getting A's.

Many of the teachers in the main high school disagreed. They believed that I was capable of taking a full course load. They did not understand why a teacher would encourage me to drop classes. There *were* teachers who understood Mr.

Mac's program, who would listen and talk with him about the students. But the majority frowned on Mr. Mac's methods. It wasn't fair that I got to break all the rules, drop classes, and come in to school late. What they didn't see was that students benefited from making their own rules, designing their own educations. It was good for students to be able to shed the tight constricting collar of the seven-period school day.

Mr. Mac's ideas came from a different place of understanding.

A paperweight Mr. Mac had on his desk exemplified his attitude toward the status quo—he called it a rock concert. It was a bunch of pebbles with smiley faces painted on them. The rock concert was holding up a sign that said HAVE A NICE DAY—which Mr. Mac was wont to say as a general dismissive statement.

"'They' [the high school teachers and administration] think every student should fit into a seven-period-a-day routine. Have a nice day."

"The Math Department head came in waving papers and saying your math work was atrocious. I told her to Have a nice day."

"They want me not to write any more Heritage passes. But have a nice day." He sometimes wrote Heritage passes for students to come in late to class. If a student was having a small or big crisis, whether personal or academic, he would give the student time to calm down on one of the couches in the Heritage "Outback." He felt it more important to sort the crisis out than to insist that the student be in every class on time.

One spring, Mr. Mac and a couple of students took a course called The Heroic Tradition in Northern Europe at the Harvard Extension School. They went to class each week, but the material was extremely esoteric. It didn't help that the course had a front row of question-asking students who seemed to be descendants of the original Vikings. Have a nice day.

"They don't know what to make of you wrestling. I told them to have a nice day."

Mr. Mac grew up in Melrose, north of Boston, and went to Boston College, where his father had gone. "My father thought the school was too big, but I insisted," Mr. Mac told me. He wanted to major in biology, but the dean told him that his high school record was too mediocre. "I felt like they thought I was stupid," Mr. Mac said. He spent a year as an economics major but couldn't give up his dream of doing biology. He felt lost at BC because it was so big. Another student mentioned the smaller St. Michael's College in Vermont, suggesting that he might like it better. He contacted St. Mike's and asked the dean there if he could major in biology. He said that he could, so Mr. Mac transferred there the following year. He worked hard to meet the biology requirements as well as take extra classes required for a teaching license. He graduated and wrote a letter to the dean of BC to tell him that they had been wrong in their estimate of his abilities.

Mr. Mac believes that schools should be smaller because students like himself would be overlooked at bigger schools like BC and QHS. If students have strong dreams and desires, he believes these students can complete any goal they set for themselves, regardless of past performance and regardless of teachers' and the administration's recommendations.

Heritage would not be a place where any students would be told—in so many words—that they were too "dumb" to do biology or anything else.

*

To make up for the classes I dropped, I took Chemistry that summer at Quincy College, a course that was easier to manage than the QHS advanced class. In the spring I took World Religions at Harvard Extension. I took the train to Harvard Square once a week, saw the variety of people there, listened to the chanting of the Hare Krishnas and the Guatemalan band that played on the street. The men had long dark hair and bright embroidered robes. One strummed a guitar while playing a harmonica. Mr. Mac saw the experience of travel and independence as more valuable than trying to squeeze another class into a tightly packed, stress-filled school day.

During the next three years, I took other classes at Harvard Extension. I was interested in religion and took classes in Buddhism, biblical theology, and a class in psychology and religion. I also took classes in logic and nutrition at Mr. Mac's suggestion that I "broaden my portfolio." By high school's end, I had taken eight Harvard courses.

My high school education differed significantly from a typical college-bound program. I did not take any math after tenth grade. I finished that year with D's in my math classes. Other students went on to take precalculus and Advanced Placement calculus, but I had an aversion to mathematics after that year. I did not take as many AP's as the other students, and I never did have perfect attendance. Instead, I devoted myself to activities I really loved: running and wrestling, volunteering at an elementary school, and spending time with friends.

*   *   *

Mr. Mac keeps in touch with many former students. They sometimes visit years later and tell him what an impact he made in their lives. Mr. Mac and I have remained friends. In

June 1998, Mr. Mac told me to pack my bags for a two-day trip and meet him in front of QHS at 9:00 A.M. on Friday. I found him there, loading several of his students into a big red rented van.

"It's Vantastic," he said, "You get to be the navigator." I climbed into the front seat. He gave me a box of Barnum & Bailey animal crackers and a map to help me navigate. I set them on the dashboard. "Just consult the frasmus map," he told me.

We pulled away from the high school, listening to show tunes. We were going to New York City, where Mr. Mac takes groups of students twice a year, to go to the theater and walk around the East Village, take in a museum or two, visit the Statue of Liberty, or walk over the Brooklyn Bridge. Those who could afford to paid a certain amount, those who could not, like myself in high school, didn't. The city is only a four-hour drive away from Quincy, but many Quincy students are from working-class families and have never been to New York.

In the van Mr. Mac told me about bareback riding at the G Bar M Ranch in Montana, one of his favorite places. He goes there almost every year with a group of students.

"My horse had no mane," he told me, "only four hairs. So I called it Rhode Island." I looked puzzled.

"You don't get it." He shook his head at me, turned to the other students (who looked mystified too). "She doesn't get it."

"Rhode Island. Rhode Island."

"What?"

"My horse had no *mane* (Maine), only four hairs to hold on to; I called it Rhode Island. Oh, it was rough." He shook his head again.

The show tunes ended and we moved on to a tape of

LeAnn Rimes and then Celine Dion, choices of the girls in the back. Mr. Mac sang along with Celine.

To pass time, he had the students make up funny phrases out of the town names. He pointed to a sign that read, VOLUNTOWN, EXIT 10.

"The name of that town was Can't Stand Up. Get it? Voluntown (Fallin' Down), Can't Stand Up."

We drew near to the city and passed by a huge cemetery— the grave markers looked like a miniature city of skyscrapers, only inches of grass between rectangular marble markers.

"Is that a graveyard?" asked one of the students.

"No, those are very small condominiums," said Mr. Mac. I marveled that the markers were so close together. Mr. Mac said, "They must bury them standing up."

"How do they turn over in their graves, then?" I asked.

"They don't. They do pirouettes."

The same summer we went to New York, Heritage was in its tenth year, and the school administration began to question the program's validity and structure.

The program had enormous success, and many of the school's brightest students were in Heritage—it boasted alumni who went to Harvard, Brown, Cornell, Sarah Lawrence, BC, and other prestigious universities. It had also helped many low-achieving students to graduate. Heritage students went on to remarkably diverse college programs, including music and art, acting and creative writing, and even culinary school. Even so, many teachers and administrators had trouble accepting the program because the principles were so different from those of the main high school. Some felt that Mr. Mac did not do enough "work." He taught only one class, and they did not understand the importance of the things he did all day to make the students' lives smoother.

The school decided to move Heritage's location and to require Mr. Mac to teach four classes each day. That summer, most of the Heritage furniture was thrown out, and what was left was moved into a new, less comfortable space. I was devastated when Mr. Mac told me that the janitors had thrown out our favorite Heritage character, Log—the piece of a tree trunk that we dressed in silly costumes throughout the year.

Mr. Mac was distressed because he felt these changes showed a lack of respect for and understanding of his work. He continued with Heritage but could not be as effective when teaching class most of the school day.

The next year, the administration decided to move Heritage again—this time into the school's front wing, next to the principal's office—to change it into a leadership program intended for Advanced Placement and honors students. It wasn't the program that had been Mr. Mac's labor of love for the past eleven years. He resigned, heartbroken.

Mr. Mac planned to retire, since his work with Heritage had ended. He had completed the Boston to New York AIDS Ride twice, in memory of his cousin. He decided he would bike cross-country by himself—to reflect on his thirty-four-year career and raise money for a Heritage scholarship.

Mr. Mac showed me the journal from the two-and-a-half-week ride from Montana to Des Moines, Iowa. "I think you'll like some of what I wrote," he said. "I was surprised, rereading it.

"I thought I would write a lot," he said, shaking his head. "Boy was I wrong. After ten hours on the bike, I would sit down at the restaurants—I hated that, you know, eating supper alone, sitting there by myself. . . . It was okay, though, I just pulled out my little book." He mimicked pushing his dinner plate aside and opening up the journal. "Most nights, I would just write a couple of pages—I was too tired from the bike. But one night, I wrote eight or nine pages. I was surprised. I just kept going."

I sat down to read . . .

Why did I teach? Not because I couldn't do anything else as some people joke. Teachers are people who want to help others; and go into teaching to try, despite community pressures not to spend money on salaries. Qualified teachers should not have to go hat-in-hand begging for raises. I'm ashamed that my good work was never rewarded as it is in so many businesses. Teachers are not aggressive by nature. They are patient and often do not get what is fair. But honestly, I did not become a teacher to get wealthy. I became a teacher to work with and for "kids" and I would not change the choice I made thirty-four years ago if I could. I tried one year and stayed.

. . . Students respect their teachers for a number of reasons. No teaching style is the best for all. You know it works when they listen, rarely miss class, and are disappointed when you are not in class. When students arrive on our doorstep they come with baggage. Sometimes that baggage is very heavy and patience and understanding is needed. A good teacher listens to what isn't said. The look in the eye, body language, simple comments and behaviors tell a lot about how the student arrives in the class. Teaching is not the passing on of facts/dates, formulas, and vocabulary. It is an adventure that has those items— but needs more. . . .

I will miss working with the kids. But, for most educators and administrators, Heritage was frustrating and confusing. Maybe I was lucky—eleven years—eleven excellent student-based/trust-building years. I would not change anything.

Mr. Mac hoped to retire, but because of a change in Massachusetts law, he had to work two more years to receive retirement benefits. He taught Applied Biology and Principles of Technology in Quincy High's vocational-technical wing.

I went to observe his new classroom. He met me after he got off cafeteria duty, which he described as "making sure the French fries don't land too close to the rubbish barrel." It was odd to think of Mr. Mac doing "caf duty," because in Heritage no one ate lunch in the cafeteria.

His lunch shift finished, Mr. Mac and I walked through the long school corridors, over the covered bridge to the Vocational-Technical High School. I liked the inspirational posters and murals and the groups of high school kids walking through the roomy, echoing hallways. "It's not all bad," said Mr. Mac.

He said to me then, "Remember your speech in Ohio— you said that strong relationships could pull kids through?" I had given a speech the previous year for NASCEHCY—the National Association of State Coordinators for the Education of Homeless Children and Youth.

"Yes . . ."

"I've been thinking about that, and you're right. But it's so hard. What I do now, teaching five or six classes a day. I see the kids forty-five minutes at a time. There's not much I can do. I feel like my feet are in cement."

Artifacts and photos—memories of his years in Her-

174

itage—covered the walls of his classroom. It was filled with visual experiments—student-made bridges created from pasta and a large wooden catapult he built for students to see technological development during medieval times. On his desk was a can of tuna fish, a macaroni and cheese box, an aspirin bottle, and an old car steering pump. In one corner of the classroom was a black trash barrel, full of huge holes and dents.

I observed Mr. Mac's lesson from the back. The students' desks were arranged in a circle. Mr. Mac stood in the center, held up the tuna fish, mac and cheese, and aspirin, and asked, "How do you get these to every cell in your body?"

They gave various responses: "You eat them." "Digestion."

"What about your heart?" he asked. "How is the heart involved?" He had the students make fists and squeeze and release for sixty seconds. Most of the students' hands tired after about thirty seconds. They shook their hands, trying to get feeling to return.

"This is what your heart does," said Mr. Mac, "seventy to eighty times a minute, two and a half billion times in an average person's lifetime. The heart never rests; it is always working to get food and oxygen to every cell." He showed the students the car steering pump.

"This pump does basically the same thing your heart does, but it has to be replaced every two or three years." The students stared with amazed looks. "How does the heart do it?" they asked.

"Why doesn't it get tired?"

"How does it last so long?"

I thought how lucky these students were to have a teacher like Mr. Mac, whose lessons are so visual, so exciting. At the end of the class, the students gathered their books and filed out in clumps. A janitor came in to empty the trash.

"Hi, Paul, how's it going?" Mr. Mac asked.

Paul pointed to the old battered-up trash barrel in the corner. "You want me to throw this out? You don't need it," he said.

Mr. Mac picked up the trash barrel. "You know what we do with this? We take it outside, the kids bang on it, and we measure the speed of sound. We see how long it takes the sound to reach three hundred yards."

"Well then I won't throw it out, if you use it, then," Paul said with some confusion. He smiled and left. We left, too, Mr. Mac locking the door behind him.

Mr. Mac and I meet for lunch a few times a year, and we always have too much to talk about. I am eager to hear his stories about "the kids" and updates on students I graduated with. Many of his former students keep in touch with Mr. Mac. And he is ready to listen to what is going on in my life, too.

As we sat down at the booth in the restaurant, I told him about the triathlon that I was doing to raise money for the Leukemia Society. I was worried that I would be one of the slowest people. Swimming was new to me, and the race included a nearly mile-long swim in the ocean through a giant kelp bed. But more than that, I was worried about my bike. It was a ninety-nine-dollar bike that my housemate Marion had given me in ninth grade. It was almost eleven years old. It was not a racing bike. It had thick, slow tires and a heavy frame. It was difficult to switch gears. Mr. Mac offered to let me use his bike, but I decided to stick with my own. I was more comfortable on it, and the race was only a week away.

"Just do your best," Mr. Mac told me. "Don't worry about

competitive cyclists with their expensive bikes. They're in a different kind of shape. They're in 'Have a nice day' shape. Even if you had the best bike in the world, they'd still be faster. You're not doing it to win. You're doing it to honor Lily and your uncle [who both died of leukemia]." He gave me a small pin in the shape of a shiny red apple. It said, I MAKE A DIFFERENCE——I TEACH.

"I'm giving this to you," he said, "because——*you* teach *me*. *You're* the teacher. You're teaching other people how to do something to help." I proudly pinned the apple onto my book bag. Whenever I look at it, I think of Mr. Mac and how unique he is, that he sees his mission as not only to teach but also to learn from his students.

"Hey, fruitcake! Bring your crash helmet?" Mr. Mac asked, on the day of our first driving lesson.

The first time I got behind the wheel of his little faded red Toyota Tercel, in a parking lot in Marina Bay in Quincy, I had scant knowledge of how a car worked. I had to think about the order of doing things. First, the key in the ignition, adjust the seat and mirrors. Okay, what's next? Put the car in drive or reverse, check the mirrors again. "Which one's the brake and which one's the gas? Oh, I thought it was the other way around. Do I use both feet or only one?"

"Oh, boy," said Mr. Mac.

For someone who was twenty-four years old, and a Harvard graduate, I was still a kindergartner when it came to cars.

When Mr. Mac began giving me lessons, I was terrified of driving. A car was a dangerous weapon. I could kill someone if I didn't know what I was doing.

Mr. Mac started me out on small side roads. We stopped and switched places when we had to go through busy intersections.

"It would be unfair to have you drive here when you're not ready," he said.

I was taking a driver's ed course at the same time. My driving instructor, unlike Mr. Mac, took me to the busiest areas of Quincy. He yelled directions at me moments before I had to execute them and did most of the driving for me, grabbing the steering wheel from the passenger's seat as we turned the corners and pressing down suddenly on the brake on the passenger's side in the driver's ed car.

"How am I supposed to learn when you're doing it all for me?" I asked him impatiently.

The first time I ever drove on a highway was with Mr. Mac, several weeks into our lessons. I was prepared and knew what to do, although I was still intimidated because I had never driven over forty miles per hour. As we advanced along the ramp, Mr. Mac's voice guided me. "A little more speed, a little more. Okay, good." I took a deep breath, feeling calm because I trusted Mr. Mac. I knew he would never make me do anything unsafe. "More speed, more, okay, good." Whew, I was going sixty miles per hour.

Mr. Mac retired last year. He intended upon his "retirement" to continue working a forty-hour week at Sears, where he had worked twenty hours a week while teaching full-time at Quincy High (in order to put his two sons through college and not sink into debt)—but he just couldn't leave teaching behind.

He quit Sears, and in his "retirement," now teaches literature, social studies, and religion to thirty black and Latino seventh- and eighth-graders at St. Peter's parochial school in Dorchester, Massachusetts. I visited his classroom on the last day before winter vacation—the class was in the midst of celebrating. In one corner was Mr. Mac's own artificial Christmas tree that he brought from home. It was decorated with student-made ornaments and cards.

Photos covered one wall—some of Quincy High students, others of his current students, pictures of "mini–field trips" he takes them on after school, in groups of four and five, so that he can spend more individual time with them, so they can come to trust him.

Mr. Mac came over to give me a big hug. The children gathered round, asking questions about Harvard, writing, and wrestling. One boy handed me two stories he wrote, then shyly disappeared while I read them. The students felt like they already knew me, because Mr. Mac told them so much. A *Boston Globe* article about me was posted on one wall. The students inspected my hair—which was a reddish purple— and compared it to my black hair in the article. "You changed your hair," they accused me, suspicious that I was not the real Lauralee.

Some students were playing checkers and chess, games Mr. Mac brought in and taught them how to play. "I like to give them things to do in their free time, things that make them think," he said.

Mr. Mac had some of his students write letters to me. Daniella, a tall black girl with long braids, wrote to me that she'd moved from shelter to shelter for the past year and a half. She, her mother, and her two sisters lived in one room. She didn't get a birthday present this year, neither did her little sister, but she tried not to bother her mother, because, she wrote, "She is trying the best she can for us." I wrote her back right away.

Mr. Mac stayed after school because his students just didn't seem to want to leave. They clamored around his desk, put their favorite CDs into the CD player, and asked Mr. Mac and me a thousand questions.

"Mr. Mac, what assignment do I need to do over vacation?" Daniella asked, looking over his shoulder at the grade book.

Another student tried to get his attention, standing within an inch of him. "Mr. Mac—Mr. Mac-daddy," she said, impatiently standing on her toes to be closer to him. He remained unfazed by it all, giving his attention to each child in turn.

19

"AS MY DREAM WRESTLED
WITH ITSELF AND ME"

ONE LATE FALL DAY of my third year of high school, I was sitting at the Heritage lounge, eating lunch, when Stephanie said, "I want to join the wrestling team, but I don't want to do it by myself."

"Girls can't join the wrestling team," I said.

"Yes they can! Didn't you hear about that girl in Norwood? She's the only girl on the team." Stephanie stared defiantly.

"I'll join with you," I said, to my own surprise. I was startled so by my own words that I leaned across the table, knocking over a chocolate milk carton with my elbow. I usually did indoor track in the winter, but this year it was headed by the assistant football coach, who had never participated in a track event in his life. Practice was running laps in the cafeteria for twenty minutes. I loved cross-country and spring track, but I had little interest in winter track, especially because my event, the two-mile, meant running twenty-four monotonous laps indoors.

At our high school, the only girls' winter sports were basketball and indoor track. Boys could do either of these sports and had three additional sports: ice hockey, wrestling, and swimming.

Walking home a few days later, I saw the wrestling coach, Mr. Venturelli, who was also an earth science teacher. The only time I had talked to him was when he caught me out on the high school's fourth-story roof. My friend Pam and I had climbed out the large open window on a whim. Why not? Let's go out there. We were sitting on the flat part of the roof talking and doing homework for the Spanish and French classes we were cutting. Mr. Venturelli must have heard us because he stuck his head through the window and said, "I hope you weren't planning to jump." Pam and I climbed back through the window, leaving the sunny roof behind and entering the dim third-floor hallway. Mr. Venturelli returned us to our teachers, with a pursed-lipped smile.

I called to him and said I was joining wrestling. He said, "See you at practice, Wednesday at three," his expression unchanging.

People asked, "Why do you want to do wrestling?" I didn't know so I made up answers: "It will be good conditioning. I want to do push-ups and sit-ups and use every muscle, so that I will get stronger."

Stephanie got an after-school job and decided not to wrestle. I didn't want to back out because so many people already knew I was going to join. I was determined to try it, since I had said I would.

The following Wednesday, I packed up clothes to wear at practice. My friend Patrick told me to wear a T-shirt, sweat-

182

shirt, and sweatpants so that my knees wouldn't get mat burn because I didn't have knee pads yet. I had only ten minutes until practice was to start. Rushing to the girls' locker room, I changed in a hurry. The room was as small as a large closet, with lockers all around the walls and one bench through the middle, not like the spacious boys' locker room next to us. Chattering and giggling, girls crowded together in various stages of dress with clothes piled around them. When I told them I was wrestling they gave me strange looks. I removed numerous earrings, took my nose ring out, and put the handful of metal in my Converse All-Star high-tops.

I rushed up to the wrestling room, my hair flying in all directions like fireworks. Some of the boys were wrestling with each other. Others who lay on their backs—eyes closed or staring sleepily up at the ceiling—suddenly sat up and turned to look at me. I reached up to smooth down my hair, hoping to make myself less of a spectacle, but the way I moved my hands seemed to make it even clearer that I was a girl.

Wrestling practice was held next to the weight room above the school's main gym. An old blue mat covered the floor, the vinyl worn and peeling back here and there. Students lifting weights sometimes stopped and watched us practice.

The first practice began when the two team captains stood up and shouted, "Everyone, line up!" The boys scrambled into a neat grid on the blue mat. I followed their lead, lining up in the back row. The captains faced us and called out directions: Up—one, up—two for the sit-ups. Down—one, down—two for the push-ups. I dug my toes into the mat and struggled to do each push-up. We shouted out each number as we did one hundred sit-ups and push-ups and then as many jumping jacks.

We stretched for several minutes, doing toe touches and side-to-side bends, the boys thrusting their hips out at the top part of the stretch. Bend left, touch toes, stand up, thrust hips, bend right, touch toes. Coach V hurried in near the end of the stretching. He carried his briefcase and wore his teaching clothes: a tie, button-down white shirt, and brown slacks. He promptly dispatched with the tie, unbuttoned the top button of his shirt, and kicked his shoes off. He grabbed the nearest wrestler and began yelling commands in his socks, throwing the boy off balance while demonstrating the right way to do a front headlock.

Our first drill was a spin drill. The coach called on one of the captains, Ashley Davis, to help demonstrate. Ashley got down on his hands and knees, his back arched sturdily. The coach placed his chest square on Ashley's back and spun his body around, supported by Ashley's back. As he circled he put pressure on Ashley's neck, pushing it down with his hands each time he went past. Ashley tried to keep his head and neck up, his eyes looking forward.

The purpose of the spin drill was to become quick on your feet. If your opponent dropped to his hands and knees when he was shooting in on your legs, you could sprawl, spin behind and on top of him to get two points.

I was paired with Johnny Richards, the smallest boy in the room. He had lots of confidence to make up for his size and was very talkative. He didn't seem to feel as awkward as I thought he would. He said he'd spin first, so I crouched on hands and knees, back arched, fingertips pressed into the dusty blue mat. Sweat and face makeup dripped from my nose in white drops. My back and arms strained to support the boy's weight, his chest pressed into my back. His legs flew past my head, and his arms pounded down on my neck. The coach's whistle blew in the distance. The boy switched directions and continued to spin.

When my turn came, it was strange at first to put my chest against Johnny's back. The only physical contact between boys and girls, men and women, is usually sparse and formal, or else imbued with sexual significance. This was a new sort of arena, physical contact with boys that was not sexual or formal but intense and athletic. I decided not to think too much about it and just to do it. Throwing myself down, I learned to balance myself on my chest while letting my legs fly in 180-degree arcs.

Coach Venturelli had intense brown eyes and a stiff smile. He reminded me of a plastic windup toy that was always wound up. He was a teacher and coach who made sure you stayed on your toes mentally and physically for the entire class or practice.

"I'll try it for a week," I told him after the first practice.

"Right," he said, already looking away.

That first week of practice, we did thousands of push-ups, sit-ups, and jumping jacks, as we would do throughout the season. To warm up, we also ran in endless loops around and around the mat. We did sprints across the mat, and practiced our wrestling stance and penetration steps and mock takedowns. Toward the end of the week, we had our first days of real "live" wrestling.

I kept a notebook in which I wrote down thoughts about wrestling practice and descriptions of moves I wanted to improve. As I wrote them, I pictured my coach and the words he used when describing the moves. Some of the boys had a natural gift for wrestling and learned quickly, but it seemed it usually took me longer than most of my teammates to understand them. I had to do a move several times before I vaguely understood how it worked. I was used to picking things up more quickly than my classmates and, strangely, I enjoyed having to work a lot harder than the rest.

I wrote the moves over and over, picturing my coach, then imagining myself executing the move on another wrestler. I said the words in my notebook over and over in my head.

HegoesCRACKDOWN
shoulderpressureingroin
headtoside
scissortohip
trytokickover
(andgethandoutonoppositeside)
orgetyourlegsinbetweenhis.
orhookhisankle(straightenhimandyouout)
walkitup
puthisleg(thatyouhavegripandpressureon)
onthetableofyourknee
asyoustepUpandForward

But wrestling was an utterly different type of knowledge, not linguistic at all when it was actually happening.

The physics class I took in high school seemed to fit with my thoughts about wrestling: force and movement, physical poetry that couldn't be captured in words.

Through wrestling, I became more me, added more parts of myself to myself. I stretched my leg in a certain way and I felt a muscle that I never had before. The motion of my body was like a feeling there were no words for—an expression of myself that left words behind yet was necessary to say to myself and others.

What if I had lived in a container of mind? Then I wouldn't care about my body, but would I feel imprisoned, motionless? In physics we learned that space curves like a stretchy spandex fabric—that our movement (as well as the movement of stars and planets) changes the shape of space. If we were just minds, then space would be incomprehensible to us. When I wrestled, I changed the shape of space. It stretched and bent, violently, precisely.

When my mind felt all stopped up inside—ideas and frustrations scrambled around, tangled up—I needed to begin thinking with my body. I did this through movement, letting the thoughts escape and take shape, releasing them into the physical world. Every thought was electric as it left through my body and circled back to me. If I kept thoughts boxed up in my mind, they stayed shallow and unreal, unable to interact with anything solid.

When I sat still for too long, my mind stirred itself into circles, sore like a too-tight muscle.

"So you're leaving," Mr. V said after the first week of practice. I, sweat soaked, disheveled, bruised, looking like a hit-and-run victim with skid marks on my face, stared at my coach.

Standing there before the coach I remembered being in second grade and playing kickball. I remembered standing in the row of children, and then eventually standing all by myself as one by one the other children were chosen. I had shuffled my feet and looked at the gravelly blacktop, feeling ashamed that the other children were fighting over who would be "stuck" with me.

When the game finally began and it was my turn to kick, I was terrified of kicking at the ball and missing it. As I stood there, I thought again about being picked last, and the sweat broke out on my face, sending my glasses sliding down my nose. Inevitably, I swung my leg over the ball and through empty air.

As I waited for the ball to be pitched again, all I could think of were the thick glasses sitting askew on my face. As the ball rolled toward me, I thought of the inch of space between my foot and the ball as my foot swept over it, the ball continuing to roll past me. This inch of empty space grew and expanded until it was all I could see, over and over. A field of empty space, and my leg heavy like lead, cutting through air. The air grew thick, as in the stuttering second before my foot missed the ball I looked up to see the faces that laughed.

Standing in front of the coach I also remembered being in sixth grade, running outside around the school track, and two boys who passed me on the right said, "You run like a chicken." It was true, when I ran my back was bent over in an arc and I practically trailed my fingers along the ground, eyes fixed on the black turf of the track. My elbows and knees flew out at awkward angles, but I was running. It was a good thing I couldn't see myself. I only felt myself running, and to me it felt like flying. Did chickens fly? I wondered.

*

My third memory was of biting my fingernails while playing basketball on the seventh-grade B-team at Astoria Middle School. I saw a blur of bodies barreling about, this way and that, and objects whizzing about in the space around me. My teeth gnawed anxiously at my nails' rough edges, as I turned first one way and then the other, struggling to keep up with the motion of the game.

Afterwards, on the school bus home, Carey, who used to be my best friend, leaned across the aisle with a sneer. Her hair was dirty blond and tightly curled like sprung wire. Her cadet blue eyes popped out of her flat, freckled, and pale face. She put the ends of her fingers to her mouth and started laughing. I looked down in shamed silence and turned dumbly to look out the bus window.

I focused on the well-known trees and rows of houses sliding and bumping by. When Carey and I were friends we would talk about boys. Carey's first "boyfriend"—a wise-cracking boy with a spiky blond mullet—told Carey that her ass was hard as rocks.

"What does he expect?" she said, grabbing her own butt in her stretch pants. "For it to be soft?" She laughed, her face as hard as her ass.

I looked at my coach's face, thinking, What does he expect? For me to be soft?

feet Ready to sprawl
move back
outside single
scooparoundStandUpdriveacross
tripsidelegkickitout

"No. I'm staying," I told him, taking off my knee pads. "I love it."

"Good," he said, shuffling some papers into his briefcase.

*　　*　　*

"Come on, Lauralee! You're wrestling like a girl!" yelled Dave Bogan one day in practice as he watched Rich Testa and me wrestle. Everyone thought Dave's comment was a really funny joke. I appreciated his encouragement, and his confidence that I could "Go on out there and rip his head off." I thought I could win and still wrestle "like a girl," since that was what I was.

If the physical language of wrestling expanded me, the actual language of wrestling was determined to resist me. "Like a girl," that phrase meant females are innately inferior to males in the sport of wrestling. I was too scared that I would be told I couldn't take a joke or how men are just naturally stronger than women physically. I liked Dave, had strong affection for all of my teammates, and I didn't want to alienate them from me, so I said nothing.

The team's slogan had been "Quincy High Wrestling: Men at Work" for almost twenty years. Even the blue corduroy baseball caps we got at the end of the season had this slogan embroidered in white across the back. People asked me, "Don't you find it offensive? It should say WOMAN AT WORK." I usually said that the slogan didn't bother me so much. What mattered more was that I was allowed to be part of the team. I believed that the actions had to change first, and the language and words around wrestling would start to change later.

When we did jumping jacks, our assistant coach yelled at

us, saying we weren't loud enough when shouting out the numbers. "See what that sign says? You're supposed to be the Men at Work! That includes you, Lauralee!" he shouted. "Start over, louder this time! We are the Men at Work!" So then I knew that when with the wrestling team I ceased in some way to be a girl. This was liberating as well as crippling. It meant that I was part of a masculine space. It also meant that I learned to disdain femininity, that I had to "be a man" because girls were weak and soft.

Once they saw that I was there to stay, my teammates got used to me. They fluctuated between treating me as just another wrestler and treating me as someone special, set apart. Sometimes they felt they needed to take care of me, wait with me outside the boys' locker room until I could get my uniform, be gentler with me, and defend me from harsh comments made by guys on other teams.

Brian Woodberry—a smug ninth-grade wrestler of about my own weight—however, was rough. In practice, he caught me in a headlock again and again, slamming me down with a thud so loud that other wrestlers would turn and say, "Are you sure you're not hurting her?" "Take it easy, Brian." It was harder to develop affection for Woodberry because he was so cocky and harsh, but I respected his unwillingness to give me any breaks. He demanded that I survive the same rigorous treatment he gave other wrestlers. After I passed his tests and wore the proud purple bruises uncomplainingly, he gave me a small measure of respect. The bruises faded to blue then brown then greenish gray, but my determination to be treated as a full-fledged wrestler became clearer and more pronounced.

A wrestler on another team once congratulated me by

saying, "You have balls, man." Actually, no, I don't. Why is the language of courage masculine? Why was I taught that women's courage is not aggressive, that women are brave only when we are patient and enduring?

One day in practice, I was wrestling Rich Testa and had escaped and gotten reversal points for an aggressive switch, and I found myself with an opportunity to get Testa in a tight half nelson and pin him to the mat. I hesitated as if unsure what to do next, not knowing why I would suddenly pause when placed in a position of power in the midst of a match. I later realized that I was afraid of how I would be thought of once I had proved myself as a competent wrestler. No longer would I be the cute little girl who tries really hard but is not a threat. I was scared that if I actually beat boys, they would begin to feel antagonistic toward me, a reminder of their inadequacy in proving their superior male strength. Instead I was sometimes content with scoring a few good moves, improving, yet losing the match in the end.

I thought that overcoming social disapproval would be the biggest obstacle I would meet in wrestling. I didn't know that it would be even harder to refuse to be a token. People told me that it was all right that I wrestled, but other females were discouraged from trying it. My coach didn't really want his team to be taken over by girls who wanted to wrestle. Other girls were told not to try out because they were too sexual, they might be harassed. It was hard for me not to revel in being unique, to want to remain the only girl. Many women in positions usually reserved for men enjoy the glory and power in being a token woman, not seeing that by allowing themselves to be perceived as "the exception" they are preventing other women from succeeding.

I also feared that another girl wrestler might be better than I was, more aggressive, more competitive. As long as I was beaten only by males, that was okay, it was understandable, I was admitting that I was at a disadvantage. But to be beaten by a girl, by someone as "weak" as myself, could there be anything more shameful? It just didn't seem as exciting a challenge. The dilemma that boys wrestling girls face is that to beat a girl is no proof of manhood. The boy at best comes out looking like the bully. But to lose to a girl would be an altogether worse fate, to be called a wimp and a loser and a weakling.

Occasionally after being thrown down in a headlock with fingers choking tight across my throat (as they ought to, this is what the move requires)—or being slammed down again by an onslaught of well-meant but patronizing words—I would cry. I cried from the shame of being a girl—weak, never good enough, never strong enough, intrinsically flawed, pushed down time after time. I kept wrestling, hoping that the tears would mix in with the sweat, that the redness and puffiness of my eyes would blend in with the rest of my face, which was red with exertion, that anyone who happened to glance at me would think my eyes were watering from dust shoved in them when my face was pushed into the mat. I feared having a thirty-second rest period, during which my tears would continue to flow and might be noticed. My coach would come over and ask me if I was all right. I would say, "Yes," not looking at him, just sniffling a bit.

Far inside me was a place where fallow fears grew like marshmallows expand in a fire, full of air and not reality. Even though I cried, if I kept wrestling, my fears deflated and became manageable.

*

Our matches were every Wednesday at 7:00 P.M. and every Saturday morning at 9:00. Mr. V was conscientious about getting me at least one JV match each Wednesday and Saturday. He always called ahead to tell the other coaches that he had a girl on his team and what my weight was, so that the other coaches could set up a match for me with one of their JV wrestlers. One of the first meets we had, the boy who was supposed to wrestle me decided he didn't want to, so the match was counted as a forfeit.

A high school wrestling match is six minutes in length, with three periods of two minutes each, no rest between. During those six minutes, the wrestlers never stop moving, so by the time you are done you feel as if you've run at least a mile.

For matches I dressed in the skintight spandex wrestling singlet with a sports bra underneath, my new wrestling shoes (my mother had scrimped for the $29.99), and old knee pads and headgear that Coach had distributed for everyone on the team. I was so nervous at my first matches, with everyone watching as I walked to the center of the mat. I was sure everyone was looking at my butt. At the center, the referee would tell us to shake hands. Then my opponent and I assumed wrestling stance and stared at each other with looks meant to communicate "I'm going to annihilate you." I soon got used to being on the mat, and once the ref blew the whistle, everyone in the gym vanished as if a curtain were dropped in front of them, and the only thought in my mind was wrestling.

Most of the other teams did not have girls. If they did, then I would wrestle the girl. Many of the girls were around my weight or slightly heavier, since girls tend to weigh less than boys. But even if the girl weighed 160, I was still eager to

194

wrestle her. Whenever I wrestled girls, I had an extra burst of adrenaline and fear because I knew I needed to win.

During my first season I beat all the girls and lost to all the boys. I was winning in one JV match against a boy, but he quit halfway through, saying that he was hurt. As he held his side and grimaced theatrically, I wondered if he really were injured.

I trained all season and had come a long way from the first practice, when I knew nothing. In a match near the end of my first season I had finally learned to run to the center of the mat. (Run out there! Don't walk—our coach told us—run out there like you want to win!) Even though I ran to the center of the mat, my shoulders were still rounded. Keep your back straight, Lauralee! I admonished myself. My opponent was a thin wiry boy a little shorter than I. He had curly sand-colored hair, freckles, and green eyes. He looked even more nervous than I did. We shook hands. I stared into his eyes, and suddenly the whistle blew. Jolt—and my rounded step circled, around and around, into molten motion. My motion told a story, my shoulders turned to this serious ground and straightened up. I faced myself. I faced my fears, embodied in my quivering flesh and the hulking frightened flesh of my opponent. Jolt—the whistle sounded and I stepped.

My forehead was rubbed raw from all the head butting in practice. An aggressive reptilian part of my brain pushed forward. It collided with the feminine submission that had been part of my psyche for aeons. My raw forehead had absorbed decades of dominance. I was thirsty now, no water left in me, I had sweated, cried it all out. I was thirsty and my thirst burst from me like a sun bursts in a glorious fury over the placid line of the horizon. Thirsty, I felt a befuddled prowess birthing inside me. A power rose from me like steam, when I thought I had no more water to give. I was steamed—I had all the power of atomic molecules but no solid shape. "My honesty gets me in hot water, I hope it boils me until I dissolve into steam"— the words of Henry Rollins came into my mind. The steam rose inside me, steam I had quietly absorbed for decades, centuries, millenniums—and it needed release.

I was crushed by the boy's tight grip and shoulder pressure in my side. His hips flew out, and I swung slamming to the mat.

When I began wrestling, my soft side was the most noticeable part of me. But my soft side had been crushed by my coach's words: "Be aggressive! Come on, Lauralee, take him down." Softness was trodden right out of me, like the soft muscles between my ribs, which I had twisted so that I could not do sit-ups without pain, my intercostal muscles— which lay over my ribs—hidden like so many matchsticks waiting to ignite into pain. My soft side was crushed by a skin touch.

In my wobbly glory I shook inside, shot down to the mat, not knowing what he had hit me with; I was thrown out of bounds. "No points," said the ref as he blew his whistle. "Back to the center." I picked up and ran to the center of the mat. My opponent's sculpted muscles were glazed with sweat-sheen, but this was only the surface. He was trying to show a seamless story. But it was not the surface that mattered, but the action, the desire that was congested inside.

"Shoot—Lauralee! The more you shoot in on his legs, the less he can shoot in on you," shouted my coach from the corner of the mat. I went for a double-leg takedown. I torqued my neck muscles, pulled in and up with my arms locked behind his thighs. I stood up, drove across, raised with the power of my legs. My neck muscles bent, imploding into his soft side. I drove across and he was—fallen.

The ref called out, "Takedown, two points." He knelt on the mat as I held the boy down. "One, two, three—three points, near fall." No pin and we were up again.

My eyes were blinded by his hairy armpit, the smooth rock of his triceps as he "cross-faced" me. Even so, I slipped in a blind underhook and twisted him, pushing back on his forehead with my other hand in this nonsexual intercourse with another body. I was winning, rocking from heel to toe, my arms slippery with his sweat.

During my match, my team left the bench, left off warming up for their own matches, and gathered around the edge of the blue mat. This was one of the first times I had been in a position of possibly winning a match against a boy. They were all screaming at once and jumping up and down in excitement. "Go, Lauralee! Double! Double! Turn him over! Your right leg!" Froelich made big gestures with his hands, imitating the moves I was to do. Woodberry pounded his fists on the mat. My coach grabbed Johnny Richards and threw him around, demonstrating moves and pinning combinations. "Put your right leg over his and drive across!" I looked over, sweaty, wild hair coming out of its ponytail and sprouting straight up out of the top and sides of my headgear, like a waterfall. "Your right leg!" shouted my coach again, and the ref blew the whistle to signify the end of the first period.

I chose the bottom position and escaped, and the boy and I circled each other again. My teammates were beginning to encroach on the large white circle that delineated the out-of-bounds line. The ref turned to them. "Stand back, clear the side of the mat!" They retreated for a few moments, but soon they ringed the mat once more and continued to roar like a rioting mob. I pressed down on my opponent's sweaty neck-line. My hands made stories out of boxed-up action. I snapped his neck down, spun around, and the hushed riot stirred inside of me. He escaped and went for a single-leg takedown. I hopped on one foot, hoped on one foot, as he held the other cupped in his armpit. I kicked, lunged, broke free, and whirled to face him.

Third period he chose bottom, hoping to escape and get points, but again I controlled his wrists and kept my weight on him and tried to work pinning combinations. He got to his feet once, but I held on to his left wrist and forearm with both hands (called a two-on-one), lifted him up onto my hips, and dumped him onto the mat, keeping control.

The ref's whistle signaled the end of the match, and I released my hold on the wrestler and stood up. He stood up, and the ref met us at the center of the mat. The boy and I shook hands again, and then the ref took one each of our hands and lifted mine up high to signal that I was the winner, then turned us to face the other half of the gym, lifted my hand up again. I was in shock that I had actually won.

After the ref released my hand, I was engulfed by my teammates, hands pounded on my back, gave me high fives, embraces, hugs. "All right, Lauralee!" After a few minutes of this they dispersed to warm up for the varsity match, which would begin shortly. I walked around for a few moments, my whole body shaking. I found a corner of the gym and sank against a wall near the girls' locker room. I was still shaking wildly. My whole body throbbed and quivered.

During one afternoon practice near the end of my last wrestling season at QHS, the sunlight illuminated every piece of fuzz and dead skin on the dusty mats and in the warm, sweaty air. The coughs of the wrestlers echoed as we waited for our captain, Ashley Davis, to bark out "Begin!" so that we could start practice with the two hundred militant jumping jacks. In that hushed moment, the world seemed to be no more or less than a winter afternoon's dim sunlight, the acrid yet delightfully familiar smell of mats mixed with sweaty male bodies, and movement. I wondered why I loved wrestling so much and what it had taught me. These practices were the only time of day when I felt that my mind and body no longer were separate, but two parts with one purpose. One reason I liked wrestling was that it was so human, so physical, mental, and emotional. I would not have kept wrestling if it were merely an academic exercise in feminist theory. I mostly loved it because my actions felt real, and I was surrounded and nourished by the true affection and love of my teammates.

20

CUTTING

DURING THE SEASON, we ate, breathed, thought, and slept wrestling. Even my dreams each night were filled with images and sensations of a red mat upon which faceless wrestlers tirelessly practiced endless moves. When I woke up, my body and mind would ache with tiredness, just as if I had not slept at all.

This obsession was evidenced one day at a match in mid-season. I sat on the bleachers with the rest of the JV wrestlers. We were absorbed in watching two lean wrestlers whose skin stretched so taut that the contracting, the abduction and adduction of every tendon and muscular tissue, was clearly pronounced. Their bodies were complex and beautiful machines in action.

The crowd bellowed commands, pleas, praises: "Sink that half." "Get your head *up*." "That's the way, John." The voices tangled like wires of a car's engine, one's exhortation becoming indistinguishable from another's admonition. As the roar lost intensity (between matches), I heard the voice of Mark

Froelich saying, ". . . four grams of fat!" I turned to see him reading from an empty yogurt container. My teammates were grouped around the yogurt, their eyes open, aghast at such a large quantity of dietary fat. We broke into laughter at our own trained reaction to food, at the unity of our response.

Being wrestlers affected each of our thoughts, our choices about food and weight and fasting and bingeing ("going crazy," as Coach Venturelli would say). Eating was insanity. Abstaining from food was virtue. We were more careful, more obsessive, more concerned about how much or what or when we ate, than a gaggle of anorexic teenage girls. As we stood awaiting the scales' verdict before each wrestling match, our weight was measured more precisely than a baker measures the flour for biscuits.

My second season of wrestling—during my senior year—my coach sometimes put me in the varsity lineup if I was able to make weight. I was in the 112-pound weight class, mostly because we had enough 119-pounders. I was small enough to get my weight down to 112. At the season's start, I weighed about 125 pounds, a healthy weight for my frame. But I thought the hunger and exhaustion would be worth the power I would have when my muscles were tightly clad with skin, their definition undiminished by "excess" fat.

I began the day with a glass of skim milk. For lunch, I had a salad from the school lunchroom. I either discarded or gave away the roll and cheese that came with it. I ate only the lettuce and tomato wedges, and the cottage cheese, for protein. This meal gave me energy for three hours of wrestling practice, the nonstop sweating and cardiovascular strain that took up every afternoon. My dinner was a light meal, some soup, or perhaps just a banana and an apple. I don't know how I managed to make it through the day without fainting. I also ran two miles each night in the dark, freezing air after practice. I applied the same amount of perseverance to the goal of making weight that I did to any task I was bent on completing.

Once, after a match, I ate half of a small peanut-butter-and-banana sandwich, and I felt guilty because I had eaten so much. So much real food, a whole half of a sandwich. My stomach felt heavy with guilt and a dread of not "making weight."

Before matches, I sometimes had to weigh in in my underwear in the hallway. My fattened lines were gone; they gave way to sinewy sensuality. They gave way to thinness, emaciation, and strength. What was health and what starvation? Johnny was the only underweight teammate, at 90 pounds. He had to get to 97 to make the lightest weight class. He wore lead underwear to make weight; that was the joke. He ate a whole loaf of bread, drank a gallon of water, couldn't take a shit, all so that he could weigh in. He was our foil, as were our heavyweights, Mark and Mike, who could eat as much as they wanted.

Before I started wrestling, I didn't use every part of my body when I moved, and that bothered me. Sometimes I felt like my body took up the wrong kind of space—that it was spilling out in every direction.

I remember standing behind one of my teammates who was leaning on his wrists over a water fountain. His inner forearms were ridged like potato chips, tubes full of rushing liquid like slides at a water park, like a 3-D map of blue rivers and tributaries against cloud white skin. The veins seemed to support the weight of his body as he leaned forward. I wanted to have veins like his.

Before I started wrestling, my arms were useless slabs of

flesh. They were never really part of me. Hanging strangely at my sides, limp and soft. What were they, whose were they? I couldn't wear sleeveless shirts because my arms were so foreign to me.

When I became a wrestler, I started using my arms more. I did cartwheels before practice, handstands during warm-up. I did push-ups, pull-ups, and lifted weights. One day I realized I had shoulder muscles, and triceps that made lumps on the outsides of my arms, swelling up, hard underneath the skin. Currents of blood flowed and made blue veins that ran down and up through the crooks of my elbows. Cerulean veins pumped ecstatic oxygen through every limb; the veins and arteries stood out on my arms like tree roots blue-white in dark soil.

I went to see the trainer at one point during the season. It had been three months since my last period. He had me take a body fat test, squeezing the plastic pincers against my stomach, thigh, and the backs of my arms. He told me that most women athletes have between 18 and 22 percent body fat, but that my body fat was only 14 percent, below the point at which most women are able to menstruate. He also said that if a woman's body fat is low, she might grow more body hair. I was still jealous of my male teammates, some of whom had 3 to 7 percent body fat, low even for boys.

Because of what the trainer had said, I imagined each day that there were more dark lines of hairs rising from their tiny pockets than the day before. On my arms I could glance down the page of my body's text.

I heard my coach's voice in my head. One day in practice he told us to be men; have some balls; this takes balls. I laughed; this was a joke, surely? It was just a manner of speech. I didn't really have to have balls, did I? Looking at my arms, the new hairs growing there, I was not so sure.

I'd had control over my body up till now, or thought I had. Not eating, when even the scraps of food in the trash looked edible, and not stopping running at six miles.

Now I had an adolescent boy's taut three-tiered stomach; from the side it was ridged and sunken in, held in. I had exterminated my woman's body, the soft spilling parts, the excessive folds, the cushioning. No evidence of my former girlish body remained—it melted, disappeared, and sat in my stomach's silky lining, comforting me instead of food. My soft awkward, spilling desire sat inside, my female desire unborn.

But desire surfaced, one way or another, and I could see it on my arms as they grew hairier each week, gradually. What trick was this? Was the sport masculinizing me?

One night before an important tournament, I had to cut six pounds or I wouldn't make 112. "Don't worry. Six pounds, no problem," one of my teammates in the 189-pound class told me. Six pounds is a lot more for a 112-pounder to lose than for a 189-pounder, is what I thought.

After practice ended at 6:00, I did without my sparse dinner. I stayed at the YMCA until almost 9:00 P.M., running 186 laps on the indoor track, nearly eleven miles. I piled on two T-shirts, three sweatshirts—two with hoods—and a heavy knit hat. Multiple layers of tights, leggings, and sweatpants ensured that I would sweat, drop by drop, ounces and pounds of the salty liquid from my overheated pores. The other runners and fitness fanatics at the Y looked at my attire as if I were slightly crazy. I looked only at the clock and the wooden track and the approaching water fountain. I chewed Extra sugar-free gum, piece after piece. It tasted exactly like toothpaste and, because I was dehydrated, was chalky in my mouth like mint-flavored dust. I saved up a small reservoir of gum-flavored juice under my tongue to spit into the water fountain every second lap. I kept count of exactly how many laps I had run by the number of times I had visited the fountain. Occasionally, I rinsed my mouth out with the cold, deliciously torturous water, careful not to swallow any of it.

This was all a game, a deceitful way to "lose" six pounds of water weight overnight. I was left feeling weak, dizzy, cold, and unstable. I finished the endless laps; my layers of clothes were heavy, drenched with the cherished pounds. The sweat turned icy cold as I stepped into the fifteen-degree January air. I did not know if I could manage the walk through piles of ice to the subway station, encompassed by cold wet clothing. I had never felt so drained and nightmarishly unreal as I did stumbling into my living room, with barely enough energy to change into three new layers of clothing and collapse deliriously under numerous blankets into a night of sticky and hot oblivion.

I worked myself too hard. But I thought it was all worthwhile the next morning, after I jogged the mile and a half to school at 7:00 A.M., after the two-hour bus ride, doing sit-ups frantically in the green vinyl seat. It was worth it when I stepped on the scales in my shiny blue and white singlet that clung to my strong yet emaciated body. The scales balanced, miraculously, at 111 pounds.

I could drink water, and it had never tasted so good. I could now eat: yogurt, sweet and creamy on my dry throat, and a few grapes, too. I became the first female in history to wrestle in the Lowell Holiday Tournament. Over sixty teams were in the huge six-mat auditorium, and I was the only female in full varsity uniform.

Before I began wrestling, I ate when I was hungry or when I wanted to eat. I felt pretty good about my body's shape. I was almost always active, running long distances and biking to and from school. I had my occasional "fat" days, when I had a negative body image, but I felt fairly confident about the decisions I made about my body, what I put into it and what I got out of it.

This confidence, however, was skewed during and after I became a wrestler.

This distortion began with the first M&M I had eaten in several months—a vast explosion of chocolate and sweetness. It was all I had dreamed of and desired during months of denial. As my mother used to tell me, for every action there is an equal and opposite reaction: Newton's third law of physics. I had denied and starved myself for so long that once I was allowed to eat, I wanted to binge. The M&M had gained a dangerous power—it was coveted because forbidden, unattainable. And when it became allowed, I could not stop. The second M&M was a smaller explosion of chocolate, not as dramatic as the first. Each M&M I ate thereafter had a half-life of chocolate: it was only half as satisfying as the previous one. Soon I was gobbling the candy pellets as I might have before I started wrestling. But instead of stopping at one handful, as I would have then, I could not be satisfied. I ate handful after handful compulsively, trying to make up for all those months of deprivation. I felt guilty. What I didn't realize was that, no matter how much I ate, it would never make up for the months of denial. It was only going to make me feel stuffed and guilty. My body ballooned, or it seemed to me it did. I had no clear sense of my body's true boundaries or limits. Food was no longer just nourishment; it was emotion. Food became a way to fill all that was lacking within myself. I was trying to fill myself up emotionally by eating, but I never could succeed.

It took years for me to become balanced, but in the end I emerged a healthier person. Since high school wrestling, I have never gone on a diet. I had to learn that I deserved to eat and enjoy food, and that eating what I wanted was not going to make me humongous. Only then was I able to stop, satisfied by one handful, savoring each morsel of chocolate and not continually chased by guilt.

I also learned to appreciate both the masculine and the feminine aspects of my body. I realized that I could love the soft parts of my body. I stroked my rounded thighs and spoke words of love to them, welcomed the fat back into myself, into my concept of myself, instead of touching and looking at my thighs with revulsion and painfully severing them from me. I learned that when I exercised and ate well, I felt strong and healthy, and that this health was more important than the exact dimensions of my body.

21

HOMELESS TO HARVARD

MY UNCLE RON had a long career as a high school guidance counselor. I was the youngest person he counseled. As a precocious six-year-old I asked him: "Uncle Ron, what is the best college?"

"Harvard," he said.

"How do you get to go there?"

"You have to do something unusual," he said, "that no one else does, like mountain climbing." I thought about it but couldn't think of anything unusual about my six-year-old life. I didn't think I would ever do anything as strange as climbing mountains.

I didn't think about going to Harvard again until my senior year of high school, eight days before the application was due.

I had no intention of attending college close to my home in Quincy. I was tired of New England winters and saw higher education as an opportunity to see a new part of the country. I looked at sunny pictures in the college brochures and was enchanted by the shiny new campuses, the fresh spring days, the glittering and unknown skylines of far-off cities. Although I would miss my mother, I wanted to go someplace I had never been, like Nashville, Tennessee; Salt Lake City, Utah; or Atlanta, Georgia. I did not want to go to Harvard, at the other end of the Red Line.

I applied to the New School for Social Research in New York City, and to Brown University, both known for being especially liberal. Even these schools seemed too nearby. I applied to Vanderbilt in Nashville, and Emory in Atlanta because their locations were exotic to me.

In late December, all my college applications were already sent in, and I went to an end-of-term dinner for my Harvard Extension class (The Dynamics of Psychology and Religion). It was at my professor's house in Cambridge.

I prepared two dishes—one was a Swedish recipe of yogurt, granola, and apple slices, and the other was an eggplant dish called ratatouille. I dressed in my favorite Christmas outfit, a red and green plaid dress that my mother bought at a yard sale and shortened to miniskirt length for me. I wore it with black stockings and combat boots, and my hair was dyed green to match. As I approached Professor Austin's house, I was intimidated by its size and elegance. A wooden trellis, taller than I and covered with ivy vines, surrounded the house. I felt tiny and homemade in my little flannel dress, as if I were five years old, a shiny, apple-cheeked kindergartner meeting her teacher on the first day of school. I rang the doorbell that said, "Ring here for Dorothy Austin and Diana Eck." The other doorbell was labeled "Ring here for Erik Erikson." Upon seeing that, I was even more intimidated. We had read Erikson in class. He had been one of Freud's protégés and contemporaries. I felt like I had been invited to the house of someone who existed only in legend.

Professor Austin, whom everyone in our class called Dorothy, answered the door. Her beautiful silvery blond hair framed a big welcoming smile. She helped me take off my winter coat. The house was already buzzing with students. She took my dishes, exclaiming "How wonderful!" as she set them on the large mahogany dining table with the other food.

I began mingling with the students, all of whom were older—from early twenties to white-haired seventy-year-olds. At one point in the evening, when I was talking to Dorothy, she exclaimed that she hadn't known I was still in high school and was applying to colleges.

"Are you applying to Harvard?" she asked.

"No," I answered. "I don't think I would get in. And I don't think I'd fit in with the students." I thought Harvard was only for valedictorians and students who had taken calculus and all AP classes and who had never missed a day of school. Harvard was not for *me*.

"Oh, no, you must apply." She assured me that Harvard was a diverse place and that, although it was known best for its long-standing traditions, it was also a place where all kinds of people thrived. "You can pick up an application tomorrow." She focused her gaze upon me and said, "I'm going to introduce you to my roommate, Diana. She's the chair of Harvard's Comparative Religion Department." She vanished upstairs for a moment and returned with Diana. I had taken several courses in world religions at the Extension School and was interested in being a religion major.

When I told Mr. Mac about what Dorothy and Diana had said, he was dumbfounded. He called Mr. Daniele, my guidance counselor, up to Heritage for a conference. They had not thought of my applying to Harvard, because they didn't think I was the "Harvard" type. Quincy was not an elite high school, and even those ranked first and second in a graduating class weren't always accepted at Ivy League universities. I was twentieth in my class. My sophomore-year grades were mediocre—many D's and F's—and I'd barely passed my classes for the year. My junior- and senior-year grades were better—but I didn't have anything close to a 4.0. But Mr. Mac said, "Well, if they think you should, you'd better do it."

Mr. Mac and I, and a few other students, were going that afternoon to visit our friend and former Heritage student Lily's grave at Mount Auburn Cemetery in Cambridge—she had died of leukemia the previous year. So we stopped by the Harvard Admissions Office and got the application. It was December 24, and the application was due in one week.

I visited Dorothy and Diana the next week. This time it was morning, and the grand house was filled with sunlight and empty of students. It was just the two professors and I. I felt honored that they would take the time to look over my entrance essay and help me edit it. Dorothy said she would write one of the recommendations for me, and I later found out that Diana also sent in a recommendation.

On New Year's Eve, I took the completed application to the Admissions Office on Garden Street. The office was closed, but I left the thick brown envelope in the drifted snow on the doorstep and hoped it would be found when the office reopened in the new year.

My last year of high school brought many unexpected events. In February I was chosen out of twelve finalists for the Boston Garden Good Sport Scholarship and was honored at halftime during a Boston Bruins game.

My winning this scholarship prompted a *Boston Globe* writer to ask Mr. Mac if he could interview me. The reporter came to Heritage and interviewed me in the "Outback" for over an hour. He asked me questions about my family and background as well as about wrestling. I was open with him about my childhood.

A month later, the reporter called to tell me that the story was coming out the next morning. I was full of nervous anticipation as I rushed to the subway station before school and bought a paper. I sat down to wait for the train. I was surprised that a small picture of me was on the front page of the paper and that the article took up almost the entire front page of the sports section and two other full pages inside. Weren't there any big baseball games going on? I wondered. There were pictures of me wrestling, but what surprised me the most was that the story was not just about wrestling but about my whole life. I couldn't bear to read it. I shut the paper and stuffed it into my book bag. That day and throughout the following week, many teachers and students told me how much they enjoyed the article. I said thank you, but I didn't read the article myself until several weeks later because I felt so exposed.

I didn't find out if I'd been admitted to Harvard until early April. It was a relief to get the thick acceptance packet in the mail. I decided to attend Harvard because Dorothy and Diana showed me that many professors there took personal interest in their students. I knew Harvard was a great school and had many resources that other colleges might not have. It also gave me the most financial aid, because it had the biggest endowment. I put aside my misgivings about going to school so close to home. Little did I know that Harvard, just a "T" ride away, would prove to be a much more foreign environment than I had anticipated.

Once I got the acceptance letter, I knew I was in for one of Mr. Mac's chief congratulatory rituals for Heritage, known as cake in the face. When one of us accomplished something important—getting into a college, starring in a school play, passing a difficult class, or pulling off a student-run fashion show—Mr. Mac would sneak up on the unsuspecting individual and smash a Suzy Q snack cake into his or her face. "Wuf," Mr. Mac would say, delighted at the gooey white-frosting-eyelashed looks of surprise we wore underneath our chocolate cake masks. Far from dreading such occurrences, we looked forward to them. "Mr. Mac caked me," we would say. "Did you get caked yet?"

Even the girls who came to school with immaculately made up faces did not mind but were proud when Mr. Mac caked them, after an initial panicked run to the bathroom to wash the gooey mess off and reapply makeup. Mr. Mac kept a box of snack cakes stashed under his desk year-round, along with a bottle of shampoo to wash the frosting out of our hair.

Mr. Mac, of course, did not go unscathed. We delighted in catching him unawares. "Hey, Mr. Mac," one of us would say, and as he turned he got a Little Debbie in his face. "Wuf," he would say, taking his glasses off and looking around for something to wipe the frosting off with.

In May, Mr. Mac got another call from an Associated Press reporter who wanted to do a feature on a graduating senior. I agreed to the interview but was more hesitant this time.

The AP story ran on page six of *The New York Times*, in papers throughout the country, and even in a few foreign papers. There was a color picture of me on the front page of Oregon's major paper, *The Oregonian*. My aunt Jane cut it out and sent it to me. Even a national tabloid ran an exaggerated version of the story a few weeks later.

I knew my father lived in Oregon. I wondered what he would think if he read this article. Would he know I was his daughter?

The response to the article was overwhelming. My phone rang thirty times a day, and mail from people I didn't know flooded through my mail slot. Reporters from ABC's *Prime-Time Live*, *Dateline NBC*, *Good Morning America*, a few talk shows, and all the local news shows called and wanted my mother and me to appear on their programs. *People* magazine wanted to do a story. *Seventeen* magazine wanted me to write a story. A dozen movie producers called to discuss the film rights. A few people wrote or called to ask if they could write about me in their books of inspiring stories.

I received many letters, cards, and news clippings. Many people, especially older people, sent me checks for fifty, one hundred, two hundred dollars. All together, it was more money than I'd ever had in my life. It was a lot of trouble to cash the checks, because I didn't have a bank account and my mom didn't either. Most check-cashing places would not take personal checks, and we went to three places before we could cash them. I felt weird about having the money. I couldn't send it back, but it seemed like fake money, because I didn't feel I had done anything to earn it. I spent most of it on bubble gum for my friends, and bus tickets for my mom, myself, and a friend to travel to Oregon to visit relatives.

I also got many other odd things in the mail. The picture in the paper had shown me playing the violin in my room, and one man from New York sent me sheet music for my violin and said he would pay me to play and record it to add to his collection of famous recordings. I received many letters and gifts from religion enthusiasts, including the Christian Science Bible and a book on the power of myth by Joseph Campbell. One young man from North Carolina sent me a care package that included a mixed tape he'd made for me (I still listen to it), packets of hot chocolate, incense, dried flower petals, holographic stickers of the Japanese band Shonen Knife, photographic portraits of himself, and a letter saying that he, too, had never really known his father and hadn't seen him since he was three years old.

There were three camera crews at my graduation, one from *PrimeTime Live,* one from *Dateline,* and one from *Good Morning America.* They shadowed me, and I tried to ignore them as my classmates around me asked the cameramen questions and tried to get on camera.

Just as the superintendent of schools began to make his opening announcements, the sky opened up. The rain didn't start gradually. Sheets of water poured down like silk curtains, like heavy wet cotton. The camera crews opened humungous umbrellas to protect their equipment. Again my classmates crowded around, this time to stay dry. My blue graduation gown and the rainbow-flowered dress I wore underneath were soaked in just a few minutes. The school officials skipped all of the announcements, and the valedictorian didn't get to give her speech. They commenced right away with reading the three hundred graduates' names in as quick succession as possible.

My mother and I tentatively agreed to meet with some of the media people. I appeared on all the local news networks and *Good Morning America.*

After our experience on *Good Morning America,* we

decided to say no to the other offers. We were wary of people making films, because we didn't know their credentials and were afraid of having our lives exploited. I was tired of receiving attention and worried that when I began school in the fall I would be known as the formerly homeless girl. I knew that I was going to meet people at Harvard who I would know for the next four years. I wanted to be known for myself, not for the media's portrayal of me, an image that seemed larger and smaller than life.

It seemed that everyone wanted a "take" on my "story." So many people wanted to write about me, tell the story in their way. It astonished me because I thought of my life as normal. There were millions of other people in this country who had lived, who were living, the life I had. I did receive two letters from editors at publishing houses who asked if I'd ever thought of writing about my experiences. I tucked those letters away for future reference. Having had so much experience with being written and talked about, I now knew that if my "story" were to be told, I wanted to be the one telling it.

22

MOVING IN

MY CLOSE FRIEND Diane and I were sitting in Donut 'n' Donuts at the Quincy Center T station when I opened another envelope from Harvard. We drank iced cappuccinos at Donut 'n' Donuts almost every day that summer. The shop's name was painted on the storefront's huge glass panes in hot pink and orange bubble letters so that it looked deceptively like a real Dunkin' Donuts. It was owned and staffed by a multigenerational family of Greek immigrants. Homeless people took up many booths, their bags stuffed into the benches next to them—they looked bundled up in layers even in midsummer. Big-haired girls from our high school occupied another booth. Two of them toted babies in strollers, like little dolls. Diane and I joked about the redundancy of the store's name. "It's not even Donuts 'n' Donuts. It is just one Donut, 'n' all the other Donuts." She giggled. Diane wondered why the owners didn't call it Mad Muffins 'n' Donuts or Donuts and Other Assorted Pastries or even Coffee 'n' More Coffee since coffee was the only thing we bought there and we never tired of it.

The beauty of Donut 'n' Donuts was that it was the center of everything. At least it was the center of everything in Quincy and everything in our lives that summer. "Everyone shows up here eventually" was how our close friend Mary stated it. Even the nonsense of the store's name seemed inexplicably Quincy-ish.

So this is where I was on the day I got the envelope that told me who my roommates would be. The paper said I was in a suite of six, in Weld Hall, Number 37. I was going to be the local girl, since all the other girls were from out of state. There was Hatcher, Mary S., from Atlanta, GA, and Goffard, Sandrine, from Sarasota, FL, and Katopodes, Fotini V., from Ann Arbor, MI. The other girls were Lin, Jenny, from Florham Park, NJ, and Osseo-Asare, Abena, from State College, PA. The names were different from those of my Quincy friends, who had names like Diane, Mary, Pam, Patrick, Jack, and Dave, and whose last names were mostly Irish or Italian.

"No one at Harvard has normal names, do they?" asked Diane. We sat sipping our coffee and tried to imagine what each of these girls and her hometown might be like. "Maybe that's how you get into Harvard," said Diane. "You have to have a weird name."

None of the names except for Mary Hatcher was a typical WASP name. Sandrine sounded French, Fotini might be Greek, and Jenny Lin was Chinese. Abena Osseo-Asare had an African name, and her parents must have been liberal because her name was hyphenated. I was excited to meet them. Later on, my roommates told me that they had wondered if I was transplanted from the South because my name was Lauralee.

In early September, my friends Mary, Joe, and Jeff helped me move. Jeff had a station wagon, so he and Joe came over and picked up Mary and me. I had two trash bags filled with clothes and bedding, a few beat-up backpacks full of desk supplies, a large red crayon bank filled with pennies, a pink beanbag chair, and my skateboard and violin.

We drove through the center of Boston, down Mass Ave, and through Cambridge until we reached Harvard Square. It wasn't really a square at all. It was a few interlocking circles of streets and cobblestone sidewalks. We often went there to hang out and shop. The sidewalks were crowded with tourists, beggars, sidewalk performers, students, and professors. On every street corner, homeless people and colorful street youth called out for spare change or lectured on topics from nuclear physics to Charles Dickens. It was even more hectic and crowded than usual with students moving into the dorms. Taxis zoomed by, and crowds of people rushed through the streets.

My friends hadn't ever been inside Harvard Yard because it was separated from the circus of the Square by high curving brick walls and black wrought-iron gates. Freshmen Move-in Day was the only time that cars were allowed in the Yard. One of the larger gates, Johnston Gate, was opened to allow cars to enter. A uniformed guard waved our station wagon in and pointed us toward Weld Hall. We drove slowly, following the other cars.

"Where do we park?" Jeff asked.

"Pahk the Cahr in Hahvahd Yahd," Mary said, and we all giggled. She had dark auburn hair dyed with bright blood red streaks. She was Irish American and her parents had thick Irish brogues, but she had a thick Boston accent. Her eyebrows arched, and she laughed. "How many people can say they actually parked their car in Harvard Yard?"

We parked just behind Weld Hall, a five-story redbrick

building that looked like a castle. It had a tall tower in the middle that I later learned was an observatory. I was impressed by its turrets and large W's engraved into stone circles on each side of the building, and the gold weathervane with a W emblazoned on its metal flag. The building's beauty intimidated me.

The four of us started unloading. I felt happy and safe because my friends were with me. Joe tucked the fluorescent pink beanbag chair under one arm and the big red crayon bank under the other. The beanbag was to become a staple in our Weld 37 common room. My suitemates used it when talking on the phone, and our smallest suitemate, Jenny Lin, would curl up in it for hours at a time, head bent over a huge psychology textbook. I had found it years before when my foster sister Terri and I saw it set out on the sidewalk for trash and excitedly rescued it. I had fallen asleep in it numerous nights during high school.

Mary carried a trash bag filled with blankets and sheets in one hand and a bunch of pillows in the other. Jeff had the violin and assorted backpacks, and I carried another big plastic bag and my skateboard.

Anxious parents carting large sealed boxes, expensive luggage sets, and assorted furniture filled the building's hallways. Some of them gave us strange looks. We must have looked funny. We were four punks carrying what looked like a toy collection.

Upstairs, we opened the door to number 37. A tall, muscular girl with long honey-colored hair introduced herself as Maggie. This was the Mary Hatcher from the roommate list. Jenny was there as well. She was under five feet tall, a Chinese girl with black hair to her waist and small gold-rimmed glasses. A girl with medium brown skin and a shaved head and a young man with black curly hair and freckles were trapped in the corner of a tiny back bedroom trying to move a very big bed. The girl was my suitemate Abena, and the boy introduced himself as Neil from New Orleans. He was moving in down the hall and had come by to visit. Joe and Jeff volunteered to help move the bed. I could see that they were immediately taken with Maggie, who was very beautiful, and were trying to impress her with their strength and chivalry.

After I settled in, my friends left me on my own to get to know my roommates. "You just missed Sandrine and Tina," Maggie said. "They left with their parents for a while." I guessed that Tina must be a nickname for Fotini.

The suite had four small bedrooms, a bathroom, and a common area. Maggie, Abena, Jenny, and I discussed our study and sleeping habits to determine who would be compatible to share bedrooms. Maggie and I were the most laid-back, so we decided to share a double. Jenny and Abena decided to share a room as well, so that Sandrine and Tina could have their own. That way we could begin moving in without waiting for them.

The first night in the dorm, I dyed my hair fire orange. Throughout high school, I had dyed my hair when in the midst of a mood change or a change in perspective. Changing my hair from blond to orange symbolized for me that summer was over and the autumn had begun, a new season and a new school. I really stuck out in this group of people, because I was the only one with neon hair, colorful clothes, and a skateboard. I didn't mind looking different, but I did feel conspicuous and detached from everyone.

Maggie and I had the biggest room and shared it for the

whole year. It had two big corner windows. The room was narrow, with barely enough space for our bunk bed, desks, and other school-issued furniture, but it had twelve-foot-high ceilings, so all we had to do was look up when we felt the need for more space.

I decorated the walls and my bottom bunk, making it into a cozy cave of pictures and words. Maggie also decorated the wall above her bed. I had a collection of sugar packets from all over the country that I stuck to the walls. Later on in the year, Jenny brought sugar packets from Thailand and China, and Mary, packets from Ireland. I even put up one empty sugar packet from Diane with a note written on it: "Sorry, I had to use the sugar."

Diane and I bought Raggedy Ann and Andy fabric at a yard sale and spread it out between the underside of Maggie's mattress and the metal bed frame to cover up the plain blue stripes of the mattress. I woke up each day to see Andy hauling a wheelbarrow, and Raggedy Ann planting a big orange and yellow flower.

It was the first time in my life that I felt frighteningly responsible for my own mistakes. I was an adult now. I was worried about balancing the two worlds—Harvard and Quincy. I longed for the comfort of my old friends. I went through each day wondering where Diane was and wishing she were with me. I had lived with her over the summer because my mom had become homeless again, and we had spent almost all our time together. We even worked at the same job. It didn't feel right to be without her.

Four of my suitemates had their own computers, as did most of the first-years. Maggie didn't, even though her parents could easily have afforded it, and that made me feel better about not having one. The Science Center had a large computer lab that was open all night, so Maggie and I made many trips there in the wee hours of the night to work on our papers.

I also didn't buy all the required books, as most students did. The Coop charged outrageous prices, twenty dollars for small paperbacks, forty for larger ones. Some of my classes had ten or more required books. Instead of buying them, I checked them out from Widener Library or photocopied chapters I needed.

During the summer, Harvard President Neil Rudenstine had sent all incoming students a required reading packet, including his speech on diversity. He mentioned race, ethnicity, political and sexual orientation, and physical handicaps—their effect on the composition of the student body. He didn't write about how isolated people unfamiliar with middle-class culture like myself could feel in a university setting.

During the first week, we attended many orientation sessions about diversity. At one of these gatherings, the speaker asked the audience of two hundred to raise their hands if they were from working-class backgrounds. I looked over the heads of the mass of students and saw seven raised hands, one of which was my own. Only seven out of two hundred Harvard students were from working-class families. My mother and I were not even working class; we were welfare class. During Freshman Week, I met many students whose parents owned companies, had millions of dollars, or were faculty at other elite universities. It was a shock to learn that such people existed in my own world.

Some students had mothers, fathers, and brothers who had all gone to Harvard. For them college simply meant a choice between Harvard and Yale. One classmate's parents had donated a million dollars to Harvard, the cost of about thirty college tuitions. Another classmate had roomfuls of designer clothes and expensive imported electronic gadgets, like a three-hundred-dollar fold-up cell phone from Japan. This was before anyone had a cell phone; it was the first cell phone I'd ever seen.

During Freshman Week, we also had a Diversity meeting with our proctor group—all the students on our floor of Weld Hall. We met in a small conference room. A distinguished African American minister dressed in a suit and tie—a Divinity School professor—led the discussion. All the students sat in a large circle. The minister asked us to introduce ourselves and say how we had experienced diversity in our lives thus far.

As each student spoke, I grew amazed. One boy named Cedar was from Washington, D.C. He had grown up as the only white boy in an all-black neighborhood, and had played street basketball with all black teammates. He said that even though he was white, it felt strange to him to be surrounded by so many white faces. A Californian boy with long bleached blond hair was Jewish. He was a surfer, and his speech was interspersed with the words *gnarly, totally,* and *dude.* Abena's mother was from Sweden and her father from Ghana. A petite blond Mexican American girl was from Texas. I had thought all Mexicans had dark hair and skin. There were many Jewish students. There were students from Wyoming, Georgia, England, and France. Sandrine's family was French American, but she had lived in Guatemala when she was young, so she spoke fluent Spanish as well as French. The students defied whatever expectations I had of them based on their appearance. I knew I would learn so much from these unique and intellectually alive people.

But as student after student spoke, I noticed something else. Many of the students came from elite private schools.

They sounded very young and naïve. It turned into a self-congratulatory session—students proudly described how they had improved race relations at their schools and what groups they had been involved in. As the introductions went on, it seemed that "diversity" had become a monolithic structure, that in the minds of these students diversity had only one facet, that of race or ethnicity. I felt scared, and adrenaline rose within me. They didn't seem aware that their experience of diversity was limited. All of the people they knew, of whatever race, were "upper" class. No one mentioned people who were physically or mentally challenged. Two of the girls in my proctor group had lesbian sisters, but they didn't bring that into the discussion, and there weren't any out gays or lesbians in our group.

Going around the circle, I was the last student to speak. My voice was shaky as I told them about my mother and my upbringing, and about how Neil Rudenstine hadn't written about class diversity. I told them that I felt lost. Unlike an ethnicity, being homeless and poor didn't seem like an identity I could take pride in (not at that point). I broke down into tears. I felt alone, dirty and ashamed, tired, and invisible. I was angry. Even in this diverse group, people couldn't identify with me as my working-class friends from Quincy did. Afterwards, several students, including Neil from New Orleans, gave me big hugs. They were glad that I had said what I did. I felt torn apart. Why did I have to be the one who was the most different, the most outside of everyone else?

My five suitemates and I tried to figure out why the Freshman Dean's Office placed us together. There was ethnic and geographic diversity but a few similarities. Four suitemates were Christians, and three of us played the violin—Tina was the most talented.

"Is that a CD?" Maggie and I asked when we heard violin music from behind Tina's closed door. It sounded like a flawless recording of a difficult Mozart concerto, perfectly tuned notes resonating up and down the scale, becoming loud and then soft.

"No, that's Tina. Isn't she fantastic?" Sandrine said. She and I also played violin, but not with Tina's dexterity. Tina played in the Harvard-Radcliffe Orchestra (HRO), the most prestigious orchestra on campus.

Most of us were athletic, but only Maggie played a collegiate sport—Radcliffe rugby. Jenny astonished us by running eight miles each day along the Charles River. She was modest and shrugged off our amazement, saying she ran very slowly. Each day she returned with an ecstatic smile, energy exuding from her petite frame.

Maggie and I thought we were put together because of the goofy pictures we sent with our rooming applications. In mine, fluorescent orange hair cascaded over my face and I wore a striped, multicolored silk shirt with a tie. Maggie sent in black-and-white photos from a photo booth in which her eyes were crossed and her face stretched out of shape by the fingers in her mouth. These pictures were also in the leatherbound Freshman Facebook, a book that all first-years used to identify and speculate on their classmates. When I met other freshmen and told them I roomed with Maggie, they would say, "Oh my God, you know her? Her picture is so cool. Can we meet her?" She developed a cult following among our classmates.

I liked Maggie right away because her energy filled the whole room. She was five feet ten inches and 165 pounds of solid muscle. The guys we knew admired Maggie's leg muscles and wished they could have legs that big. She didn't shave them and had beautiful soft fuzz covering her legs. I thought about growing out my leg hair, but I knew if I did that it would be sparse and scraggly, dark hairs popping out in scattered bunches. Maggie's arms were also muscular. She told our other roommates and me that she always wanted to be little and cute and be able to curl up somewhere and go unnoticed. But she wasn't little so she couldn't help being big and bumbling. Our room was so small it seemed that every time Maggie moved—pushed back her chair, stood up, stretched out her arms behind her head, or leaned over the edge of her bed to talk to me—everything in the room had to shift space imperceptibly to accommodate her. The room just looked entirely different every time she moved somewhere in it. I thought it great to have so much presence—to make such an impact with every gesture.

One day during the first week of school, I came back home to our room and looked up because I heard a muffled sniffle coming from above, and there was Maggie, crying. I asked her what was wrong and she really started bawling, so I climbed up the side of the bunk and sat with her. I didn't know that people as big and strong as she was could get so upset. She was crying because she had been placed in Expos 10, a sort of remedial writing class for first-year Harvard students. All students must take one term of expository writing, but those in Expos 10 must take two full classes. All of us first-years had to take a placement test to see if we knew how to write essays. I thought it strange, because we had all gotten into Harvard—how could we not know how to write?

Maggie was a creative, imagistic writer, and she thought writing was one of her strengths, so it was disheartening for her to be told she needed extra help. The essay topic was "creativity," oddly enough. Maggie had used a blender as a metaphor for creativity and had written about "creating" different kinds of drinks. She was trying to be "creative," so she hadn't followed a traditional essay format. Instead she had circled around the topic, written a "blended" essay in which the form echoed the content. I had read some of Maggie's writing, and it was lovely. This writing placement test and its categorization of students into "good" and "not good enough" writers seemed just another example of how Harvard seemed to have an elitist mind-set about everything.

Harvard felt impersonal, but it had a definite presence among its students, who talked about Harvard as if it were a person with thoughts and a personality that was larger than life, a personality molded by tradition.

I remembered walking through Harvard Yard with Mr. Mac one evening after our Extension classes, the spring before I was to start as an undergraduate. It was before everything in my life revolved around the school and Harvard Yard became "the Yard," the place in which I lived and slept, the serene bubble that I walked through every day to get to class. I remembered that night with Mr. Mac looking at the dark brick buildings and feeling scared and awed. Scared that I was soon to be officially identified with them, that I was to become *part of* these buildings, part of their fear and mystery.

Harvard's name itself carried a thousand images and assumptions. For instance, it was a good thing I didn't decide to go to Yale. Or Princeton. Or Dartmouth, Columbia, or Vanderbilt for that matter. Because what would they have done for newspaper headlines, unable to rely on the alliteration of "Homeless to Harvard"? Vagabond to Vanderbilt might have worked. Poor to Princeton? Destitute to Dartmouth? They just don't have the same ring to them. Part of the reason that it was so important that I attend college at Harvard was not merely the alliteration. The name Harvard, the idea of Harvard stands in for privilege, knowledge, power, wealth, tradition, excellence, reliability. When you say you go to Harvard, people back away. Something in their eyes changes suddenly, and they don't look at you *at all* in the way they did before. They say the name back to you (in a drawn-out fashion) as if it is a magical word that can invoke all kinds of powers: Haaaaarr-*varrrhd*, ey? *Har-vard.* You have gained a mixture of respect, fear, distance, and possibly contempt from them.

If you are in the position, as I have often been, of being a small person keeping to herself in the window seat of a plane or a bus, with purple hair, a nose ring, maybe toting a skateboard, then you know you're in trouble when the innocent person next to you, in the middle of a pleasant conversation about the weather, plane flights, and how good some peanuts would be right now because aren't you starving, asks: "Are you a student?"

"Yes . . ."

"Where do you go to school?"

"Boston, um, Cambridge, actually."

"Oh really," and he might get sidetracked and talk about how his niece goes to BU and isn't Boston a lovely place to go to college, and that she's very happy there. Then he'll remember that you still haven't told him where you go to school, and he'll ask again and you'll have to say it.

"Harvard." And the bomb has dropped. Watch out civilians, bystanders, farm animals, and fellow plane passengers. Prepare yourselves for a heavy moment of silence, and then . . . but I've already told you. The backing away, and the sudden distance.

*

Even after I was enrolled in school that fall I was sure that it was an accident that I was a Harvard student, and that one day someone would find out that I was a fake, and I would be asked to leave. Our student IDs were also key cards that let us into the dorms. Anytime I slid my card through too fast and a little red light would come on (access denied), I panicked and started sweating, sure that I had been found out—that I hadn't paid my term bill, that I was being kicked out.

Sleeping there in the middle of the Yard inside of Weld Hall was strange. It was as though the Harvard administration wanted to impress the fact that you were a Harvard Student upon you at every moment. Maggie and I would wake up to parades of tourists—Japanese, American, and English, people from all over the world—outside of our windows at eight in the morning. They walked in double file down the narrow pathways, glancing around curiously at our building, following the tour guide.

Rushing to class, I felt that my life was on continual display. I avoided the crowds of tourists in front of the John Harvard statue, walking around them on the grass. They swiveled their heads in one motion when they saw me hurrying by. *Shhshh* is what they said to each other. *There goes a real Harvard student. Shhhshh, is that what they look like? So happy!* they said. *Everyone here is so happy because they go to Harvard and how could you not be happy?*

The way the newspapers write *Harvard,* and the way the people say *HARVARD,* they make it seem that it is big and imposing, written up in capitals with lights and stars. When I wrote about Harvard in my journals, I did not capitalize it, and I abbreviated it to *harv.*—so that it would seem like the name of one of my best friends—so that it would not intimidate or have power over me.

Even so, as I lay in bed at night, I would have half-awake thoughts, sensations of being a tiny creature in a factory-like world that was Harvard Yard. I was tiny, and I slept in a matchbox bed, stacked in a building with other small people living in matchbox beds, arising each day to churn out paper after paper of words spit out in rows across the page. I dreamt that the papers were printed out through the windows, out of each window in Harvard Yard, more and more papers, more and more words, tiny words that would be sifted through, and someday, somehow a few of these words would mean something very important, and that this was the reason for the factory's functioning.

It was not until I really got to know people, and especially Maggie, that Harvard started to seem more manageable and comfortable and real.

At night as we lay in our bunk beds, I would talk to Maggie about how I felt fragmented and unsure because I didn't do any of the things I used to do, the things that made me *me*. I didn't think I could continue wrestling, because the men's team was varsity—Division I—and I didn't know any women wrestlers at the school. I didn't play violin anymore, because all the orchestras were highly competitive and meant for violinists who had had years of private lessons. I was a skateboarder, but the sidewalks in Harvard Square were cobblestone and too bumpy and littered with sidewalk artists to ride boards on.

I talked about my mother to Maggie as we were falling asleep in our bunks. "Maggie, whenever I'm with my mom, I get so angry and horrible, and I'm not sure why." It made me want to cry. "She's done more for me than anyone, she gave up so much just to make me happy." But her mere presence made me anxious and frustrated. My anger didn't surface with my friends. But my mom reflected everything I was anxious about.

"I want to push her as far away from me as I can. I'm terrified that if I'm nice to her, if I accept her for who she is, that I'm going to be just like her, that I don't have what it takes to succeed here, where everything is so intimidating." Deep inside, I felt that I *was* my mother. She was in my blood, and she was the antithesis of all that Harvard cared about or understood. I felt that, in order to succeed at Harvard, I would have to identify instead with my classmates and the Harvard environment.

Maggie struggled to stay awake and listen. She apologized in advance in case she answered my questions with snores instead of words. I didn't mind if she started snoring, because the snores were soft, gentle, and long drawn out. I was used to falling asleep to them each night.

"Another part of me just wants to hold my mother close. I get so angry and protective of her. They will never understand—will never know or care about all the truth and beauty inside her. And what is my response? I treat her like a piece of dirt, I get angry with *her* instead. I try to twist her shape into something deformed and mangled to make her conform to what people here at Harvard see as normal. . . ."

Sometimes when I was elaborating on questions or stories, they branched off and then again were intertwined. They seemed to grow legs and tails, fingers to scratch their heads in bewilderment even. As I spoke, my questions grew from small embryos to full-fledged thoughts and problems, fleshing themselves out. I got lost in watching them as they became embodied and tentacled, like strange beings wrapping themselves around in my head. I would keep talking, thinking out loud, until at some point I would suddenly realize that I was talking to the sound of Maggie's snores.

I would grow quiet, but now all of my questions were as huge as people, multilimbed, and they weighed down on me, entangling me in their messy complexity.

23

BLUEBERRY HONEY

THE VAULTED CEILING was engraved with the Veritas motto, and the chandeliers were hung with enormous elk antlers. An impressive sight, yet the ceiling seemed distant to the Harvard freshmen who ate at tables forty feet below. This was the Freshman Union, a building next to Harvard Yard where all first-year students ate their meals.

The Union was grandiose and austere, as are most of the buildings on campus. The walls were paneled in ornately decorated dark wood and hung with enormous pictures of distinguished, unsmiling Colonial men in coattails. The chattering eighteen-year-olds seemed incongruous in this setting. A first-year student's most difficult challenge, according to Harvard lore, was to get a pat of butter stuck to the ceiling of the Union. This wasn't easy, but many pats of butter were already stuck to the ceiling, and when you looked up, you could see them, little yellowish patches against the ebony-stained wood. People tried everything, from rubber band slingshots to a spoon used as a catapult. Most efforts were unsuccessful; hence it was no shocking thing suddenly to see a yellow splotch land in your food or feel it in your hair.

A great variety of food was served at the Union: a full salad bar, a vegetarian as well as a meat entrée, several dessert choices, including ice cream every day, fixings for peanut-butter-and-jelly sandwiches, and anything you could want to drink, from coffee to soda pop or any kind of juice. We even had the option to have cereal—there were at least twenty different kinds—with any meal.

Almost everyone complained about the food, maybe just for something to talk about, or maybe because they got bored of the same choices every day, or the food wasn't quite as good as their mothers made it. But to me, the plentitude was amazing. When people complained, I would flash back to something my friend Dave said to me earlier that year. Dave was one of my skater friends from Quincy. Baggy clothes hid his skinny vegetarian body. He wore huge pants that flared out at the bottom and made him look triangular. With his dingy green Mohawk and devil's lock, and thick-rimmed glasses taped together with duct tape, he wasn't someone whom teachers at my high school expected me to be friends with, but he was someone I could count on for simple wisdom.

We had just skated three miles from his house to mine, and I offered him something to eat, telling him that all we had was bagels and the only thing to go on them was peanut butter. "Sounds good to me," he said, as he bit into it with great relish.

Reflecting as he savored a mouthful of peanut butter, he said, "You won't forget me when you go to Harvard, will you?"

"Of course I won't, Dave," I said, smiling at him in amusement because he was so earnest. And I didn't forget him.

He shook his head at me and said, referring to Harvard students, "Dude, they're like, 'My second Rolls-Royce broke down, bummer.' How can that compare with 'There was nothing in my house for two weeks but peanut butter and bagels'?" I understood where he was coming from because we both came from similar homes, the kind of home I felt most comfortable in. The kind of home where none of the furniture matches, and the curtains clash with the couch, and everything appears to be a little bit dingy and worn-in, comfortable. The kind of place that is dark and crowded, because the ceilings are not high nor are the windows big. The kind of place with nothing in the kitchen to eat except for peanut butter and bagels. The kind of place that always felt like home to me.

These were the thoughts that would flash through my mind as I sat in the Union and listened to the complaints about the food.

One day in the Union, as I was sitting surrounded by friends, Maggie pulled a jar of honey out of her pocket. "Try some," she told me. "This is special honey. My dad sent it to me." The label said it was blueberry honey. It came from bees that gather nectar only from blueberry flowers. Special bees, select flowers, and not your ordinary field clover. Honey that was pure and sweet and probably expensive. I hadn't heard of this sort of honey. "Does it really taste so much better?" I asked, curious. My friends explained about a farm, and blueberry groves. I made a joke about elitist honey but received only blank stares. There was a hint of irony to my words, but I meant them lightly.

The silence was rearranged with complaints about the upcoming problem set in Behavioral Biology, nightmarish Chem 7 lab reports, and English 10a readings that kept on piling up.

*

I grew up on peanut-butter-and-honey sandwiches. The peanut butter and honey were free. They came from the food bank, and their white labels said USDA GOVERNMENT SURPLUS in generic black letters. The cloudy honey came in a ten-pound plastic bottle. No one could use that much honey quickly enough. It dried into crusty layers of grainy sugar, forming a brown solid lump at the bottom of the bottle. In fifth grade, when I lived at Blue Ridge—"the Village"— Cathy and Jenny's mother produced sandwiches en masse for all the children in our neighborhood. She lined up the Wonder bread, slapping peanut butter onto half the slices, dribbling honey on the other half. She threw the sandwiches together, handed them to us as we ran off. We ate while we played, our honeyed fingers turning black with grime.

As a child, I didn't really know I was poor. I thought that all children ate honey from plastic bottles with white government labels.

If I was unaware of children who ate blueberry honey and their world, I'm sure they were unaware of me and my peanut-butter-and-honey sandwiches (and also unaware that I called my mom each night at a shelter pay phone to make sure she was okay).

The honey seemed to be a starting point. Social and economic difference affected even small, unimportant exchanges among my friends at Harvard. It was hard to talk about class differences directly. A casual comment—maybe just mentioning a foster sister, or something that happened once at a shelter—could provoke innumerable questions about "what it was like," something I would not have had to discuss with my friends from home. I longed not to be different, but I didn't want to be like these students. I envied their comfort in being with people like themselves, and I missed my friends from home.

When I was with friends, a chance would arise to talk about class, or just to talk about our different experiences and how they shaped us, and I didn't know how to approach the subject without sounding like I was bitter or angry. And I was afraid that to share a part of myself might arouse their pity.

Maggie was aware of her privilege; she knew that she could count on her father's allowance each month. For me, even the word *father* was painful. My father had money, but he had no face. I'd never met him; I hadn't seen his picture. I hadn't heard his voice or seen his handwriting. (And I'd never seen his money.)

Maggie's father's check each month ensured that she wouldn't need to get a job during college. She was free to concentrate on schoolwork and rugby. My allowance came from cleaning dorm bathrooms for two hours a day, five days a week. As I headed to work, seeing Maggie at her desk or heading to the pool or rugby field, some afternoons I was jealous of her freedom.

Still, as I muscled the last layer of brown scum off the shower tiles, my thoughts found their own freedom.

But Maggie was not an elitist, not snobby, not a hoarder of wealth. She was often uncomfortable with the subject of money. She worried about what she spent her money on. She talked to me about feeling guilty because she could spend forty-five dollars on a weekend of snowboarding when I could not. Sometimes when she saw a homeless person asking for spare change she would cringe, feeling that she should not have so many advantages. I told her that she couldn't help being born with money just as I couldn't help being born poor. I told her to enjoy her opportunities. She could use her privilege—a voice more easily heard by society than voices of women who did not enjoy class status—to help enlighten people about class difference as she became aware of it.

Like the bees who gather only blueberry nectar, many Harvard students had tasted only one kind of flower. I was there to dance them the directions to orchards they had never been to—orchards where common clovers grew alongside the blueberries.

24

PARENTS' WEEKEND

DURING MY FIRST YEAR at college, if I wanted to talk to my mom I had to call her on a pay phone at Father Bill's shelter, and only between 7:00 and 10:00 P.M. Often the line would be busy and I would call several times before I could get through. I would ask, "Is Elizabeth Summer there?" A man who sounded slightly deranged or drunk would look for her, and I hoped she would be there (or else I would worry). The pay phone was in the shelter's lounge next to the TV and the couches, so there was always a lot of background noise. Usually my mom was watching a basketball game with the guys in the shelter. She followed the players and game scores closely. The pay phone had a ten-minute time limit because people were waiting to use it, so we could never talk for long.

When I got her I loved her stories about her friends at the shelter, about Joan and James and Ray, and going out for a beer, or watching sports games and eating donuts with them. I'd often wished she would go out more or make more friends. She preferred to spend her time gardening and reading and doing what she thought was watching out for me. But she didn't mind staying home, even alone. She has always preferred her own company, and always will. No one can understand her in the way that she understands herself.

When she wasn't at the shelter, I worried whether she had found a friend's house to stay at or not. One morning after I had been unable to talk with my mom, I rose from my soft bed. Sun slanted through the tall windows thickly framed in dark wood. The phone rang; I shook sleep off and answered. She was a little tired, my mother told me on the other end of the line, because she had been awake all night in Dunkin' Donuts. She said this with a laugh, as if it were not out of the ordinary. This was where she went when the shelter was full. I felt a sudden fondness for Dunkin' Donuts that were open twenty-four hours. How many times had black coffee and an orange plastic booth saved my mother from freezing?

Parents' Weekend was supposed to be a chance for parents to see their children who were newly away from home, and to see what their college life was like, their friends, dorm rooms, and activities. It was in early November so that parents and students who were homesick for each other wouldn't have to wait until Thanksgiving to reunite.

On the Friday of Parents' Weekend I met my mom at the train station at 9:00 A.M. She was carrying many heavy bags, because Father Bill's shelter wouldn't let her leave her things during the day. She had bought a wheeled cart for nineteen dollars—but the wheels broke off after a week, so she had to go back to carrying the bags on her back. I helped her carry them through the busy Square. She looked happy but a bit frazzled, with her hair going everywhere as usual. I told her she could leave the bags in my room so she wouldn't need to carry them around. "Oh, thank you," she said as if it were a privilege.

From the moment I met her at the T station, where she emerged laden down with her duffel bags and layers of clothes, I knew that *my* Parents' Weekend would be a lot different from anyone else's. As soon as we put her bags down, my mom pulled out the brochure about Parents' Weekend I had given her a few weeks earlier.

It was my eighteenth birthday, but I had to send my mom off to do the parents' events by herself because I had an Expository Writing paper due at 5:00 P.M. as I did every Friday. "I want to go, for sure, to the talk on Shakespeare," she said. She expected that I would go with her, but I had to finish the paper. She said she didn't mind going by herself, but I felt bad. I felt resentful of students who had two parents, or at least a parent and a stepparent—who could occupy each other's attention. Even though I was glad for my mom to be visiting, I felt like it was such a burden, because I had to make sure she was happy and busy all the time. By the end of the day, after turning in my paper, I was so irritated. I just wanted her to leave, but she wanted to stay. I was on the verge of tears, seeing all my suitemates with their perfect families, overjoyed to see their parents after the time apart. One of my friends, also a first-year Harvard student, had emigrated from Iran with his parents when he was in elementary school and had spent most of his life as an illegal alien. He said of Freshmen Parents' Weekend, "It's an opportunity for all of us children of dysfunctional families to watch functional families walk around."

To myself I added *and do functional things, like buy clothes, go to classes, get taken out to dinner, et cetera.* I couldn't relate to my mom in that way. I felt exhausted and angry, and as usually happened, this anger surfaced in my being short with my mother. She couldn't understand why I wasn't having a great time. I was so angered and embarrassed and sad. I wanted to push my mother away, ignore her, and pretend that she didn't exist. I wasn't conscious of why I felt this way, but I felt extremely guilty about it. I just wanted to curl into a ball in my bed and pretend this whole world of Harvard didn't exist, that my swimming headache wasn't real, that the fury and nausea at the unfairness didn't matter.

She had to leave soon after I turned in the paper, and couldn't have dinner with me for my birthday, because she had to check in at the shelter at 6:30 P.M. in order to get a bed for the night. It felt so horribly wrong on Parents' Weekend to be sending my mother back to the shelter. I felt that I should ask her to sleep there with me at Harvard, but I couldn't do it. I didn't know what to say to my suitemates or their parents—who were all staying in hotels—if they came in and saw my mother sleeping in the common room. I was so mad at Harvard. I felt like "they" had created this whole situation just to mock me, that it was an evil sadistic parade.

25

SLEEPING OUTSIDE

"POOR DIANE," Maggie would murmur from her bunk at night. "I stole her roommate." Maggie and my other suitemates called my friend Diane our honorary roommate because they all liked her so much. Diane often came to stay at Harvard for the weekends. We would both sleep on my bunk, in opposite directions, with her toes next to my head and vice versa. She was such a crazy and fun girl. My suitemates could see how much affection I had for her and how happy it made me to be around her.

One day Diane and I had been skating through the Square. Diane's board hit a kink in the sidewalk and flew right into an artist's display of paintings laid out on the cobblestone. The board broke a glass-framed picture of a smiling sun with orange and yellow dreadlock-like rays. The artist grimaced at the offending skateboard. But he was happier when I said I would gladly pay for the picture and the frame. From then on I skated only at night, when the streets were still and dark and empty of people.

On such nights, I was revived by the loud sound of my skateboard against pavement, glad to be free of the sterility of Weld Hall and the desolate Science Center.

Out here with my board I was free, and my movements swift and unconfined. The smooth black road, the sloping concrete hills, my eyes following the yellow line that kept the daytime cars divided in neat rows. Now, in the early hours of morning, only occasional headlights emerged through the deserted dark. I disregarded the yellow line, as the small hot wheels of the skateboard slid over and back across the painted divider. I built momentum by zigzagging in wide loops on the slick black street. No one was present to observe my exhilaration, and that was fine.

Some nights, though, Diane came with me. We were caught reverently in mutual quiet, coasting down Mass Ave. I would rather be free than safe, I thought then, remembering the stifling panic I felt when staring at the white walls and clean corners of my dorm room.

At Harvard I often needed the sound of wheels burning against pavement, the wind rushing by in a furiously swift wave. I missed skating during the day, but to try to skate was useless because the streets were so crowded. I *was* a skateboarder, but only at night. The few people who skated at school mostly carried—more often than rode—their expensive and new-looking boards. I loved skating through the dark over the smooth parts of Harvard Yard, going faster and faster on the little crisscrossing sidewalks. Sometimes I practiced the few tricks I knew on a really smooth space in front of Widener Library. I tried shuv-its—in which you make the board spin 180 degrees underneath you as you jump up and land back on it—and ollies—in which your board leaps up into the air with you and then you land back on it as it comes down. I had never progressed to the more skillful ollie kickflips and rail slides that my skater friend Dave had mastered.

In late November the weather got colder, the days darker. The campus population was swollen to twice its size for the Harvard-Yale game, but I did not share in the festive spirit. I had spent three months struggling to find a place in this overwhelming atmosphere and was ready to run away from Harvard. Always in the back of my mind were thoughts of my mother living in a shelter while I was living so free—for free—in a comfortable college dorm. I felt that there was no one who could understand. My mind was in constant tension as I tried to hold together irreconcilable realities. The tension mounted without my realizing it. One night that weekend, I started crying. *Just go away, everyone. Be quiet and leave me because I'm not worth being around. Why am I here?*

My schoolwork went unfinished because I had been too busy socializing and adjusting and constantly writing in my journal. I felt the expectations placed on me were enormous. The University (someone, somewhere—I imagined a wealthy benefactor sitting in his cozy home writing a check—I didn't know if he'd be forgiving or not; I feared that this person would find out he'd made a mistake with me) was paying a huge amount of money for me to be here, and my response would be to fail my classes or turn in mediocre work. When I mentioned that I was afraid of failing astronomy, one well-meaning acquaintance said, "Don't worry, they couldn't kick you out, it would look bad for them. Can you imagine the news? 'Harvard Kicks Poor Homeless Girl Out on the Street.'" Oddly, this made me feel better momentarily, because I thought it might be true. But it also suggested that people thought I could get by on that and not on my own efforts.

Diane was visiting me that weekend. Most of the students were safe asleep in their bunks and small cubicle rooms at four thirty in the morning. There were only a few whispering sounds of the latest partygoers struggling back to their rooms to fall into their beds and pass out, their bodies coming to rest gratefully against the identical soft-striped mattresses.

I nudged Diane as we lay with our heads at opposite ends of my bunk and begged, "Please, please, can we sleep outside? I need to be somewhere different. I can't sleep in this place tonight." Harvard Yard was a manicured lawn, steeped in tradition, surrounded by a tall brick wall. There were twenty gates, most of them closed after sundown. Its buildings were the oldest on campus, some built in the 1600s. It made me feel trapped, claustrophobic and false. My eyes were red and puffy, my limbs weakened from shaking sobs. Diane was willing to humor me because I was upset.

We took the blankets, the comforter, and pillows from my bunk bed and carried all of our bedding across dark triangles of perfect green grass toward wrought-iron Johnston Gate— one of the few that stayed open all night. As we walked through the huge decorative gate I felt like I was leaving a shiny bubble, bursting through a quick and iridescent surface. From the Square all we could see over the high brick wall were the tops of the old buildings.

During the day, the bustling surface of Harvard Square was several worlds of people who coexisted obliviously and anonymously with each other. There were the teenagers who flocked in from the suburbs and the street youth with wild haircuts and hair colors, their dog collars, tattoos, black leather, and tattered clothes. Tourists came to the Square for entertainment, for its carnival aspect and history. Then there

were the distinguished professors with white hair and intellectual looking glasses, and the Harvard students in khakis
and buttoned shirts in conservative earth tones and brown
leather loafers or new sneakers. I knew about these worlds and
their separateness, only because I'd been a part of all of them.

There were also scores of homeless people. Any Harvard
student will become familiar with their faces and voices, if
not their names. I came to know many, some by name and
others only as "the spare change guy" or the guy outside of
Christy's who always held the door open and insisted that I
give him a hug. There were a few men who slept every night
on the grates on Dunster Street, next to the Garage—a mall
in the Square that was built out of a converted parking
garage. Warm air from the mall flowed up and out of the
grates, but after my first year at Harvard, the city built cages
over them to prevent people from sleeping there. To me, this
was sadistic and cruel. Why shouldn't the homeless people use
the warm air from the grates? No one else was using it or
wanted it. Where else would they go? Did Harvard, which
owned the property, think they could eliminate the problem
of homelessness just by removing it from their immediate
sight?

We crossed Mass Ave and went to where the subway
entrance was located in a brick circle about the size of a small
pool, three or four steps lower than the surrounding sidewalks
and streets. This area was called the pit. It was a central place
to meet friends or sit on the encircling steps and watch people.
During the day, it was filled with the "punk rock" kids—a living art exhibit for tourists and students to gawk at.

We placed our pillows and blankets against one of the
raised concrete barriers that curved around the edge of the
pit. The ground was cold, but the concrete slab gave us a sense

of shelter. We wrapped the blankets around us and shut our eyes. I lay there cold and light as a grungy cloud floating across the stars above in the sky. The ground felt bumpy and made me real again. I was glad I was here, anywhere rather than inside that bubble that was Harvard. We half slept for a couple of hours. I felt it getting light but didn't want to open my eyes. The street-cleaning machine chirred and roared by like a gargantuan insect. A man asked Diane for a cigarette, and she fumbled around for one. I still didn't open my eyes. I didn't want to wake up, but this man—from the corners of my half-open eyes I could see that he was older and had a gray beard—kept trying to engage Diane in conversation. I pulled the blankets more tightly around me, ignoring him, but Diane was much nicer than I was and answered most of his questions. I pressed my face into Diane's back and wished he'd go away. The small of my back started to feel like a piece of ice or part of the ground. The sky got lighter and lighter, and a few people began to come out. We got up and dragged our blankets back through the Square and the Yard like we were coming back from an all-night sleepless slumber party. Or maybe we looked like two small children dragging their leaf-covered dismantled fort back from the backyard, struggling with the big blankets. It didn't feel like coming home exactly.

The concrete and cold ground had reminded me of shelters and being on the street. I felt held by the concrete in a way I could never be held by a person. There were people sleeping like this every night. I felt connected to these homeless people and held by the thought of them sleeping outside, feeling as lost and cold as I did inside. In feeling closer to them, I felt closer to myself, and stronger. Most of all I felt so free and real, throwing off all the pretensions and protective barriers that held the people inside the Yard together. It made me feel free to think, free from the structures, motivations, and processes that were so alien.

Back in my room, I felt tired and dazed, bedraggled and dirty. The sunlight didn't feel real. But it was a new day that didn't seem as terrifying and cold as the nighttime before. I wanted to go back to sleep, to have sleep float me out into sweet oblivion. As I pulled the covers over my head, I honestly appreciated the soft bed and being able to crawl back into it. All I could do was lie there with the blanket over my ears, rocking back and forth and feeling the tension spin me into a tight and tighter ball. Something pressed inside my brain, making me shake and feel like I would explode. I was aware in a bad way of every particle of skin, every itch and irritation, every sound and voice. Diane had stayed in the common room, talking to Jenny and Abena.

Maggie came in quietly, closing the door behind her. She had seen Diane and me come in. She sat down next to me, saying nothing. She had often given me back rubs, which were the only thing that would help me go to sleep when I felt tense. She put my head in her lap and started rubbing my shoulders and my hair. I curled up toward her and quietly began to weep. I pulled the fuzzy sky blue blanket over my head and just lay there crying and holding on to her ankles. Her legs were fuzzy just like the blanket.

Everything came tumbling out from inside with deep heaving gasps and sobs. I took a few deep shaky breaths. "Maggie," I told her, "I wish I could die or live my life backwards and end up in the womb again." And I was thinking that this being in Maggie's lap with the blanket over top was the closest I was going to come to the womb. I wanted to go back to someplace comforting and dark where I wouldn't feel exposed to the flooding light of such an unforgiving world. A world in which I had to deny my mother, become motherless in order to succeed. All my thoughts formed little circles and pinwheels in my mind. I tried to explain to Maggie how I felt all at once, and then I tried to tell all of it to her in order. I felt that if I could just get it all out, she would understand because anyone who had a lap like hers would understand.

She stayed and held me and I felt the first glimmer of how the warring parts of me could find peace at Harvard. I felt that I had to make a decision that would determine the rest of my life. The decision revolved around the question: Why did I want to be at Harvard? For many students, the question was easy to answer. They wanted power, wealth, security, and knowledge. They wanted to be at the top of the totem pole. But what I had seen of Harvard disgusted and alienated me. I didn't want to be part of this culture that seemed so wrapped up in itself, distant from the world's poverty and sorrow. Why was I here? Was I complicit in the oppression, keeping poor people in their place?

I dreamt that I could leave Harvard and be a hermit living at the bottom of some faraway mountainside. I lived on the street with my mother and other homeless people who could not function well in society. I was at the bottom of the power pile, with uncertain happiness. I was "free" to do what I wanted when I wanted to—but that freedom was a deception because without power inside of society it was hard for us to be completely free. In my dream, we had to struggle every day for our basic needs. My life was curtailed without all the benefits and comforts that society provided. I would be only as free as my mother was.

That morning, talking with Maggie and crying, I decided that I would stay at Harvard. I could abide by its outward rules as much as was necessary—something Mr. Mac had taught me—while still existing according to my own standards. I could still embrace my mother. Perhaps I could take my Harvard diploma, and the power it gave, and instead of using it to be comfortable I could use it to make others uncomfortable enough to want to change, or I could use it to advocate for poor people. When I had a Harvard degree—even though I didn't agree with the elitism and exclusion that, in many ways, it stood for—instead of using the power and recognition it gave me for myself, I would use it to have a voice that would be a catalyst for change.

26

THE UNIVERSE AND
EVERYTHING

I HAD TAKEN the astronomy class because the title—The Universe and Everything—sounded humorous and interesting. The catalog described the course by saying, "We will apply a few basic principles to the origin, evolution, and fate of the universe. We will go on to examine our Galaxy; we will discuss the origin and evolution of the planets, stars, and black holes. We will ask what the universe looks like and how it got to be that way." That the course would involve convoluted astrophysics did not occur to me. The professor raced through many equations in each class. I understood the basic concepts and thought I would be able to catch up with the math. I went for extra tutoring with my teaching assistant. I copied the formulas and problems over and over but still wasn't getting the right answers. I went to my Weld proctor for advice and told her I was worried about failing. She told me not to worry and gave me astral meditation tapes to reduce stress. She told me to keep trying and said I could drop the class later if I needed to. But the proctor was misinformed, because the deadline for withdrawing had already passed. So I had to stick it out.

I knew I would fail the final, but as long as I went to the exam I could receive an E, which was a failing grade but not as bad as an ABS, which was what I would receive if I were absent from the examination. I had to stay at the exam for a minimum of an hour. I tried to answer the first few easy problems, but the harder essay questions confounded me. The week before final exams, in mid-January, a senior had hanged himself in his dorm room. This event was on my mind as I was sitting in the exam room. There was one question asking us to write about our experience of Astronomy 14. I wrote that I knew I would fail the class, but that I survived. I wrote that I was glad I had enough perspective of the universe to realize that failing a class did not make me feel hopeless enough to end my life. I left as soon as I was allowed, turning in my little blue exam book to the proctor at the door.

The next day, the dean of freshmen called me. She said that the astronomy professor had called her because she was worried that I might consider suicide. Ironically, this was the first time the professor had noticed me. I explained that I was fine, I had written the opposite.

I joked about the class title, laughing that there was not much else I could fail at now that I had failed The Universe and Everything. I felt a lot freer. As Janis Joplin sang, "Freedom's just another word for nothing left to lose." I took that attitude with me into my second term at Harvard.

To cope with the foreignness of my surroundings that first year in college, I read poetry and wrote in my journal. I filled five big journals. I wished I could write good poetry, but I laughed at my own poems when I wrote them because they were so bad. I decided to take a poetry workshop in the spring, but it was by application only. Even the creative writing classes were exclusive. If you couldn't already write poetry, there was no chance you could get into even a beginning poetry class. As I applied for the poetry class I saw something about a course called Creative Nonfiction. I applied for that too, and I got in.

My classmates were several senior undergrads, two mid-career journalists who had won Nieman Fellowships to study at Harvard, and one former U.S. congresswoman. I enjoyed being in a heterogeneous class that wasn't limited to wealthy eighteen-year-olds. The class let me write about things important to me: running, wrestling, living in a foster home, and my friends from high school. I got C's in my other classes that term, but I received an A in writing.

On my own, I read a book of postwar Polish poems. They were so full of hope seasoned by the experience of war and death. The poems looked at the simple things of life with a new sense of appreciation. The poet, Adam Wazyk, wrote a poem about his brother that reminded me a bit of my mother. Wazyk's brother had gone crazy from years of trauma and unemployment after the Second World War and had jumped out of a window. Wazyk wrote:

> *I did not visit him in the morgue,*
> *I wept only when I knelt before his drawer,*
> *looking at trifles as useless as he was:*
> *a lighter out of order, little inventions,*
> *magic tricks which he liked very much—*
> *for him they took the place of assonance and rhyme.*

This poem made me cry and think of my mother's collection of newspaper articles and toys from McDonald's, the things that everyone else would call useless, things she couldn't have with her at the shelter.

Over a year after I enrolled at Harvard, my mother got her own apartment through a program called Shelter Plus. After fifteen months of homelessness, it was a big deal.

She loved the "wallpaper" that my sophomore suitemates Veronica and Alena created by covering the walls with tissue paper and metallic paper and wanted to make wallpaper for her new apartment. I bought her some dark blue paper and gold metallic poster board. She created an entire galaxy, a universe displayed on a wall. Although I had failed at The Universe and Everything, I knew that no one could fail in my mother's universe. Grades and comparisons with others did not enter into her thought; this idea was something she had taught me all my life.

In the back of her new apartment—an apartment she still lives in—is a hallway leading to the bathroom. Along one side of the hallway, her universe is displayed. Each sheet of the night blue tissue paper was smoothed out flat on the wall and stuck there by double-sided Scotch tape. The edges of each big sheet of paper overlapped so that—from floor to ceiling— none of the original white-painted wall showed through. Upon this homemade canvas was my mother's mind-art, her stars, moons, and planets.

The first time she showed it to me, she pointed out each constellation and comet. Some of the stars glowed in the dark, some were stickers, and "Some of my favorite ones are from the inside of a potato chip bag," she said, showing me a couple of small irregularly shaped holographic stars. "Some of the best ones." The floor was littered with scraps of paper, gold foil, rolls of stickers, sheets of stars, scissors, and the said potato chip bag with its glitzy interior.

The major planets glowed in the dark and were three-dimensional, half-spherical shapes. She bought them at the Science Museum in Boston. They seemed to be embedded in the wall, emerging from the vast space of the night sky. Small animal stickers walked across the bottom of this firmament, dwarfed by the vastness above.

The wall was confusing and spectacular, covered by thousands of decorations. It was impossible to notice them all at first glance. Tiny rocket ships zoomed past cratered red moons. There were facsimiles of real comets here, too, my mother told me—photographs she cut from astronomy textbooks I had given her after I failed the class.

She shut the hall door so that we could view the wall in darkness. A string hung from the lightbulb in the hallway's center. Hanging from the string was a man-in-the-moon-shaped glow-in-the-dark piece of soap. "Soap on a rope," she said, pleased with her literal sense of humor.

It was only after my first year at Harvard that I was able to see that my mother would build her own structures, her own way of life. She would do things in her own way, and that was okay. Before, I had seen only that she was different, and that she didn't fit in with the elite universe I had been thrown into.

One night, a week or so after seeing my mom's wall, I was walking across the Yard with my friend Naima. The leaves on the ground looked so inviting, brown and crackly. It was a windy night, warm for early December. Naima and I lay down on the expansive carpet of leaves to gaze at the soft deep blue sky. Naima gave me a push, and soon we were rolling in the leaves. We rolled and rolled until we came banging into a tree or each other and then we changed directions, back and forth across the Yard in wide ecstatic diagonals.

"Try it with your eyes closed," Naima said. We rolled through empty blackness. We opened our eyes again and the lamplight spun in wide circles. The tops of the tall, grand buildings looked like castles from a long, long time ago. We could see more of the sky than was normally allowed.

There was only motion, feeling grass and truth. The wind was delicious and fierce. I felt safe and free, looking at the tiny wisps of incandescent clouds spinning with joy far above me. The blue blue sky dark and studded with infinite bright stars. I felt I could go anywhere, do anything, be anyone, and still be enclosed by these buildings in Harvard Yard as if it were my own backyard. I felt lucky, enclosed by a place that had once seemed so foreign.

27

DISCIPLINE, PART II

AS WE LOUNGED in the common room, my first-year suite-mates discussed where they learned their study habits and discipline.

"My parents had a strong Protestant work ethic," said Sandrine.

"Mine emphasized strict study habits," Jenny chimed in.

"My parents made my sister and me do our homework directly after school," said Abena. "There was no discussion."

I panicked, remembering how I often had typed the last pages of my reports at ten in the morning, late for school, while my mother helped me hurriedly paste pictures onto the report's cover. I remembered many times of being awake at two or three in the morning working on my biology lab reports. I feared I had no real work ethic, no strict discipline.

When I tried to fit my ideas and my schedule into neat boxes, my mind felt as messy as homes I had grown up in. I liked to gather knowledge in broken bits and pieces, paste, and build according to some innate sense. Like my mother's endless files of clipped newspaper articles, my knowledge might not make sense to anyone but me. I swallowed the lump in my throat. Where would Natural Consequences leave me here, at Harvard, where all the students seemed so self-assured and capable?

In my first year of college, I learned a new meaning of the word *discipline*. A *Discipline* at Harvard meant a branch of study or learning, such as history, psychology, or sociology. Each discipline had its own set of rules and tools. In classes, we read books on how to confine, organize, and determine knowledge.

I tried to approach learning in the way the disciplines dictated, but it did not feel natural. At Harvard I was expected to categorize, enumerate, and evaluate topics from an objective distance. The rules of each discipline stung me and hemmed me in like the leather belt with which my mother had once futilely chased me around our apartment.

I remembered elementary school, the rain coming down in streams, huge drops of water plummeting to the blacktop. It rained so often in Astoria that a large plastic canopy covered half of the playground. On wet days, all the students huddled inside the covered area, playing foursquare basketball, and jumping rope. My friend Donna and I, however, loved to escape the discipline of foursquare. We stood out in the open, underneath the purple and gray cotton ball clouds. We took turns standing beneath the drainpipe on the edge of the covered shelter. The water hit our half-dry clothes in a hard stream and there was no going back. I stood under the pipe and my hair smoothed instantly to my face. My clothes turned dark and clung to me like draped robes, my shoes filled with water, and—suddenly!—I was transformed. Donna and I danced in circles, twirling, making ourselves dizzy, shooting water out in spiral streams. Eventually a teacher came and scolded us, herding us back into the school like imprisoned second-graders and not superheroes any longer. Our sneakers squeaked and squelched and left streaks of dirty water behind us in the school's big empty hallways. Back in class, our feet turned cold, and colder, surrounded by wet socks and water.

The word *discipline* derives from the Latin *dis-*, "apart," and *capere*, "to hold"—"to hold apart"—at Harvard, learning within a discipline meant holding the knowledge apart from oneself. It meant watching water pour from the drainpipe from a distance, counting the drops, not being baptized by the wetness. I remembered being a young girl and eating 320 gummy worms in one night at a slumber party with my friend Lorraine. We were not well-disciplined children. To me, studying within a discipline meant looking at the gummy worms one by one under a microscope, not touching them, not eating them.

I wasn't sure what I wanted to major in. My favorite classes during my first year of college were writing classes. In addition, I was confronted constantly with the perplexing question of my identity—surrounded by students and professors whose class backgrounds differed from my own. I felt my difference from them even in the ways we thought and approached life and learning. Studying these differences interested me, and I thought I might major in sociology. I took a class called Poverty, Public Policy, and Controversy.

The class taught me a lot about welfare reform, but I felt constrained by the discipline of sociology—its methods of searching for knowledge (categorizing, enumerating, observing) and the types of knowledge (detached, conceptual) it found useful.

Many Harvard classes taught me that knowledge was a box outside of myself. I could walk around knowledge, poke at it, squint my eyes at it from all different angles, but I mustn't ever step inside of it.

I remembered the large cardboard box that I played in when I was three years old, and small. Then, my neighbor Rhonda and I climbed inside. We played house in the box, and my mother cut windows for us with cardboard shutters that opened and closed. Blue-green light filtered through the quilted blanket that covered the box top. Knowledge was a dim blue dream. If knowledge was a box, I wanted to step inside. I sought the beginnings of my own knowledge: how I came to know what I now know, and how I go about knowing and learning.

Learning—for me—had to be personal and practical. I needed to run with the learning, carry the new knowledge for long blocks like bags of laundry or groceries. To feel its weight and movement in my body and mind. To eat knowledge up, devour the 320 gummy worms at a sitting and painfully digest them. I wanted knowledge to pour over me like water from a drainpipe; I wanted to feel its cold wetness shrieking against my skin. My knowledge was on the side of body and chaos.

Which is why I became flabbergasted when sitting in Poverty, Public Policy, and Controversy. Single mothers and their children were discussed and tabulated. I wanted to think about poverty in connection with my own experiences. Yet the discourse of the class did not create a comfortable space for subjective knowledge. When I spoke—of my mother and her life, of living on under five thousand dollars a year—I spewed words from inside me into a dampening space where they fell flat like dominoes collapsed in a line. The other students grew silent.

*

I thought about when I had been homeless. That lack of a roof and walls, that open field, that living was painful, but it gave a place to view the world, living on the edges of the woven world carpet, hanging on, tied into the fringes. That point of view was like being wedged between the floorboards and the wall moldings, hidden like the dust in corners of a room, swept out of sight. I lived inside the empty spaces on the margins of the page. I lived on the top and the bottom, and on either side, all around the words. The words of power were written on the middle of the page, the words of the Constitution, the words taught in schools, the words of welfare laws. I grew older, and I learned to crawl inside the straight snakes of words. I was inside the words; in the university I could write words. But it was not the same as always having been inside.

My experience in courses at Harvard led me to create my own concentration (major), which I chose to call Children's Studies. My sophomore year, I applied to the Special Concentrations Department, stating that I wanted to study poverty's effects on children's development and include classes from psychology, sociology, Afro-American and women's studies, education, literature, and creative writing. In choosing a course of study outside of traditional disciplinary bounds,* I chose to resist the dominant ways of thinking and talking within the university. The smothered voices of poor people

---

*The boundaries that border knowledges constitute divisions between particular *disciplines*. They divide knowledge according to historically specific categories as well as the inside and the outside of the subject (psychology as analysis of "man's" interior and sociology as an analysis of "his" exterior); self and other (anthropology); the universal and the particular (philosophy and history, respectively); appearance and reality (literature or visual arts and natural sciences); and so on. Although the boundaries are not *immutable*, enabling some cross-fertilization between disciplines,

and children cried out from behind rows of tables and graphs, from inside the long polysyllabic words. I wanted to write in language that would be read by people whom I most wanted to speak with: poor people, single mothers, and homeless families—as well as by more academic types.

I put together a plan of study and went to look for an adviser. I called and met with all those who taught classes or did research in poverty or children's issues. Many professors were interested, but most already had their allotted advisees within their own departments. They did not have time to take on another student. Each professor gave me the names of other professors. Then I would meet with each of them.

I met with Professor Sara Lawrence Lightfoot. I had been in one of her classes at the School of Education. She was a tall black woman in beautiful purple African robes, her long hair gathered into a bun with an ornate comb. I was so petrified and awed by her presence that I burst into tears before I could even begin talking to her. She was kind and had compassionate eyes. Like the others, she could not take on any advisees and gave me names of other faculty members.

I met with over forty professors in various disciplines, including professors at the JFK School of Government and the Law and Education Schools. Defining what exactly I wanted to learn, and explaining it to others, taught me perseverance. My ability to clearly articulate my thoughts and plans increased. By the time I met with the fortieth professor,

---

nevertheless each defines and is defined by both a mainstream or core and a periphery or margins. These margins and the *spaces between disciplines* are unable to be theorized in the terms of the core—that is within the discipline itself. (Elizabeth Grosz, "Bodies and Knowledges: Feminism and the Crisis of Reason," in *Feminist Epistemologies*, Linda Alcott and Elizabeth Potter, eds. New York: Routledge, 1993, pp. 187–215).

I knew exactly how to say what, and how, and why I hoped to learn and do. I eventually found excellent advisers in the Literature Department.

My mother's unique lack of discipline of me as a child and Mr. Mac's Heritage program, with its emphasis on individuality, gave me the confidence and courage to pursue a special concentration, to learn outside of a discipline.

28

"LOVE IS BODIES, BLOOD AND SWEAT"*

We can sit in our safe corners mute as bottles, and we will still be no less afraid . . . [I]n this way alone we can survive, by taking part in a process of life that is creative and continuing, that is growth. And it is never without fear—of visibility, of the harsh light of scrutiny and perhaps judgment. . . . But we have lived through all of those already, in silence. . . . And I remind myself all the time now that if I were to have been born mute, or had maintained an oath of silence my whole life long for safety, *I would still have suffered, and I would still die*. It is very good for establishing perspective—

—Audre Lorde**

---

*From "Poem of the End" by Marina Tsvetayeva, in *A Book of Women Poets: From Antiquity to Now*, Aliki Barnstone and Willis Barnstone, eds. New York: Schocken Books, 1992 edition.

**From "Transformation of Silence into Language and Action," Audre Lorde, *Sister Outsider*, Santa Cruz, CA: Crossing Press, 1984.

*

NEAR THE END of our freshman year Maggie told me, "You have to meet Moon; she plays rugby with me. She wrestled in high school, too." Moon had expressive dark brown eyes, pale clear skin, and a boyish haircut. Her soft brown hair flopped over her forehead, and she pushed it back as I listened spellbound while she talked about feminism and the patriarchal hierarchy of our culture. We became friends, and since we were both in Boston for the summer, we decided to wrestle at the Boston College open mats on Tuesday and Thursday evenings. It was exciting to be able to do again what I loved.

At the BC practices, we found out about a wrestling camp in upstate New York. It was run by Paul Widerman, a former Harvard wrestler who had been an All-American, nationally ranked in collegiate wrestling. The flyer said that female wrestlers were welcome, so we decided to go.

Paul let us stay in his house so that we wouldn't have to room with high school boys. Moon and I were the only women there, and we were older than most of the boys. The campgrounds were in the beautiful New York countryside near the mountains. Paul took all of us on hikes up the mountainside, and on runs around a nearby lake, in addition to the three wrestling sessions each day. We climbed a ladder to get to the "wrestling room," which was the top floor of an old barn. Parts of the barn walls were torn away, so it was almost like wrestling outside. We could see sunshine and trees and the honey-colored fields through gaps in the old wood. Paul was small, about five foot one, and extremely strong though he weighed only 110 pounds. His personality made him seem taller. After our wrestling sessions, he taught us yoga stretches.

It was funny to see ninth- and tenth-grade boys in the postures of ancient yogis.

Paul had organized a women's wrestling club at Harvard several years earlier, but it was now defunct. He asked if we were going to wrestle at Harvard. Moon didn't want to because she didn't want to be in a male-dominated sport. She preferred women's rugby, which she found more supportive and nurturing. But it seemed that Paul and Moon expected I would join Harvard Wrestling, something that had never occurred to me. I thought the men would be more advanced than I, and the coach would cut anyone who wasn't competitive. But they convinced me that I should try.

I left the Harvard coach, Jay Weiss, a message when I got back to Massachusetts. My sophomore year began two weeks later. My two roommates and I had just moved into a suite at Adams House, and before classes had even begun, Coach Weiss called. Preseason captain's practice was beginning next Monday. He said that I should be in front of the Malkin Athletic Center (the MAC) at 4:00 P.M.——ready to run. When I hung up the phone, I began jumping up and down. "Yes! I'm in!" I shouted to myself. I couldn't believe it.

I showed up next Monday on the MAC steps, just as the loud bells of Memorial Church in the Yard rang four o'clock. Thirty boys covered the steps, stretching and talking and laughing. I found my friend Rob Durbin, who had lived in Weld Hall with me the previous year. He slapped me on the back and introduced me to several wrestlers, who shook hands with me. My hair was in pigtails, and I wore my black "40 and Feelin' It" shirt and black Northeastern women's ice hockey shorts appropriated from my friend Emily. Coach Weiss came out of the MAC. He was surprisingly young, only twenty-seven years old. He wore shorts and a Harvard wrestling T-shirt. He had strong handsome features, dark brown eyes, and a flat-top haircut, and looked young and fit enough to be one of the wrestlers. I wouldn't have known he was the coach but for his air of calm authority and the whistle he wore around his neck. He told us to run a four-mile loop on the Charles River, crossing over at the BU Bridge and heading back to the Harvard football stadium, where we would do push-ups and sit-ups. We raced toward the river in a large pack, through the big cast-iron gates of Kirkland House. I was determined to keep up, my body electrified with adrenaline. I managed to stay with several of the men near the back of the pack.

My friend Rob told me that he had been there when Coach Weiss had gotten my message. The coach was nervous about a girl joining the team and didn't know what to make of it, but Rob had said, "Yeah, I know her. She's cool," meaning that he thought I was serious and not someone wanting to do it for a joke.

Rob also told me later that some of the guys asked him, "Who was that girl running with us?" They weren't sure who I was or what I was doing there. Soon enough, I got to know all of the guys and participated in the freshman initiation at the end of the preseason practices. Initiation was held on a Friday night, in the middle of Harvard Square in the T pit. I was supposed to dress as a boy, but the captains couldn't get in touch with me that day, so I showed up wearing a red skirt with butterflies.

We met up in one of our captains' dorm rooms at 6:00 P.M. Most of the upperclassmen were sitting on couches drinking cans of Bud Light while others helped the freshmen don their costumes. The guys told me my initiation would be to get five girls' phone numbers. One of the freshmen, Matt, was costumed as an alien, wrapped in newspaper from head to toe. He was given a flashlight to carry and told to shine it on unsuspecting strangers, asking them to "bring me to your leader." Brad wore a flight jacket and aviator glasses and had a cardboard airplane built around him. He carried a boom box playing music from *Top Gun*. Scott Smider, who we called Spider-Man, wore a Spider-Man costume.

Our strange parade headed up to the pit after the freshmen drank a couple of beers—if they wanted to—to calm their nerves. Eddie, a freshman who was blind but had wrestled in high school, had a great auditory memory and knew Warren G and Snoop Dogg albums by heart. One of the upperclassmen sat with him in lotus position in the middle of the Square as he recited rap songs while wearing a toga and turban, with his red-tipped walking stick next to him. I was too shy to approach girls to get their numbers, so some of the upperclassmen, their confidence supplemented by the Bud Light, helped me with the task. Two of the lighter-weight freshmen, Kevin and Dan, wore spandex shorts and competed in a World Series of Twister in the middle of the pit. They were in great shape with well-muscled torsos and looked like miniature versions of WWF wrestlers. Rob taped everything with his video camera.

We attracted a crowd, and eventually police showed up to disperse the hundreds of people who had gathered. Our team captain ushered everyone back to the dorm, where we watched ourselves on Rob's videotape and laughed at ourselves.

Once preseason was over, I spent about three hours each day in the wrestling room. I was the only female and the first woman ever on the team. I spent more time in this all-male space than in any of my classes, or in all my classes together, more time than I spent in the company of any one friend.

This experience was a journey in which I learned to reconnect the dissociation I felt from my body and voice and the bodies and voices of men. Most of the action in this story happens inside the psyche. But I was moving mountains that represented the way I constructed relationships with others.

The Harvard Wrestling Room was a red, oddly womblike space, floor and walls crimson like blood, and soft and protective like amniotic fluid. Wall to wall, the floor was a thick, resilient crimson mat. The walls were also padded with red mats to protect bodies slammed against them. It was kept warm, ninety degrees on some days, to encourage sweating. This womb nourished and enclosed the development of a group of people.

There were high windows on one side of the room. In the daytime, sunlight fell in elongated squares on the mat. Dust and hair hung illuminated, drifted slowly down, settled on the red spongy surface. The slow particles and languid sunshine contrasted with the violent exertion and grunting of the wrestlers. Columns of lazy dust were cut through by an arm, a leg, a body moving at a high velocity. On a sunny Saturday morning, the light made us calm and good-natured, even as sweat poured and breath quickened.

The slogan "Harvard Wrestling: Earning the right to win begins here" was painted in thick red letters on the wall opposite the windows. Black-and-white photographs of stern shirtless men in rows encircled the walls above the mats. There was one picture for each year of Harvard wrestling. The room reflected a tradition of masculinity, and even the red mats spurred on male aggression. It immersed the wrestlers in a tradition that encouraged them to "be men," feel no pain, win, win, always strive to win. These ideas were built into the Harvard Wrestling Room; they seethed from the walls.

Practice was the most challenging part of my day and often the happiest and most satisfying.

Inside this room I felt free of the usual dichotomies: mind-body, men-women, inner-outer. While I was wrestling during my junior year, I was also taking a psychology class at the School of Education called A Radical Geography of the Psyche, taught by Carol Gilligan, a well-known theorist in the fields of education and women's psychology. The theories I learned in class seemed to echo the psychological process of wrestling. The goals of Carol's new psychology were to put the two halves of each duality back into relationship with each other, reunite bodies with minds, and bridge the separations between men and women.

At first, it was painful for me to assert myself and speak with my coach and teammates. I got along with them, but there was a lot that we didn't talk about. When I entered the wrestling room I followed the rules of contact between people of inferior-superior groups. I didn't make eye contact; I looked at my shoes as I put them on. I waited to be spoken to and kept to myself while listening to the boys' banter. I smiled, but didn't join in. I didn't feel that I had anything important or relevant to say, so I stayed silent.

One Tuesday in midseason, there was no one to wrestle with me. "Coach . . . I don't mean to bother you, but none of the lightweight guys are here."

He smiled. "The three of them just got sent over to see the doctor to get treated for impetigo or herpes, some skin infection."

"Oh," I said.

"Maybe you should get checked, too. Go have Kate check you."

Kate was our trainer. She checked me, but there were no eruptions, only smooth skin. The next morning in psychology class, I touched my chin and the skin in one spot melted away and opened. I felt the blood and fluid underneath, the vein moving back and forth as I stroked the skin delicately. A few head butts, slaps to my temple—a few times of my forehead being ground into the mat while I pulled fingers off my neck—made the skin rubbed raw and red. It was here that the thin skin opened, and the herpes virus gained entry.

Later that night, pieces of my face peeled back, pustules formed hard hills, maps of rough braille were written across the sensitive skin that I usually shoved into John's or James's neck and shoulders.

At first I tried to cover up the blisters with half a jar of makeup, but as the sores worsened, the makeup just made them more obvious and grotesque, so I stopped trying to hide them.

My doctor didn't listen when I told him I was on a wrestling team and some of my teammates had herpes. He looked at the sores and me with disapproval. He didn't take a skin culture, and I didn't know enough to realize that he should have.

He wrote a prescription for antibiotics, believing the red pus-filled sores were a staph infection. I took the pills for a week, but the sores grew worse. They hurt and itched and pulsated. By week's end, they covered half my face. I had a 102-degree fever, and all I wanted to do was lie in bed and cry.

The doctor looked at the sores again and gave me yet *another* kind of antibiotics. He again shrugged off my suggestion that it might be herpes. When I began to cry, he backed away in disgust. "There's nothing to cry about," he said, mocking me. "The scars will fade in a few months." It wasn't scarring that worried me. He thought all I cared about was my looks. But what had made me cry was that he wouldn't listen to me.

I took the new antibiotics for three days before finally reaching the school dermatologist. She took one look, winced, and said, "That's herpes, all right." She gave me an extra-strength prescription of Valtrex, which my teammates had been taking all along. "Did he even take a culture?" she asked. She would talk to my doctor.

Once I was on Valtrex, the blisters stopped spreading and started to bleed and scab, which meant they were healing.

I wanted to hide in my room until the sores were gone, but I couldn't. I couldn't wrestle until the scabs were healed, because I was contagious, but I still had to go to the gym to work out on the StairMaster and lift—Coach Weiss required it. And I still had to go to class. The first couple of days I wore a hooded sweatshirt and looked at the ground on the way to class, not wanting anyone to see me and think I had leprosy.

When I took my hood off in writing class, my classmates gasped and said, "What happened? Did you get in a car accident?" It was that bad. They were fascinated as I explained the situation. Our class was close, so they didn't make me feel self-conscious.

I was also on the BGLTSA (Bisexual, Gay, Lesbian, Transgender, and Supporters' Alliance) board. The other lesbians surrounded me. "What happened to you? Were you in a brawl, or what? You look tough, man." They inspected my scabs with admiration.

It was a lesson in vanity and self-confidence. I learned from my teammates, who were uninhibited and unconcerned about their sores. They were used to everything from ringworm and staph to black eyes and bruises. To them the herpes was a big joke. They made disgusting jokes and laughed it off. I learned to do this too. It was nothing to be ashamed of. People had stared enough at me in my life for having green or purple hair, or being the only woman working out with a group of men— why should I care if they stared at me for the sores on my face?

A few weeks later, I saw my doctor at the pull-up bar in the gym. He recognized me and looked away. He knew he had made a mistake and wasn't even person enough to say anything. And he could do only three pull-ups. I just smirked at him, did my set of twelve pull-ups, and walked away.

Boys—at about age five or six—are taught to hide their feelings, to be tough, not to cry. When around men, I learned to keep my feelings secret too, for fear that they would be ridiculed. I felt that my attempts at true relationship or feeling sharing would not be taken seriously, that they were not important. As I learned more about the psychological pressures that men face, I realized that they were oppressed just as I was although in a different way. As a girl, I was told I was weak, sentimental, helpless, in need of protection. As boys, they were put in a box that confined them by not allowing them to share their feelings. I began to see that we had more in common than I had thought. They were struggling to break out of a shell, or mold, just as I was, whether or not they were conscious of this yearning.

A few of my teammates' faces, like mine, were spotted with red gaping sores. Hordes of parasitic viruses had moved in and colonized beneath our skin. In Latin, *virus* means a snake's venom. It can also mean anything evil or harmful that corrupts a mind or character.

I realized herpes and the stilted relationships caused by societal norms were diseases that did not discriminate by gender. The herpes was a metaphor for men and women's relationships to each other. The vulerabilities we shared made irrelevant whatever differences there were between us.

The closer I grew to them, the harder it was for me to see my coaches and fellow players as merely white male oppressors. In some ways, I was an oppressor—because of my white privilege and because I attended an elitist university. At the same time, I could be seen as oppressed—because I grew up in poverty, raised by a single mother on welfare, and because I was a woman. Because I could see that we were all oppressed as well as being oppressors, it was easier for me to feel empathy and love for my coach and teammates, and to see the differences between us as a source for growth and understanding.

The differences between us faded when confronted by a virus that leapt across flesh. Strength, weakness, testosterone, estrogen, high, low, breathy voice all became dim in this virus's conception of the world. It accepted any host and made me know how closely related we were. We all shared the same virus of corrupted relationships, stuck in our roles of men and women. These roles had been part of us for so long that their beginning was the head of a serpent wound round and round hiding deep within.

Together we needed to cleanse ourselves from this serpent's venom.

In psychology class, we were learning about the dissociation from their bodies that most adolescent girls in our culture experience. Young girls enter a public sphere in which they are taught that their minds and emotions are unstable, unreliable. What is held in the mind must come out through the body, and so young women also learn to disconnect from their bodies' sense of balance. We learn that our bodies are frail, weak, desirable, meant for swooning, and so we learn not to stand firm. My professor Carol Gilligan proposed that this imbalance arises in adolescence. She worked with adolescent girls at the Emma Willard School and discovered that when climbing water towers and ladders, the oldest teenage girls were always the only ones who could not climb. Many young girls climb trees and railings without a thought. When they grow older they lose their sense of balance and become dizzy.

While women become unbalanced and are steered toward a more passive bodily knowledge, men often have more opportunities to use their bodies and gain their balance, exercises that in turn strengthen their minds and give them confidence. They are taught to unite their bodies and minds in hunting, sports, and hard physical labor.

Wrestling helped me to escape part of this dissociation from my body. Many women have not had the chance to explore their own inner physical balance as I have through wrestling.

A wrestler must stand with a wide stance, weight low on her hips, so that she will not be taken down with a sweeping single-leg takedown, a high crotch, or a surprise hip throw. My balance was getting better each day as I felt reconnected with my body.

If I was practicing and did not have good balance, our assistant coach, Granit Ivanovich, who was Ukrainian and just learning English, described me: "Wind come," he said, making side-to-side motions with his arms, waving the wind in. "Go 'hoooooosh.'" He puckered his mouth, made a blowing sound, and flattened his arm out horizontal, depicting me lying on my side. "Next time, no," he would say and slam me down in another head throw. The third time he did this, my body finally got his point, and I stayed upright and balanced, muscles resisting the force of his arms as they shoved me one way and another.

One day before practice, I was putting on my wrestling shoes, wrapping the long laces around the backs, pulling them tight in front. The guys sat around, stretching. I looked up. They were playing catch with a two-inch cockroach. The brown spot was scooted back and forth across the mat. The guys joked around, and the cockroach barely got on its legs to scurry away when it was again shot to the other side of the room. These laughing boys—I was amazed by them.

I remembered a similar encounter with a cockroach that had blocked the way to my belongings when I was alone in the women's locker room. I backed off, circled around it, threw my shoe at it. I really didn't want to touch it. Was I raised to be so afraid? Could I never have noticed this? Duped . . . since when? Birth? Adolescence? To circle around. Back away with caution. Stand clear. There was nothing like the sight of cocky, laughing men lounging on elbows, taut muscled, treating a cockroach as if it were a hockey puck.

One day before practice, James and I sat against the wall talking while he iced his shoulder. The guys were wrapping white Ace bandages around one boy's middle, pinioning his arms to his sides—it was his birthday—and tying his legs similarly. A group of shouting, laughing boys stood over him, dragging him around, flipping him over. My coach laughed, loud and free as the rest. They were all having so much fun. James and I grinned at each other and raised our eyebrows. Inside my head

I heard two voices. One was an analytical voice: This is typical of male sports, how shocking, how violent. The other was the voice of my senses, my intuition: But this is so happy. It made me happy to watch them playing around like little kids.

Sometimes I felt a yearning, a wish for this intangible, joyous roughness of boys that I could not quite capture in myself. Boys may be taught to be false and inhibited in some ways, but this rough jocularity, this carefree use of their bodies was something that I lost when I became grown up, or when I entered adolescence and ceased to be a crazy little girl.

When I reached out to the men I saw every day and loved, I reached out for something that I never got to be or have. I saw that they related to each other in ways women usually didn't. I wanted to have access to those ways. The men were so free, so easy in their joking, their laughter, their physicality.

Most women want to reject "acting like a man." In wrestling, I spent a lot of time with men. Does it mean I was "acting like a man" when I participated and found value in a "violent," traditionally male sport? I searched for what men found valuable in a traditionally male endeavor or a "male personality." What is of value in the ways men relate? What kinds of relationships had I missed because I was female? I searched for "the testosterone in me . . . some piece of myself as a woman that I am reluctant to acknowledge or explore."*

Granit helped me not only to improve my balance but also to strengthen my voice. When Coach wanted us to take a break from wrestling, we sometimes played "death basketball." The only rule was to shoot. Traveling, tackling, shouting, pounding

---

*Audre Lorde, *Sister Outsider,* p. 246.

your fists on your chest to intimidate the other team, all were legal strategies. Players often ended up rolling around on the hard floor of the basketball court, running blindly through the curtain that divided the gym in half.

Granit made me the scorekeeper. As I played I had to yell out the score. I had trouble making my voice loud enough to suit Granit. He shook his head every time I said the score and cupped his ears to show he hadn't heard; I wasn't loud enough. I got frustrated with his continually badgering me. But it worked. I got louder and louder. After the first few times, I wasn't too shocked by the high pitch of my voice anymore. No one else seemed too shocked by it either, so I must have sounded okay. Rob, all 189 pounds of him, hurtled by, shouting, "Nate, I'm comin' to get you. Where are you, Nate?" intimidating one of the wrestlers who was smaller. I breathed easier knowing I couldn't sound as ridiculous as he did. He wrested the ball from Nate and sank a basket. "*Twenty—Four-teen.*" My voice grew louder and more confident, and so did my playing. I jumped in, intercepted passes, and even tackled some of the smaller guys. (I stayed clear of Rob, who was twice my size and rather scary.) It was amazing that the physical sound of my voice made me capable of so much.

One Saturday morning, we had practice matches that were refereed and scored to determine the varsity lineup. Every wrestler had a scrimmage, even those who would probably not have a chance to be in the lineup.

I stood on the edge of the wrestling room in a nervous sweat. Everyone was warming up for the matches. I wanted to stay near the wall. I did not want to run around in circles and do practice takedowns. If I began to warm up, that would mean I took myself seriously. It would mean I believed I had a chance to win my match. The voices inside oozed out of my pores. They spoke in salt sweat, nervous cold, shaking disintegration. They reminded me: *You are really, really not supposed to think you can beat a man. Strive for a couple of takedowns, but you're not meant to win, and you can't do it. You'll look ridiculous trying. So don't take yourself seriously.*

My psyche is a land of many colonies. When I began to believe that my own voice and ideas were worthless, voices from outside colonized in my head. My mind was not my own. One voice told me, *You are too weak; you will always be weak.* Another colony congratulated me for being a thin woman. All these voices took over my mind.

But another, opposing voice warred its way up. It surfaced above the others. It was the voice of Audre Lorde, and my own voice, saying: *You are suffering now in silence, aren't you? Can the pain of running around this room, people watching you take yourself seriously, be much worse? And, maybe, who knows, they will be happy for you to begin to place value in yourself. . . . If I am going to suffer, I might as well be acting.* So I began to run and take myself seriously. I began to speak more clearly and strongly. I began to ask my coach and teammates for help, and I began to be heard.

I learned that the pain of reaching out to build relationships was better than the pain of silence.

On the team I sensed an unacknowledged hierarchy. I knew my coach's priority was to the men because this was what he said in speeches—the team goal was to do well in the NCAA Division I Eastern Championships. This was his job, and although he handed out goal sheets to everybody, he never sat down with me individually to discuss my goals. I didn't get his input—but I didn't ask for it either. So I just did things on my own. I felt that he didn't mind me working with the guys, but if it was going to slow down or hurt someone's drilling, then I would not have the opportunity to drill with that person. The top players came first—there was a hierarchy not only by gender but also by ability, but I was stuck on the bottom.

But in what was demanded of each of us, there was no hierarchy. My coach was conscientious. He demanded the same discipline and output from me as he did from all the other wrestlers. If I was late to practice, I did the same sprints at the end as punishment. I was held accountable to be in practice every day, and I was not given any breaks because I was female. Each time that I approached Coach with a question or asked him to do something (such as write a recommendation for me to get an athletic grant from Radcliffe), he responded quickly and honestly, attentively.

I really wanted to communicate—be in relationship—with my coach. How could I get him to see who I was and why I was here on his team? How did I know what my coach was really thinking? How did he see my role and purpose, since it was so different from the other team members'?

One morning after a Saturday practice, Coach had us lying on our backs, stuck to the mat in puddles of sweat. Rivulets of salty liquid radiated from each body. We closed our eyes and listened to Coach's voice telling us to visualize our individual victories in the upcoming Eastern tournament. "Go over every move, visualize your opponent's responses, and what your second shots will be. Plan your counterattack. Go through the whole match, and when you can see yourself winning the semifinal match at the Easterns, raise your hand."

There was no way I could visualize myself winning that tournament. I couldn't raise my hand. It would have been unrealistic for me to believe that I would beat out Division I varsity wrestlers. I felt conspicuous even though everyone's eyes (except for Coach's) were supposedly closed. The warm sticky sweat from exercising mixed with the cold sweat of fear. I couldn't raise my hand, but I hoped my coach knew that I did have goals and that I did want to win.

I went up to him afterwards, and my voice came out in a squeak. "Coach, what if I can't picture myself at the Easterns?" And he replied quickly, "You're right, you should visualize yourself at your own tournaments, or picture yourself in practice, getting takedowns." I felt much better, having spoken. He would know, and I would know, that I was raising my hand for my own goals, and not for an Eastern tournament that I would never see. Now our separate realities could merge, and we'd understand each other better. "You're doing a great job," he said as I started to walk away. "Thanks," I said, barely audible.

Finding my voice took all my strength and made me vulnerable. It shook me. But I had survived. And I felt good.

At practice not long afterwards, I was working with James and John. The three of us took turns, rotating, working in. I already felt out of place because I was the third person. I felt in the way and inadequate. I held the tears inside. Today would be hard. James asked, "Is it okay if you don't work in every three, only once in a while?" I waited for him to answer his own question, because he should have known that it wasn't okay. "You want to work in every three," he stated impatiently. "Yes," I said. I was angry. I knew I belonged here, I knew I could do this. Now, we were both so furious, and it came out when we wrestled, pushing, shoving, slapping, circling with all our strength.

After practice James asked me how I was, and then apologized for taking his anger out on me. I said, "It's all right, we all have frustrated days." We continued to talk. We started saying things we really meant and felt. "It's just that lately I've realized I have to do things for myself," he said. "I have to take my goals more seriously, and if I need a partner who can challenge me, that's just how it has to be. It's not you personally," he said.

We talked for two hours. Angry, longing tears stroked my cheeks. "Why *do* you do it?" he asked. "Why do you wrestle? If I were you, I don't know, I might just quit; it would be hard. If I wasn't completely serious about this," he said, "I could be spending my time doing something much more fun, there's a lot of activities I could take up. If I'm not serious about this, then I shouldn't be here."

I remembered a Jorie Graham poem we read in Carol's psychology class. It reminded me exactly of what James was saying, and also of how I felt about wrestling.

The anxious bird in the wild
    spring green
is anting, which means,
    in my orchard
he has opened his wings
    over a furious

anthill and will take up
    into the delicate
ridges of quince-yellow
    feathers
a number of tiny, angry   creatures

that will inhabit him, bewildered
  no doubt
traveling deep
  into the air
on this feathery planet,
  new life. . . .

We don't know why
  they do it.
At times they'll take on   almost anything
that burns, spreading
  their wings

over coals, over cigarette
  butts,
even, mistakenly, on bits
  of broken glass.
Meanwhile the light keeps
  stroking them

as if it were love. . . . . Who wouldn't want
  to take
into the self
  something that burns

or cuts, or wanders
  lost
over the body?

from "The Age of Reason"

Wrestling was like spreading my wings over ants, coals, broken glass. The tiny angry creatures were my own fears that I discovered wandering inside. The broken glass was sometimes the physical pain, the torture of bodily exhaustion, dehydration. I think that all wrestlers face these fears and physical stresses.

Wrestling was hard, it required so much. Getting a move right took intense concentration and patience. The move had to be practiced over and over, not just repetitively but perfectly, precisely. Then, when we were in a live match, the move almost never worked the way it was practiced. Over and over we attempted to get it right, searching for that instinctive moment when the body would know what to do, and would be able to counter our opponents' actions in precisely the right way. The moment this happened was like no other. Wrestling, and I imagine any worthwhile endeavor, made us dive deep into our psyches and uncover the resistances we found there.

But for me, there was another way in which wrestling helped me to realize that there is no deep enough. For me, the fear and pain that I faced in wrestling was also the fear and pain of defying the traditional behaviors and false relationships expected of women. Jorie Graham's poem spoke to me. Some days, going to wrestling practice was like opening my wings over a furious anthill of fears and resistances from within and without. Some days, the effort of speaking or acting in this male sphere where I felt so foreign, some days this effort was as torturous as "a number of tiny, angry creatures" inhabiting me. For me, wrestling was a continual pushing inside of myself and pushing without, learning to hear my inner voices and need for connection, and learning to bring these needs and emotions into outer relationship with (mostly) white males. It moved me to the edge of my knowing.

The two-hour teary-eyed talk I had with James was one of the first opportunities I had to share my conception of the world with one of my teammates. In some ways, James had a very different conception of Harvard wrestling's purpose than I did. He had been thinking about his goals and felt that it was time for him to focus on himself, look out for himself. He sensed a danger in just sitting back and letting things go on around him. He was a hard worker, self-motivated and driven.

Anxious tears ran down my face, but my voice managed to come out in a sort of warble. I took deep breaths between quavering yet resolute sentences, determined to speak it all out. We talked back and forth. Stumbling, hesitant, unclear, making associations, I attempted to figure out what I was trying to say and how to tell it to James.

It was hard, but we really wanted to understand each other. This is the key to all true relationship: this yearning and determination to listen, really listen to the resonances and vibrations coming from another's psyche, through the imperfect mediums of the voice, language, and the body. Risking not being understood, yet striving to be understandable to another with a different reality.

James espoused an objectivist conception of the world. He said that the world would work perfectly if every person was out for himself or herself. If we don't look out for ourselves, who will? was his reasoning. I agreed.

But what I saw as missing in his conception of the world, I tried to say to him. He left out the importance of human relationships: the give-and-take that is involved in working toward individual and shared goals. He worried that if we helped others too much, we would become lost, that we would subjugate our own goals to false attempts to help other people. I think that this is the position women have been encouraged to occupy throughout history. In his individualism, James forgot that we do not all start from the same place, that we often cannot achieve our goals without the help of others. And indeed one of the major values and satisfactions in human life, for me at least, is to be able to help and nurture someone else. This nurturing is a goal in itself.

In James's conception there was no room for me in Harvard wrestling, because he saw winning as the only real goal in intercollegiate sports. And yet he said, "I hate saying this. . . . I feel that I am being condescending." I respected James a lot and was glad we talked, but I left feeling uneasy, lonely, and scared.

The following week, a pigeon flew in through an open window before practice. There was a commotion as the bird flapped around the ceiling, perching hidden on a high white pipe. Joel and a couple other guys tried to scare it out the window. I felt less odd. The bird circled around the room a few times. Confused, it left at last, finding the window by accident, it seemed. We slammed the window shut securely. The daily routine returned to normal, and we started running circles around the room. I felt a strange empathy for the pigeon. Seeing the bird chased from the room, I felt there was something more displaced than I.

A few days later, I stood near the wall for most of practice and hardly got to wrestle at all. The next day I sat in my room crying for a while. My roommate Alena was there to listen. I couldn't bring myself to go to practice. I had never missed a practice before. I ran eight miles in the cold winter darkness, over the Harvard Bridge and down along the Charles River, crossing back over the river at the Longfellow Bridge. As I ran, the streetlights of Boston blurred behind my tears. I returned feeling satisfied that I had at least gotten more of a workout than I would have standing against the wall of the wrestling room. But inside I was not really satisfied.

I knew that I had to talk to Coach. I wasn't sure how to say what I felt. My fears and complexes might seem like hysteria to him.

I was full of tangled, knotted fears. Mentally my hands were tied behind my back, like Tommy's one day when Coach tied a jump rope around his arms and midriff to help him learn to keep his elbows in. I tried to overcome my fears in my own mind by shrugging, worming, and wiggling to get the knots to come slipping off. But my efforts were useless. The knotted fears grew ever tighter, a red soreness that burned. What I really needed was someone to help undo the knots. But to ask for help, I needed to speak. My fears kept me gagged as well as tied up.

I feared that I would speak and my coach wouldn't understand, that my words would be muddy and incoherent, incomprehensible when I brought them as clumsily wrapped gifts before him. But I was determined to speak.

Before practice the next day, I stood in the hallway three times and turned back, unable to go into the wrestling room. Finally I went in and put on my shoes, acted like everything was normal. I gathered strength and walked over to Coach, who was sitting against the wall with his whistle in hand. "Where were you yesterday?" he said, letting me know that I better have a good reason for missing practice. I said, in a voice that stayed constant only because I believed that it wasn't my own voice at all, "I wasn't feeling well."

"Feeling better?" he said.

"No," I said, quiet, looking at his face.

"You want to talk?" he said, rising to his feet anxiously. I nodded, really unable to speak now, holding in the tears. We walked out together, through the men's locker room and into his office.

"I don't want you to miss practice," I said.

"This is more important," he said. I was glad he thought so.

A few tears escaped. I wiped them away quickly. I'd rehearsed what I meant to say in my journal the previous night. I sat facing my coach, not crossing my arms or legs so that I would feel more open in what I had to say. My voice carried on strong. This is roughly what I said:

I don't want to be in the way. I want to have a chance to work as hard as I can—to do well in my own tournaments. Maybe we can work something out. If it's a few days before a big tournament for the guys, if there's no one for me to work out with, I could just go for a run on those days. I just don't want to stand against the wall. Do I have a place on this team? Does it matter that I'm here? The guys are supportive. I only wish that I had something to bring back to the team in return. Sometimes I feel like a beggar. I just want to do my best. I haven't turned in my goals because I had a hard time with them. I wasn't sure what my place is on this team. What do I contribute to Harvard Wrestling? I mean if the goals of this team are only to win at the Easterns, place at NCAA Nationals, then why should I be here? I am filled with self-doubt.

My coach's responses restored my confidence. He listened

so well that I hardly realized I was doing all the talking. I heard his voice and was startled by the unusual sound of so many words from Coach, coming directly to me.

He entreated me to feel that I belonged, that *everyone is an equal member on this team. You see Ed Mosely, Eastern champion, don't you? You don't see him getting any special treatment. You are a full member of the team. You belong here, you have a place here, you come to work your goals out here, too. One of the neat things I tell recruits and tell people when they ask about our team—I say we've got all these people . . . and we've got a girl with not as much experience. And we're all working on the same thing, we're working toward the same goals—together. I tell them that. It's so important. What you do here is the same as everyone else.*

That's what this sport is about, setting goals for yourself and striving to achieve them. That's what I miss the most about not competing anymore—I can't set those training goals and work every day, see myself improve. You guys don't know how lucky you are. Of course I still have goals here in coaching—and I always keep them in mind. I change them now and then—you can change them—but you don't want your end goals to change too much—you want to keep them in sight.

People in the athletic office ask me, "Is that girl still wrestling?" I tell them, "Of course, Lauralee's still wrestling, why wouldn't she be?" They can't get over a girl wrestling.

But for me, wrestling is about what you take with you through life. Things I learned wrestling, they still help me today. It's about discipline, and goals, and hard work, and keeping at it. You have to love what you do. And that's the best part for me about coaching here, is getting to work with all of you Harvard students. I really love seeing each one working through their goals, you are all such great people. Forget about wrestling, forget about what tournaments you win. What you'll really take with you is the people you worked with and the skills you'll use later in life.

Coach's words were like a soothing balm. I felt so much better. Changes happened now. Coach began to make sure that I had partners. If I got stuck in a group of three, he rearranged wrestlers, so that everyone would have a good partner. No longer did I stand silent on the side. If I had no one to work with, Coach himself would sometimes work with me. We negotiated and communicated much better. Yet talking with him left me with a lot more that I needed to say. And more that I wanted to hear. When I turned in my goal sheet a few days later, it was five pages long.

I wrote:

Harvard Wrestling has three sets of goals. The most tangible is the goal of winning.

There are also two other major goals that are not antagonistic to the first but complementary to the first goal. The second goal of Harvard wrestlers is the efforts of each team member to be self-disciplined and uncompromisingly persistent in pursuing individual improvement in skill, endurance, strength, and mental attitude.

The third goal is for a team community that supports each of its members in the pursuit of their individual goals and contributions to the team goal. For team members to work together and nurture each other means to speak and communicate honestly when individual goals come in conflict and to acknowledge that and work out a solution. Support means to bolster each wrestler to increase their output and precision through verbal support and physical intensity and concentration at all times.

Community means understanding when a teammate is having a bad day or is tired and helping him or her work through that, not beating down on people with negativity but building up their self-confidence.

All three goals are interdependent. For the team to work well together and foster achievement in each other, each member must be internally driven to bring the most he or she can to practice. For individuals to pursue personal goals, they need the support and respect of their team members. And for the team to achieve the tangible goals of winning matches and tournaments, both of the underlying goals must be acknowledged and in effect.

The day after I gave Coach my goals, he gestured me over after practice. "I read what you wrote. Thank you. That was the most moving thing I have read in my entire wrestling career. I cried." *Yay,* I thought, jumping up and down inside my head.

We were both breaking free of traditional gender roles. As a man, he wasn't supposed to cry or admit to crying—yet he was strong enough to cry and tell me about it.

He asked, "Can I read parts of this to the team? You've written what my vision is for Harvard wrestling . . . exactly. I wish that more of the guys understood what you wrote. Sometimes I get frustrated. They don't reflect, they don't listen and help each other." I asked him to read it when they were on the road, because even though he'd keep it anonymous, I was afraid I would turn red if I was there. But I was glad that he would share it. Many coaches might not have felt comfortable talking to their teams about other goals just as important as winning.

*

Since I did not have the experience or physical strength to compete against male Division I wrestlers, I had to find my own opportunities to compete. USA Wrestling, the national organization for freestyle wrestling, had men's and women's divisions and held many tournaments throughout the country. The closest women's tournaments were in New York. Sophomore year I could afford only two tournaments. Junior year, at our annual team banquet, several of the wrestlers' mothers suggested that I apply to Radcliffe for funding. During the next two years I received grants from Radcliffe, the Harvard Undergraduate Council, and the Radcliffe Union of Students. The grants gave over two thousand dollars to spend each year on equipment, travel, lodging, meals, and entry fees. This money was enough to compete in the major regional and national tournaments, seven to ten tournaments each year. I traveled to tournaments in New York, Michigan, Arizona, and Florida. I did well and gained a lot of experience in wrestling other women. Going to Nationals was a dream I'd had since high school. Junior year I broke my hand two weeks before the Nationals, but senior year I attended the Women's Nationals in Orlando, Florida.

In that season's goals, I wrote that I wanted to place in the top six at Nationals. I placed sixth, and although I felt I could have wrestled better, I was happy that I had achieved my goal, especially when I reflected on all the emotions and physical training and effort it had taken to find funding to get there.

The week after turning in my goals, I pummeled with Coach one morning. I used my chest and head position to bully my arms underneath his armpits and behind to his back. Once I had an underhook, I could use this leverage to throw him where I wanted him to go. Of course, my coach was much stronger and bigger than I was, so he gave just enough resistance for me to use my full effort to get control of him, and then he would fight back and regain control. So we went back and forth. Because I felt trusted and valued by him, I worked hard, reached deep inside, and made as much of an impact as possible. I pummeled back and forth, head moving to each side of his neck. I felt my coach's strong yet yielding muscles through the cotton T-shirt. Pummeling was like swimming into his body, swimming into a new understanding of relationship.

29

MEETING HIM

AS I KNELT on my bed in my sophomore year dorm room, I saw the letter that Kristi, my mother's daughter and my half sister, had sent me over a year ago. The letter contained my father's address, and it lay dusty and crumpled, underneath my bed next to the wall. Kristi worked at the courthouse in Oregon where my father was a judge. A year ago she had asked if I wanted his work address and I had said, sure. Maybe I would write to him one day. I hadn't yet, though.

When I was in high school, reporters, looking for a good story, had asked me, "Are you going to look for your father?" This question frustrated me. It was his choice not to recognize me as his daughter. My mother had sent him a letter and pictures when I was four years old, and he had never responded. I had no desire to meet such a person. But the newspapers or the TV clips always ended by saying, "Lauralee's next project is to find her father," or that I "had another quest: to contact [my] father."

By the time I was in college, my thoughts had changed slightly. Although I still did not feel an overwhelming urge to write to or know him, I had an image of a white-haired man in his sixties, getting older every day. What if he suddenly died, and I had never even tried to contact him? I had a vague curiosity about the person who had given me half of my genes. I knew I would regret having given up my one chance to satisfy that curiosity.

I rescued my sister's letter from the dust and realized— there never would be a perfect time. I would never have the perfect words. I would never have more to say to him than now.

I sat down at my desk with a piece of white paper, a small piece because I didn't feel that I had much to say. I wrote three neat paragraphs: a short biographical sketch.

28 january 1996

Dear Robert Morgan—

Hello. I am your daughter, whatever that relationship implies. I guess that I can't really want or expect anything from you; I just wanted you to know that I exist. I've never seen a picture of you, and I don't know much at all about you.

I'm a sophomore at harvard, that's not an important thing to know about me. Hmmm . . . I wrestle on the varsity team here. It's fun, the best sport, I think.

Anyway, I'm enclosing a picture from a year ago. My roommate is a good photographer. (she took the picture.)

If you want to write back or something my school address is

———— Adams Mail Center
Cambridge MA 02138-7520.

Sincerely,
Lauralee Summer

(I've wanted to write this for a long time, and I can't seem to do any better)

(If you write back I would be happy to send more pictures and explanations)

My nonchalant tone hides the importance of the content. I didn't expect anything to come of it. I didn't know if he would reply. I didn't want to care.

I decorated the paper with ink stamps of flowers and stars. I put it and the photo in an envelope and sealed it. I did not decorate or write my address on the outside, because I didn't want anyone, including him, to guess who it was from. I didn't want him to throw it out before opening it.

I wondered how surprised he would be. Did he ever think of me?

*   *   *

My classmates exchanged stories about how their parents met, at Harvard, perhaps in the stacks of Widener. Stories about when we each became something more than the proverbial twinkle in a father's eye. Instead of celebrating his birthday, my eccentric friend John had a party to honor the date of his conception. But my conception involved conflict, heartache, miscommunication, and two people, only one of whom I knew. The story must include lovemaking, but that was not the part that I ever heard about from my mother.

My first year at Harvard, in a dim room late at night, people were dancing, grooving to mellow music. "My father does these African dances," said Abena. "He just looks so funny." Naima replied, "I think all fathers look goofy when they're dancing." The others mimicked their fathers' awkward, outdated dance steps. As they laughed, I sat in silence.

I told myself it didn't bother me too much that my father didn't want to know me. I couldn't take his denial of me personally. He never knew me. It hurt less to be rejected by a stranger. I had never known life with "a father," a dad, so I couldn't really miss it. My life seemed complete as it was.

As a child, I sometimes tried to put things back neatly into cases, sealing the lids shut. For a week or so, I would be compulsive about rolling both socks into a little ball before putting them in the laundry basket, and could not leave loose earrings sitting on my dresser for more than a minute before I put them in my jewelry box. The box was a wooden case. When it opened, music played, and a ballerina in a pink tutu began to dance and twirl. When I shut it, the ballerina went back into hiding, and my earrings stayed safe. If I left them on my dresser as I usually did, papers piled over them, they lay undiscovered, they were swept into dustpans, into trash bags, out of my room. The earrings were like my life had always been: getting lost, losing people and things.

I wondered if my father was imaginary, if he had gotten lost, swept into someone's dustpan. Maybe my mother lost him because she didn't have a case to keep him in, in fact the only case in this story was the child support case in which my father denied paternity.

*

When I was twelve I wanted to be a model, as many girls do at that age. I entered one contest sponsored by a magazine to win a "model makeover." I filled out several dozen entry forms, spending all my money on stamps and big, brightly colored envelopes, hoping that they would be chosen in a drawing. I made faces in the mirror, practicing to be a model. Sultry faces, playful faces, serious faces, faces with All-American smiles. When I tired of this I became silly, squinching all my features inward and sticking my tongue out or making my eyes big and pulling the corners of my mouth out with my fingers. Then I would stare for a while and try to picture what my father looked like. I would note all the ways that I resembled my mother and then narrow my eyes and imagine my mother's features erased so that I could imagine that this must be what my father looked like.

In high school, my mom and I shared an apartment with a family who had a TV. One day I stood watching a video by the metal band Poison. I was infatuated with the lead singer, Bret Michaels, who had long blond hair and a red bandanna tied around his head.

My mom walked by, paused, and said, "He reminds me of your father." After that I interrogated my mother: Why? How do they look alike?

She became impatient, saying, "Oh, I don't know. They just resemble each other."

I knew nothing of him save a few impersonal bits of information: he was several years older than my mother, he had white-gray hair, he was a judge, and he lived in Oregon. I treasured these few facts as prized belongings, little pieces of myself that connected me to the unknown. But even with an energetic imagination, I had trouble identifying him with a twenty-something pop singer in leather pants, screeching "Talk Dirty to Me" with his bright blond hair held back in a red bandanna.

My father remained a man with no face.

There's a song by Buffalo Tom called "I'm Not There" that goes, "Maybe it's only 'cause I'm so poor, that you don't count me anymore. . . . I'm so much closer, but you're so tall." I made a tape of this song for my father when I was fifteen. I fantasized about sending it to him—but I didn't have his address, so it remained a fantasy. (I felt that I could have found his address, had I a strong desire to do so.) He had been a lawyer for many years and was now an important judge. No matter how much I tried to make myself important (in school and in sports)—no matter how much closer I got—he was still going to be taller, he was still ultimately far away from me, and I was still going to be a useless, helpless, voiceless baby. Yet in the song, the singer says, "I'm screamin', 'cause I'm tired / I'm a little bit lonesome / But I'm no baby, I'm no child / Hear me callin' / Down your stairs / Count your babies / One's not there." I wondered if my father ever heard a ghostly voice, a calling from his missing child, if he ever noticed the absence in his life.

I wondered if he handled cases as difficult as the one described in the Bible, in which two women come before Solomon and claim to be a baby's mother (I Kings 3:16–28). Solomon asks for a sword and commands, "Cut the child in two and give half to one and half to the other." Solomon had a wise and discerning heart. He determined that the woman who did not want the child killed was the real mother.

When parents go to court now, it seems they sometimes have little regard for what happens to the babies, who gets cut up or what. When my mother and father went to court so that my mother could get child support money, I got cut up, but it wasn't a noticeable thing. I didn't know until a lot later when I realized parts of me were missing. It was like big pieces of flesh were falling from me every time I looked around. Except there weren't any pieces to pick up, no blood to see. The pieces had been gone all along. It was only just now that I had noticed.

A week after sending the letter to my father, I received a card from Dallas, Oregon. I didn't recognize the scrawling handwriting on the outside.

"Dallas? Who do I know in Dallas?" I assumed it was from one of my great-aunts who didn't write often. Opening it, I saw pictures of four adults I didn't know, sitting in a restaurant booth. My heart beat faster because I figured out that the letter must be from my father, because of the unknown address, the photos of unknown people. I shut the card. I didn't want the first time I saw a picture of him to be when I was rushing off to class.

That evening I had the clean exhausted feeling that I got every night after wrestling practice and a good shower. Every limb in my body felt stretched out, used, strengthened. Maybe I was ready to open the card. My two close friends Nadia and Naima stopped by. I took a deep breath, and told them that there it was on the desk, he had written back, but I was too afraid to open it. Naima opened the letter for me and read it out loud while Nadia looked at the pictures and then passed them to me.

2-6-96

Dear Lauralee,

Thank you for your letter— What a surprise— You come across as an unpretentious, warm-hearted human being. It's terrific that you're going to school and are active in sports too. I have emotional and ambivalent feelings having received your letter— I don't want to visit hurt on you or me or do anything that would interfere with your life. I fear that contact between us could unleash an avalanche of recriminations and negative feelings. Can contact be positive and be good for you??

I don't know what you know of me, I suspect perhaps what you have heard may not be very good, but maybe, hopefully that is not the case. Life is too short to replay the pain of the past or things one has no control over.

I do know I want you to be happy—to be the very best you can be— If contact with me can help and be positive for you then I perhaps would write to you if you desire that. It's hard to talk about oneself but I am a very caring person; when my close friends or family bleed I bleed too— Perhaps if I send you a few of my opinions (court decisions) you would have a better "feel" of who I am besides the less important things like my life and career.

Thank you again for your letter— You have so much to live for—two and a half years more at a great school— I know my 4 year college experience was wonderful— I have dear friends to this day that I went to school with so long ago (1954–58). Enjoy every minute—they are golden days.

My address is   P.O. Box ————
                   Dallas, OR 97338

My wife Dawn knows of you, as we are very close (married 4-9-95).

Thanks for the photo— I would like to know more about you, your likes, dislikes, etc.

   Love,

   Bob Morgan ☺

P.S. My penmanship and spelling have never been super B

Naima and Nadia laughed because he signed his name with a smiley face and decorated his letter with stickers just like I did. Tears welled up in my eyes. I was relieved but also hurt that he said he had "emotional and ambivalent feelings."

When I wrote in my journal that evening, it felt strange to write those alien words "my father." Now that he had written back, the faceless myth he had been had vanished. I now had a "father" that was more than a name. I wasn't sure I wanted to write back. I didn't think I even wanted him to be real.

A few days after receiving his first letter, I received a sticker-bedecked package from the address I now recognized as my father's. Inside the package was another letter and a mixed tape also decorated with stickers.

His tone in this second letter was much less hesitant and he seemed more eager to get to know me. I listened to the tape in my Walkman many times while on runs and sweating on the StairMaster at the Malkin Athletic Center. As I listened, I felt a father's love pouring into my ears through the headphones' intimacy. Surrounded by the Harvard undergrads in the gym, I smiled and wanted to shout in joy.

I loved the tape, which my father said represented "some

of the best music of thirty years of the rock era." My suite-mate Veronica loved the Beatles songs, "I'm Happy Just to Dance with You" and "Words of Love." We listened to the tape with my wrestler friend Rob as we roasted marshmallows in the fireplace of my dorm room.

My father wrote and told me that he thought about me at work, at home, when riding his bike. He thought about me as he drove to and from work, even at Trail Blazer games with his nine-year-old stepson, Aaron. He believed that we have limited control over our thoughts and our dreams, and that his thoughts and dreams mirrored who he was and who he would like to be. His dreams told him that he and I had a lot to learn from each other. He thanked the fates and me again and again for granting him a second chance. He hoped that he had not hurt my feelings with his first letter. He wrote that he saw the first daffodil of spring when he was bike riding in early February, a few days after he received my first letter. Spring came early to Western Oregon, and spring came early for my father and me because we were budding as a father and a daughter, flowering in tentative love for each other.

I wrote and told him that he had not hurt my feelings (even though he had, a little bit—at first). I was happy to receive a reply—especially so quickly. I loved his cards—the fun pictures and stickers. But his words were the best part. I told my father that I didn't wish to violate his privacy in any way. I would not mention him to anyone but my close friends.

I told him that I loved to bike just as he did. While he rode on back roads in the beautiful Oregon countryside amidst green fields, small towns, tall pine trees, and rolling hills, along the Willamette River Valley, I rode through the busy streets of Boston. From Quincy, down Hancock Street to Neponset through Dorchester, and then through Roxbury down Mass Ave to Boston and all the way over the Charles River into Cambridge. Some people didn't like riding in the city, but I loved it, I told my father. It was exhilarating, dodging potholes and car doors that suddenly opened, the wind on my face, seeing all the people and sights. I loved seeing how all the neighborhoods melded into each other, the faces changing as I passed through different ethnic communities, pedaling through wealthy and poor areas alike, the sweat evaporating behind me, seeing how the different parts of the city connected.

He wrote back and told me not to worry about his "privacy." I could tell anyone I wanted to about him—that would never, ever be a problem for him. His openness and willingness not to hide his past mistakes made me feel he was honorable.

I sent him more photos: wrestling in the barn in upstate New York, my college friends and Diane, my messy room in high school, and copies of the few pictures I had from when I was young, one when I was in kindergarten, and one at age four at my aunt Jane's house.

My dad wrote back and said that he had cried when he saw pictures of me as a young child. They made him feel happy and sad. Happy because I looked happy in the pictures, but sad because he hadn't known me when I was young. He wrote that he couldn't control the past—"you can't unscramble an egg, or unring a bell"—but he did have some control of the present and future. He called his home each day to see if a letter from me had arrived. He tried to hold his emotions in check. I had done well without help from him. He wanted to be part of my life but knew that could not occur automatically. He had to earn it, and I had to want it too. He picked up the telephone several times to call me, but his courage failed him.

My father and I continued to write letters, about one every week. When he discovered that I was interested in working with children and children's rights, he sent me several of the court opinions he had written for juvenile cases.

I expected the opinions to be dry, filled with legal jargon— but instead they read like stories, the stories of the victims woven in with the stories of the people accused. I read them to my friend Joanie when we were in her kitchen. By the time I finished reading the twenty-page document, Joanie had tears in her eyes.

The stories were interspersed with bits of poetry—both poetry that my father quoted from and the poetry of his own words. His paragraphs were woven with metaphors. In his opinions, my father referenced figures as diverse as Oliver Cromwell, Christopher Columbus, Napoleon, Joan of Arc, and Thomas Jefferson—and quoted everyone from ancient Greek philosophers to Voltaire to Grantland Rice, a modern sports-writer, and poets such as John Keats and Oscar Wilde. His opinions showed his compassion and emotion, his knowledge of and fidelity to the law and the history of the law. He spoke of truth and justice. I could see the workings of his mind as he weighed each piece of evidence against each part of the law. His opinions also demonstrated his courage in taking risks to interpret the law in ways that others before him had not sought to do.

He oversaw many long and complicated murder trials. One trial involved five youths who had brutally murdered a 103-year-old man. He sent one youth to adult court "with a heavy heart," and tried the youth's accomplices as juveniles. He told me in his letters that his twenty-four-year career in law was rewarding because he had a sense that he could make a difference in people's lives. He also enjoyed working for himself. Although it meant he had to work early mornings, late nights, and weekends, he had an inner satisfaction he would not have received elsewhere.

I wrote to him about one of my friends who was the first openly transgender person at Harvard. I was unsure how he'd respond. I knew he was open-minded, but I was surprised by how forward thinking he actually was. He wrote back that he thought my friend courageous. He himself had represented several transsexuals during his career. I felt proud that my father was so admirably open to all types of people.

After we had been writing letters for a couple of months, my father wrote that he felt awkward signing Bob. He felt more than that. I wrote back and told him that he could sign the letters Dad. It was a relief to me, because it felt odd to address my father as Bob. So from then on I called him Dad.

A short time later, I found I would be speaking in late April at an Oregon Shelter Network conference in Bend, Oregon, and so I made plans to meet my dad for lunch while I was there.

The morning I left, my mom insisted on meeting me at six at the subway station to help me carry my luggage onto three trains and one bus before arriving at the airport. Perhaps it was important to my mom that she see me off, that she be involved in some way in this first visit to my father.

On the plane on the way to the conference, I looked at my legs. I thought they were big and muscular. I was proud of them. When I was a teenager, I'd tell my mom, "I have football players' legs, like Bruce." Bruce was a cousin I admired for his strength, kindness, and compassion. He was one of my favorite cousins because, even when I was a small child, he always seemed to take me seriously, to look at me with clear, attentive eyes.

"No you don't." My mom laughed and shook her head when I said this as if to say, Don't be ridiculous. But when I looked at my legs, I still believed them to be football players' legs.

I fell asleep on the plane, and in my dream my cousin Bruce carried me. I was a football tucked underneath his arm. He held me safe and tight in the hot hollow of his armpit and pinched with his elbow. He ran and ran across the green field next to my aunt Jane's house. His thighs were big and muscular, hard curved muscle. His legs were firm like tree trunks; they were a football player's legs.

I woke up, rubbed my eyes, looked out the window, and saw that we were landing. Looking down at the mountains dotted by tall Oregon pines, and the square shapes of green farmland, I was reminded of the green fields in my dream, of Bruce running and running. I remembered the feeling of being held, safe and tight, while the green and blue world rushed past me. I wondered when I met my father, would he hold me tight and safe.

I waited in the lobby of the resort where the conference was being held, wearing a summery sleeveless dress borrowed from my roommate Veronica. It had a red and black sixties flower print. My dad and Dawn were driving out to Bend, three hours from their home, to meet me.

I waited nervously, sitting, standing up, walking around, taking a peppermint from the hotel desk, and sitting back down. In a short time, a young tan woman, in jeans shorts and a sleeveless sweater, appeared at the lobby's entrance and began looking around the room. I recognized her as my stepmother, Dawn, from the pictures my dad had sent me. She was about five foot three, had shoulder-length brown hair with blond highlights. She exuded health and athleticism. I stood up, and she said, "Lauralee?"

"Dawn?" She smiled and enveloped me in a big healthy hug.

"Your father's outside," she said. "He's really nervous. He can't wait to meet you."

We went outside into the bright warm sunlight. He looked smaller than I had pictured him. He wore faded blue Levi's, and a pale blue polo shirt, and his hair shone white and brilliant in the sunshine. He stood nervously, with his hands in his jeans pockets, rocking back and forth on his heels. His face was flushed red. He took my hand and then gave me a big hug. As we walked to the car he kept looking at me and smiling, as if to reassure himself that I was really there. He later told me that his heart pounded and he could feel the blood race in his ears. When he saw me smiling, the whole world seemed to stand still. He gave me another hug and whispered into my ear, "I like your earrings," looking at the four piercings I had in each ear, rhinestones in a row going up my earlobes.

It was easy to talk with my dad and Dawn. They made me feel comfortable and were good listeners. My dad gave me a watch and some stickers. He was nervous about giving me the watch, because he didn't want me to think he was trying to buy my love. He just really wanted to give me something— some token to show that he loved me. My dad and Dawn kept telling me how wonderful and special I was and how much they loved me. I wasn't used to so much verbal affection. At first, it felt strange. I wondered if they were sincere. I soon came to learn that they were. My dad was the same in person as he had been in his letters—thoughtful, kind, and optimistic.

The next summer, I went to stay at his house in Oregon. Now that we were getting to know each other and we got along so well, neither of us wanted to waste any time. I wanted to really get to know my father.

On my first visit to their home, I arrived in midafternoon. As soon as I set my bags down, my dad was eager to walk me around the property. He led me on meandering trails through the woods around his home, pointing out types of trees and birds (he could identify over fifty different birdcalls), leading me over one-plank bridges across bubbling creek beds—and out of the woods again to the large duck pond. It reminded me of books I had read, like Jane Austen's *Pride and Prejudice*, in which the wealthy suitors live in homes that have "grounds," lush gardens and paths which one could walk on for hours. He took my hands and squeezed them.

He had been a fairy tale, an imaginary figure for so many years, so when I met my father how could he be anything but ideal? I couldn't help loving him; it was the natural thing to do.

My dad and I would leave for work early in the morning, after the dawn broke and the morning birds began their hymns. But now it was 2:00 A.M., and I lay awake with an insomnia I inherited from both my parents.

I heard my father's footsteps as he headed for the kitchen and felt comforted by his habits. He, like me, wakes in the middle of the night and craves ice cream, cereal, or perhaps peanut butter. It is a weakness we share. I heard the creak of the kitchen cupboard, the box of cereal pulled out. I pictured my father in his bathrobe as he opened the wax cereal bag, the cereal rattling into the ceramic bowl. I wondered on the mysteries of life and the strength of heredity.

We were alike in so many ways—not only physically, although many people have said we look a lot alike. I look most like my dad and his oldest daughter, Tonya. We all have the same deep-set eyes and strong eyebrows, the same jawline.

My father and I also shared many interests. We were both exercise addicts and loved to play sports. My father played football in college. That summer, he swam twice a week, we biked together almost every day, and he sometimes played tennis or basketball with his stepkids, Aaron and Erica. Now I knew part of the reason why I've always loved sports: running, biking, swimming, and wrestling.

We were both very driven people. My father believed in his ability to be a lawyer and had a very successful career. I had always been very goal oriented and determined to complete any task I undertake.

My dad and I were both very emotional. We cried often.

I was so surprised—I did not expect to be so like him. It may be that I was more like him because I never knew to be influenced not to be like him. Had I been raised by him, I might have rebelled or tried to differentiate myself from him during adolescence and adulthood—to form my own counteridentity.

Conversely, perhaps because I did not know my father, I may have unconsciously strived to become (or become like) him in order to regain or recover him. I may have worked hard in school and had a drive to succeed because I wanted to become like my father, who I knew was a successful, wealthy lawyer. Maybe because I had no father, I strove for the attention I lacked, strove to become worthy of attention and approval, worthy enough not to be abandoned. Perhaps that is what drove me forward.

The first day of my summer job in Oregon he came into my room at 6:00 A.M. and wrapped my still asleep hands around a mug of strong black coffee. In the twilight state between sleep and waking, I was aware only of warmth, the spicy aroma of coffee, and my dad's smiling face above me. "Good morning," he said and quietly stepped out of the room and closed the door, leaving the particles of steaming coffee to gently caress my face and senses into wakefulness.

Another morning, he sat on the edge of my bed and rubbed the soles of my feet through the bedcover. "Honey, are you awake?" he asked.

"Mmgh, yes," I replied, rubbing my eyes, stretching and sitting up, wishing I could wake each morning with my father rubbing my toes to wake me up.

That summer, my dad and I left for work each morning in his little brown Toyota truck. The truck had over 300,000 miles on it and he still drove it to work every day, although he had five other vehicles, including a newer truck, two SUVs, and a 1980 white MG convertible in which he has driven cross-country. The truck is still his favorite vehicle, and he will drive it until its engine sputters and dies, all its parts fall off, and it can't be driven anymore.

For Father's Day, I bought him a white T-shirt with a little brown truck on it and the caption LIFE IS GOOD.——because this is something he likes to say, sometimes at the end of letters (*I love you Lauralee and I am happy when you are happy— You're extraordinary in 1,000 ways— Life is good— Love for forever, your dad xo)* or when he is sitting in his much-used beach chair on the beach in Maui, where he has a second home.

Sometimes during the summer I had Fridays off of work and I would go to my dad's office with him. We would walk up the back stairs and hallways of the courthouse, passing by the other judges and courtroom staff, to whom my father would introduce me, proudly, as his daughter.

His office was at the far back of the courthouse—a large and sunny room with an oak desk and lots of light. As he sat down to review that day's case, I sat in an armchair next to his desk and he gave me a wooden clipboard with his name, ROBERT J. MORGAN, engraved on it. He smiled at me writing in the chair using the clipboard. "You like that? You can have it. I never use it." He couldn't know how much it meant to me to have this piece of wood with his name on it, the name I had known and pondered for so long, without knowing the person behind it. And now I had this solid thing with his name— proof that I had a father, a *dad*, who knew and loved me. I have used it ever since then even after the spring broke during a move.

Meeting my dad was like being reborn at the age of nineteen. I was reborn as my father's daughter with a past life to be learned and filled in. To each other we mean redemption: his redemption as a father and my redemption as a daughter. We are conscious of this in every moment of our interaction. An amazing second chance, a rebirth for him at age sixty and for myself at age nineteen.

During our morning commute that summer, my father told me many stories about my new family history. . . .

*   *   *

Two months after his second birthday, in February 1937, my father was diagnosed with pulmonary tuberculosis. He and his brother Norman, a year and a half his elder, were admitted to the Niagara Sanatorium in Lockport, New York, twenty miles north of Buffalo and twenty miles east of Niagara Falls. It was a tan brick, many-storied institutional building, surrounded by woods and fruit trees, home to many deer and woodchucks. Their father, my grandfather, Norman Witney, was already a tuberculosis patient at the sanatorium. My father's brother left the sanatorium after four years, when he was seven, but my father stayed on for five more years. It was the only home he remembers before the age of eleven, when he was released.

My dad woke each day in a ward of six to twelve boys, their cots six feet apart. Each morning he hung his clothes on the merry-go-round in the center of the common shower room with the other boys' clothes. The nurses were like family to him. They were very kind and feared for his health. His meals were brought to his cot, along with castor oil in tomato juice twice a day. He tells me now that he doesn't know if it did any good or not, but he knows for sure they didn't like it.

Each morning they had school from nine thirty to eleven thirty. Then they had lunch and were ordered to bed for daily "cure" until two thirty in the afternoon. My father hated being confined to bed, for he longed to play outside on the playground, on the teeter-totters, or on the ball field. After their "cure," the children had school for another hour. My dad believes his penmanship suffered since he didn't go to regular school until sixth grade, but he says maybe that's not it, maybe some people just naturally have better handwriting.

After school each day, his temperature was taken. He was finally free to play outside for an hour, as long as he wasn't "running a fever." If he was well enough, the playground, the ball field, apple trees, and acres of grapevines awaited and in the winter, sledding, which was the best thing. If he had a fever, he was sent to bed and couldn't go outside. There were times when his brother was too ill to come outside, and he played outside without him.

Some boys, like my father, had tuberculosis of the lungs. Others, about a third, had bone tuberculosis. Some of these boys had to lie in bed with what my dad describes as a rope harness and pulley with a sandbag hung on one end as weight to keep the leg stretched out so it would grow. My dad wonders now if this actually worked. Some boys had spinal TB and were not mobile. They could not walk much except with crutches and elevated shoes. They would have to lie on stretcher frames that were curved up in the middle to stretch their spines.

Sometimes my dad and his brother visited their father in the adult sanatorium, adjacent to the children's building. On one such visit, he was in a corner behind the door in his wheelchair. They walked right past him, and he said in a joking voice, "Where you guys going?" They looked over in surprise, and he smiled and pulled them both into his lap. My father remembers his father coughing incessantly and often spitting into a change purse that he always had with him. He had had some of his ribs taken out so that he could breathe more easily.

One day when my dad was seven he asked a nurse when he could visit his father. The nurse told him, "Well, honey, he's not sick anymore." Then my dad understood. He knew his father was ill, but it had never occurred to him that he might die. "You don't think like that when you're so young," he tells me. "I accepted it. I just accepted that he was ill and then he was gone but that he wasn't suffering anymore." There were no antibiotics to treat tuberculosis until two years later, in 1944, when streptomycin was introduced. "Was there a funeral?" I asked my dad, and he said, "Well, I don't know. My mother told me he was cremated—which was unusual in those days. Not many people were cremated. I don't think there was a funeral." My dad has only a few memories of his biological father.

My father was very happy at the sanatorium; it was home to him. He was too young to be much affected by the Great Depression or World War II, but he remembers blackouts and being afraid.

My grandmother remarried a year and a half after my grandfather died. My grandmother's new husband, John Morgan, was a family friend who had often driven her up to see her first husband and my dad and his brother. He was kind and generous and caring. He adopted both children shortly thereafter and raised them as his own sons.

Some of the other boys at the sanatorium had a better idea of what *home* was than did my father. He was too young when he entered the sanatorium to remember being at home, and his parents lived too far away for him to visit them. "We talked about going home," my dad tells me. "It was like a dream—a paradise—but we still talked about it."

By August 1946, the war had been over for a year. My dad was healed and could finally go home, after nine years. He had a feeling of disbelief. There had been talk about allowing him to go home for about a year. On the day he was actually to go, he had the feeling that something might go wrong, that he wouldn't really be allowed to go after all. It was a beautiful sunny day. His adoptive father drove up, but his mom didn't come because she was very pregnant. He said good-bye, and all the kids told him, "You are so lucky." They drove home to Bradford, Pennsylvania, which was about eighty miles away. At that time, however, it took almost three hours to get there, for there were no highways, only winding back roads. When he arrived it didn't seem real to him at first. He was home. But what was home? He awaited it with joy.

Driving to and from work in the little Toyota truck, I listened to my father talk about his life, his years in the sanatorium, his fond memories of it as his childhood place. My heart leapt as he reached out to touch my hand.

Part of the joy of getting to know my dad was that he became real. He was no longer so tall and formidable, and I was no longer missing. Part of what made me feel closer to my father was learning that he was also homeless as a child, although in a different way. And he too had experienced a kind of fatherlessness as a youth.

Journeys are mysterious, and all maps show roads that converge and diverge. The world, after all, is round although it appears flat and thus sometimes it is possible for two people to walk in opposite directions and eventually end up in the same place so that they may journey on together. Or a father and a daughter could begin their journey, next to each other and walk a few feet apart in two infinitely parallel lines which never cross. They could circumvent the globe of life in endless parallel circles, but never communicate and never know much of each other. The geography of life is curious. It does not always make sense.

People have often asked: How can you reconcile the father you came to know with the man who denied his paternity, refused to acknowledge his child, and paid her mother four thousand dollars so he could forgo his visitation rights? That is a tough question, and a lot of people do not understand the answer. Even Mr. Mac was a bit suspicious and protective when I said I'd met my father. He wondered why my father wanted to know me now and what kind of person he was. I have asked this question myself many times. I imagine myself in my father's shoes. I suppose it was hard for a public figure, the lawyer and the circuit court judge that my father later became, to admit that he could produce illegitimacy. His profession, the suit and tie and confident look that he wore to work each day, his distinguished hair that turned gray at thirty, all these exuded legitimacy, wealth, and power. I imagine being forty years old, in the midst of a successful law career, a divorced man with three teenage children, who had been involved in a relationship with a woman who had unexpectedly become pregnant. It might have hurt his law career to have the public know he had an illegitimate child. I imagine that the decision was hard for him. Perhaps he did not feel he would have been able to be a good father to me, and he chose not to be involved at all.

"We make choices," he told me recently. "I lost wonderful years to see you grow up. I could have been there for you. I don't mean just financially; I mean emotionally, too. We went to court. I agreed to the lump-sum settlement. Of course, we know now, that wasn't enough, not nearly enough to provide for you. It was not a proud moment," he told me. "I'm not proud of any of that. I can't justify it. It wouldn't have mattered who you were. If I saw you, I couldn't have walked away." So he chose never to see me. I still do not understand that choice. I do not think it is one I would have made, but I was not him. But when I think about the small baby I was, and how much I grew and changed in the nineteen years after that—all that I experienced—I would not want someone to judge me based on my actions when I was two years old, or when I was nine, or fifteen. Because I have learned and grown so much since then. My father must have learned and grown just as much between the ages of forty and sixty. The choice he made when he was forty might not be the same he would have made at fifty or sixty. How could I hold him accountable, how could I feel angry for something he did nineteen years earlier? Any more than my mom would still be mad at me for something I did when I was two.

People ask: Don't you have any negative, angry feelings? I have learned that it is better not to live with anger, not to dwell in disappointment. If you let anger and disappointment rule you, they will be chains that will hold you down and keep you from growing.

And so, when I relate to my dad now, I relate to him as the man he is. I judge him only on his actions now. As he stated in his first letters, he has shown me in countless ways that he will always be there for me, whether financially or emotionally.

After I contacted him, he sent me money every month when I was in college so that I wouldn't have to work two jobs. He sends letters several times a month just to let me know I am in his thoughts. For my college graduation he gave me a luggage set in bright yellow, blue, and orange. He said as he hugged me, "They are colorful. I thought they'd suit your per-sonality." He and Dawn (and the luggage set) made the long trip to Boston for five days to see me graduate college, to meet Mr. Mac and my friends. For my graduation, he also bought me a plane ticket to go to stay at his condo in Maui. When he and Dawn went on a two-week bike trip to San Francisco while I was staying with them over the summer, he trusted me with his house. My home will always be your home, he said. When I didn't have dental insurance, he took me to his dentist and paid for an entire mouth's worth of work.

When, last year, I needed someone to drive my truck with me from Boston to Berkeley, California, to go to graduate school—a friend was going to go and decided not to at the last minute—my dad flew to Boston and made a fourteen-day trip cross country with me. It is these things that I judge him on, not on one choice he made decades ago.

My dad loves to relax in the Jacuzzi in his house after a long day of work and bicycling. He lets the hot jet streams of water massage away the day's stresses and tensions. My father and I sit in the steaming whirlpool one evening—he in swim trunks and me in my sports top and black men's swimming trunks that ballooned with water while I kept pushing them down. My dad takes my warm pruned hand in his own. His voice was tremulous: "I hope you know . . . Many times I have thought of all the years I lost with you. I've wished I could have them back. I hope you will forgive me for not being there for you. It breaks my heart. . . ." The tears spill out of his blue eyes, down the handsome lines of his face, and over the white hair of his chest.

As I sit there with him, the warm water baptizes us. It is like we are returning to a womb, floating, cleansed. He tells me the story of the day he opened my first letter at work.

"I made the mistake of starting to read it a minute before I was to go into court. Unexpectedly, tears burst from my eyes." In shock he fumbled for the black robe on its hanger on the oak door of his office. "I had to wait fifteen minutes before I could go into court. I felt so foolish." The letter brought back memories of time spent with my mother. He held the picture in his hands and had an intense, immediate longing to know and see me. He felt as if he were an adopted child who had never known his parents and had now been given a chance. He managed to get through the rest of the afternoon in court, with half his mind on the letter. He drove home from work in his little brown truck, loosening his tie and listening to the birds singing. They seemed to tell him, "Don't blow this—don't blow it. You've been given a chance, don't mess it up." At home, he sat down and wrote and rewrote his first letter to me—trying to convey the right tone, to express himself truly on the page.

"You know," he tells me now as we sit in the spiraling whirlpool, "your mother sent me a letter and pictures once, when you were about four."

"Yes." I nod in agreement, just listening. He describes the letter as an aftershock of an earthquake he had tried to ignore four years earlier. It shook him emotionally.

"I talked to a couple of friends, and they advised against getting involved, saying it would only cause more heartache for both of us. It would open old wounds. So I threw the pictures out."

I only want to let him know that it is all right. I feel like a daughter now in this moment that we share. "It's okay, Dad, I know. It doesn't matter to me." I hope he knows that this is true. How could the past, which is a dim receding universe, matter in this moment of now, when we are completely open with each other; we are almost naked in the warm bubbling water. The past in which we were not known to each other is inconceivable, it is forgotten, it is dismissed. There is no distance between us. How could there ever have been?

30

(HOW TO) MAKE A ROOM
OF YOUR OWN

For the environment to be an extension of the self, it is necessary not to act upon and transform it, but to declare its essential emptiness by filling it. Ornament, decor, and ultimately decorum define the boundaries of private space by emptying that space of any relevance other than that of the subject.

—Susan Stewart, *On Longing*

The world-embracing, metaphysical cupola that once enfolded mankind has disappeared, and man is left to rattle around in an infinite universe. Thus he seeks all the more to fill in his immediate, his physical, environment with things.

—Leo Spitzer, *Acts of Memory*

*

THERE CAME A POINT when the floor of my high school room became invisible, a barely remembered smooth wood-enness and a vague memory of green carpet. Layered over this theoretical ground were books, old homework assignments, unused or unusable notebook paper. Clothes, dishes, blankets, odd and broken bits of several months of life.

Everything had become such a mess that it seemed like less work to start from scratch and sort everything out than to shift around what was already there. I had a vision of a room entirely different from the messy although familiar and loved one I now lived in. Even if with the same old objects, the same old bedclothes, books, and papers, it had to be different.

Like lost sheep, I corralled scattered objects into a mountain in the center of my room. All the papers came off the walls: old finger paintings, their brilliant smudges of color symbols of the unconscious mind; Bible quotes, New Kids on the Block posters. Everything came out from inside my desk—pens, toys, papers, stapler, scissors, crayons—and was added to the top and far edges of the mountain. The little figurines I had, animals and toys and useful or useless knick-knacks that were placed just so on a shelf or desk, these all had to be swept down. Everything sucked, as if by a huge all-powerful magnet, into the center of the room. Even the curtains came off the windows. Whatever was on the windowsills or inside the closet was thrown into the pile.

I removed the tissue "wallpaper": silver paper clouds and blue and silver raindrops that streamed down like tears. The glue remained stuck to the wall in dirty streaks. Down came the empty calendar, all the things done on days past not penciled in, not recorded. They all joined the heap in the middle.

I sat on this mountain of all that was tentatively called mine, having climbed for three hours.

It was a visceral, physical thing, taking stock of my life through my objects or possessions. Remaking my room was the creation of a world on a scale that I could handle.

With everything stripped away, I had a canvas, four blank walls. It looked much as it did on the day I moved in, in the summer before ninth grade. I looked around with satisfaction at the clean (some paint chipping off here and there) mint green walls, wooden window frames, bare closet, empty bookcase, naked mattress, and felt satisfied.

I began to sort out the vegetation and animal life of my mountainside, making piles of papers, books, clothes, and so on.

But first, before sorting out my menagerie, I had to shut out the outside world. The sky glared like a sheet of blank notebook paper through my uncurtained windows. I imagined the stark raving white sky was a straitjacketed lunatic. In his fury, he tore the trees' vibrant leafy clothing from them, leaving them old men, cowering knock-kneed without a stitch to cover their bony limbs. They could not protect me from this madman's empty stare. The sky contained all the lunacy and openness of the homeless person that I sometimes felt like.

It was December, and a few days earlier I had found on the street, blowing in the cold wind, the red and green plaid paper the newspapers came wrapped in when left on the corner for the paperboy or -girl to pick up. I chased after and captured it. I sketched curtain shapes onto the pretty paper and cut and pasted them on my windows to make the room feel like Christmas. The curtains were an artifice, life in a two-dimensional cartoon world—yet it was a cartoon I drew myself. Christmas and coziness and wintry solitude and shut-in-ness. I drew the curtain shape the same way I had in the houses I drew in second grade. The houses were boxes with triangles on top, a brick chimney rectangle off one side of the roof spewing a scribble of smoke. They had two stories and square windows. The windows were miniboxes with plus signs drawn inside them that divided each box into four miniature boxes.

After shutting out the outside, the next step to creating your own space is to gather the boxes of yourself or, in my case, their innards piled in the room's center. In high school, staring at my huge pile, I tried to remember all of the things I had packed up and brought out again in each new apartment when I was younger. The things I endowed with significance, by placing them in and carefully taking them from suitcases or cardboard boxes: my books, my Flower Kid doll, my running shoes, my journals and letters, a stuffed hedgehog named Mrs. Tiggy-Winkle, given to me in first grade by an elderly neighbor named Ethel.

As a child, I packed and unpacked boxes in box-shaped rooms far flung from each other. All the boxes—full of complex treasures—were windows, boxes within boxes, views within views, views into myself. Then there were the boxes left behind, boxes of things sold, boxes stolen. All these coalesced into an idea of—what? Home?

From a small box, I pulled out a letter in my own nine-year-old handwriting. It was written from California and addressed to my friend Billy, who was still in Oregon. I had never mailed it: "Dear Billy . . . Merry Christmas! It is ninety-eight degrees here. For Christmas everyone had a picnic. I opened my presents on the beach. Isn't this weird?" I moved many times after that and kept taking in and in, like a tentacled, spongy creature. Each time I reached, each place I moved, I found a sensation and a space new and unfamiliar. Uncertainty exhausted and strengthened me.

I pulled the contents out of another box and added them to the pile: old socks, a gift of a rock from a third-grader. Books, stepped on, pages embossed by rumpled footprints. An afghan that I slung on top of the pile. My mother made it for me in fifth grade because she felt bad that we had left everything behind the year before. Its variegated yarn matched the pastel green paint of the walls. The afghan had a blackish brown burn hole.

Fingering the melted yarn, all plasticky around the hole's edges, I remembered living at Blue Ridge in fifth grade, sitting on a concrete slab outside: It was the porch of a duplex next to mine that burned down and was never rebuilt; instead it was a vacant plot of land, with weeds sprouting up all around us. It was the Fourth of July, and Jenny's father set off fireworks. One landed right on my afghan, and that's how it got this hole.

Our boxes—much like our lives, homes, and thoughts—are made out of other people's fragments. They are filled with secondhand items, a random hodgepodge; even so, the combination of these items is our own. The way we arrange machine-made things—the newsprint from the street, the Crayolas we love that are made by a corporation, the meaning and significance we endow these foreign objects with—or the way we embellish rooms and rented apartments—is something our own, our own meaning, our reality.

A homeless man on the T, too, had his box—but it was a big green reeking trash bag at his feet. In the subway car, I sat next to him. He was an obese man, dirty, his fingernails brown claws that extended half an inch beyond his fingertips. The bag—full of who-knows-what, an immense putridity making my eyes water with sorrow and a responsibility I felt for his terrible emptiness and ache.

He reached into the bag, shuffled an unknown edible into his mouth. I tried to escape into my book, reading the clean words strung across the orderly white page, but there was no way to distract my nose. The reeking air refused to be ignored. Then, the politest, sweetest voice emerged from his monstrous mouth, asking, "Excuse me, which stop is this?" His voice made me realize that this sad man had once been an innocent boy with smooth round cheeks. His mother leaned over him, whispering, "Say 'excuse me' when you want to get someone's attention." The same mother's voice must have taught him cleanliness, washing behind the ears, please and thank you. I wondered what he held in his bag, if it contained the clues to who he was now.

When you are homeless, you are without an empty clean room to reorder your boxes in. You have some ideas of what the room might look like, but it won't stay put, it won't be built, and as soon as you turn your attention to one empty window, a door and wall melt behind you.

You cling to a corner of a brick wall, your back against it, sitting and resting your tired feet. Still your thoughts entirely escape, caught up in an undercurrent of wind, forming the cloud shapes you stare at above you. Your dreams are liquid, they seep down your body, into the ground, and roll in crazy rivulets away from you, colluding in puddles over dirty brick. All your best ideas, unbracketed, float away and join the steam rising from someone else's cup of hot coffee. Who you are is solid, and you try to hang it in the air. You can see yourself crash down in front of you. You are homeless. You are home and less.

Yet there I sat in high school, surrounded by my belongings (my dirty green trash bag, emptied into the center of the room). I now had the sense of order—the white cups hanging neatly in a row—that I had envisioned so often when I was younger. Everything in this room—down to the particles of air—belonged to me. I could close the door and hold it all in safe, or open the door and let people in to experience it—the me-ness—or leave it behind, ordered and all together, to come back and find it still here.

I was ready to put my room in order. First, I got out my tool-box. It contained glue, tape, dozens of sheets of double-sided stickies, fishing wire, and a box of Crayolas: all the tools of creation.

Crayolas—what could be more perfect than these little colorful sticks of wax? I could pick them up in any store for a buck. Everyone had access. The artists most respected, revered, displayed, in this unique medium were children from their first joy scribble to when they knew how to "stay in the lines" but chose not to, drawing their own pictures in a complex visual language. Oil paints, charcoal, most artists' tools except watercolor, are expensive and only for a few privileged adult artists. Not everyone has access. But Crayolas are automatic art for anyone. They come in a colorful box, you can take them anywhere. Crayons made—and still do make—me happy for these reasons. A room isn't my own unless it has a box of crayons in it.

*

The next step in putting my room together was to "unpack" the pile, arrange it, create form, and release myself into the room by organizing and decorating it. I found hours of joy in alphabetizing books by author, and then having the luxury of reorganizing them by title, then subject, color, size, age level, then most favorite to least. Eventually I would replace the books neatly on the little red garage-sale bookcase. I labeled each section of my library, taping little signs onto the red wood frame. The books were beautiful.

From time to time, Marion, our housemate when I was in high school, would say, We're going to paint the walls, what color do you want? Anything but mint-toothpaste-gel green, please, I would say. But we never did paint them. That was okay, though, because I covered over them anyway. In crayon, on sheets of white paper, I wrote quotes from the Bible, Thoreau, and the Bhagavad Gita in big letters and taped them up. The winter sunlight was brief but bright. There were no tree leaves to block the sun. Once I'd finished my room, I loved to lie on my bed looking at the pattern of the paper curtains and the big shadowy X's that crisscrossed the yellow sun-squares on the wall. The X's were masking tape that my mother put across the windows in case of hurricane.

*   *   *

In another room, one summer during college, I hung Christmas lights in wide loops by poking the twisted green wires in and out of the ceiling's crisscrossing metal beams. It was a basement room, and I thought the lights might make it seem more cheerful. They arced like fireflies frozen in flight. When I blurred my eyes, the fireflies lived, swooping around my bed in a softened smooth dance. I was a spider, and I caught more than fireflies in my web. Entangled in the wire was also a doll's wooden head.

The doll's head was lost to the rest of its body, which was a *TV Guide* tree. My eight-year-old friend Caitlin (whose family I lived with on vacations from college when my mom was homeless) made dozens of them over a few months. She folded ordinary *TV Guides* into circular, freestanding shapes that resembled trees or bell-shaped gowns. For a while, every place I turned to—on coffee tables, on the mantel, on kitchen counters—a *TV Guide* tree would appear. My nineteenth birthday came around, and I was not surprised at the gift I received. But now the doll's magazine paper body was lost. Only her wooden head remained, its delicate corkscrew curls enmeshed in my wires.

An iridescent pen also hung in my web of lights. My friend Brian gave it to me to hang around my neck, because I always lost my pens. There were other objects trapped in my web of lights: a squirt gun from Emily, a picture made by Alena, and a medal won in a wrestling tournament.

From my ceiling, just above my desk, also hung a black spider with egg carton body and pipe cleaner legs. He was a present from Kimber, Caitlin's younger sister. She made him when she was five.

> *o spider*
> *you hang*
> *silken*
> *in my space*

The spider's green sequin eyes asked me: Who are you? Why do you feel an urgency to live inside a carefully constructed visual display of yourself?

I answered: I can't live in a room with blank walls. When growing up I swam and drowned in the whiteness of the walls of shelters and new apartments. Now when I'm in a room I fashion it into a piece of art. I have a ceaseless, restless desire to make each place I live my very own.

Growing up, I was continually sending out feelers into new spaces. My spongy tentacles drew in oceans of environs, people, places, and experience, saturating me. Now my tentacles reached out into this room ready to absorb some more and did not find oceans. I found only four dry walls. I turned inward—in frantic haste and vigilant care I reached inside myself and carefully placed artifacts on the walls. I decorated, embellished, created, arranged. My perceptions bounced back to me from wall to wall. I could begin to wring myself out without losing the oceans inside me into immeasurable landscapes. I would not wring myself out into a dry riverbed that became a flowing torrent rushing away and beyond me. I could begin to speak, drip words out with care. Knowing I had this watertight word-tight image box in which to arrange self.

The feeling of an enclosed space—a box with a lid—is concretely gratifying. To reach out and touch a wall opens up inward possibilities.

In the same basement room in college, at home on spring break, I began another project. I poked holes in fat waxy crayons with safety pins, stringing them on fishing wire and tying satisfying knots around ceiling beams. I enjoyed the physical act of tying things to hang from the ceiling of my room. As I tightened the wire, yanking the knot to secure it, I imagined that, years from now, if anyone came here to unearth me, to wipe me from this room, they would have a hard time. Try to move my spider's museum and they'd see that my cobwebs would not be swept easily down. I added another string of myself to this room. And the more I tied on, the harder it would be to move me out.

I lay on my back after tying the string of crayons up in a waxy rainbow. The lights and objects and the memories they evoked mesmerized me. I had entirely covered over the lime green faux 1970s wood paneling with sheets of black tissue paper, and cut red metallic hearts and diamonds out and pasted them onto the black.

In this box of basement I had woven, the tissue-papered walls spun into rich black memories. I dwelt within the empty space. I jumped into the void I feared, and became real. I spun into the darkness of my first enclosed space, my mother's womb.

There I was nourished by paradoxes. My mother smoked a cigarette. I tasted the stale sweetness as the smoke curled inside my mother and to me. I heard her voice as it read to me, talked to me. Curled fists reached out and encountered the soft womb walls. Home, enclosure, safety, an end to reaching.

My senior high school English teacher taught us the A—non-A dilemma of writing. Whatever is named, spoken, shown, evokes its phantom opposite. If I write about good, I imply that what I have not written of is evil. I describe ugliness, and I set the standards that beauty must follow. The A of experiencing home's lack creates a clearer conception, an obsession with its opposite, provoking these questions: What is home? How do I get there? Am I already there? Why can't I be at home here?

*

As a child, obsessed with drawing houses, I sometimes drew homes with circular doors—each with a knob in the exact middle, inspired by the hobbit-hole doors in J. R. R. Tolkien's book *The Hobbit*. A hobbit hole is a home burrowed in a hillside.

I memorized the first page of *The Hobbit* inadvertently through dozens of readings. I attempted to read the book aloud to anyone who would listen—my mother, my friends:

> In a hole in the ground there lived a hobbit. Not a nasty, dirty, wet hole, filled with the ends of worms and an oozy smell, nor yet a dry, bare, sandy hole with nothing in it to sit down on or to eat: it was a hobbit-hole, and that means comfort.
>
> It had a perfectly round door like a porthole, painted green, with a shiny yellow brass knob in the exact middle. The door opened on to a tube-shaped hall like a tunnel: a very comfortable tunnel without smoke, with panelled walls, and floors tiled and carpeted, provided with polished chairs.

Why did these paragraphs from *The Hobbit* stick in my brain? Because they are the first paragraphs? Or because they made me feel homey and like I wanted to be inside a hobbit hole, or because in saying all that home was not, they summed up what home *was* in one word: comfort.

When I was in fourth grade, my possessions, my "home," were sold in a rummage sale. The fifty dollars we made was to be put in the bank for a bicycle. But we had to spend the money because we had nothing else.

When I was in eighth grade, we moved to Massachusetts, and I again left most of my favorite things behind. My books,

Flower Kid doll, and my running shoes had to stay behind in a box, safe. Or I thought safe. To be sent for soon. My mom left them at a friend's house. But the friend moved far away. She said she'd leave our boxes at the church we both had attended. But they were forgotten, abandoned, locked forever in a church basement and in an eighth-grade mind. Perhaps they were also sold in a church rummage sale, my loved books, scattered.

For many years I believed I would get my Tolkien books back, and I refused to check them out from the library. Reading them from the library wouldn't be the same as reading my own books, and it would be a betrayal of my hope of finding this childhood self, this childhood home, once again.

Senior year in college, my roommate Alena and I moved into our dorms a week before classes. I had free time and no schoolwork. I bought a new copy of *The Hobbit*, finally giving in. (I had called my old church, to see if my boxes were still in its basement, but they weren't.) I took the new copy of *The Hobbit* to Gnomon Copy. I copied the first page over and over, magnifying the words times two hundred, times four hundred, until they formed an abstract pattern over the white sheets of paper.

At my desk, I colored each sheet of paper a solid green, wearing the glitter crayon out into a tiny wax stub, its paper in rags. I taped twenty sheets together and cut this huge sheet into a circle. My dorm room door had a shiny brass knob, just like the one on Bilbo's hobbit door. I inserted the paper onto the wall with dozens of double-sided stickies. My real doorknob poked through in the exact middle of the green circle.

I turned the knob and opened this hobbit hole door, and there stood the small child that had been me. Behind her, all she had lost: the frayed collection of books, the ones I had gotten crumbs in, smeared blood from paper cuts on, dropped into the bathtub more than once. There she was, surrounded by her Flower Kid doll, her books, her new running shoes, the knit Christmas stocking her mother had made—with the snowman with its three-dimensional yarn nose that looked like a real carrot sticking out.

I was able at last to accept and relinquish my losses. I knew now that this girl, this me, was there whenever I needed her, just behind the door. I had kept her and all her boxes safe, after all.

31

GRADUATION

I WOKE UP graduation morning to a room half torn apart.
Half of my decorations, flyers from BGLTSA dances organized by my roommate Alena and I, art projects I had made
for classes, humorous news clippings from *The Harvard
Crimson*, these things were still up on the walls. But most of
my books were gone, leaving the bookcase empty and dusty,
with only the black cap and gown on the shelf and still in its
plastic bag. I put on my favorite rainbow flowered vintage
dress, the one I bought in tenth grade, wore cross-country in
a Greyhound bus in eleventh grade (with jeans underneath
for nights when the air was cold), wore at my high school
graduation: the dress in which I still felt beautiful and comfortable. Its colors contrasted with the somber black of the
gown. I unfolded the gown, shaking out the wrinkles. I
threw it over my arm, grabbed the cap and tassel, and
headed downstairs to where my friends Katherine and
Amanda were waiting. Katherine was already wearing her

gown, and Amanda was helping her attach the white collar. We walked down to the dark dining hall for the traditional early Champagne Breakfast. Some of our friends were already tipsy from champagne and orange juice mimosas.

I expected graduation to be no big deal, just another day, another hassle to get through before I would finally breathe again and be settled in the real world as a real adult.

There was too much going on, amid the flurry of packing, to think about what graduation really meant. My suitemate Alena and I had to decide what to do with the furniture and how to find happy homes for our plants. We bought one spider plant sophomore year and now, from that one plant, we had a dozen gargantuan plants and numerous smaller offspring. There was too much other stuff to think about besides graduation. It was just another ceremony, formality, a tradition.

Senior Week had been a week of parties and good-byes after final exams had ended. The seniors and a few dorm crew workers were the only students left on campus. It was like Freshman Week—when our class had arrived a week earlier than the other students—but backwards. I spent the week in a calm panic, packing my belongings into the wheeled plastic bins that Joanie (practical woman that she is) gave me for graduation so I could move out, bit by bit, bin by bin, on the train to Quincy. I knew no one with a vehicle readily available to help me move.

I carted the bins to the Harvard T stop each day, passing by Stacey, a rotund homeless woman who had been sitting in the same spot on Mass Ave for the past few years. I could hear her cheery monotone all the way down the street: *Spare change....* *Spare change, sir, ma'am. . . . Spare change? Spare change. . . .* *Spare change, sir. . . . Spare change— Oh it's you!* she'd say when she saw me. Two years ago, when my hand was broken and in a cast (an injury I got playing power ball with the wrestlers), she would ask: *How's your arm?*

Much better, thank you. And I'd babble some trivial piece of news about my day or life as I passed on by. I never gave her any money, only talked to her. Each day on my way to practice or class there were several homeless people asking for spare change. And since I couldn't give to all of them without going broke, I rarely gave anything. Sometimes on my way out of Store 24, I'd buy a hot chocolate or Coca-Cola for the homeless man holding the door open for me. I didn't feel right about giving money, since I wasn't sure if it would be spent on something hurtful or helpful. I often thought, There has to be some better way, there must be a solution to this problem of homelessness, but I can't (or I'm too busy to) know what it is right now. I thought maybe this attitude was hypocritical or selfish, but I didn't know what else to do.

Over four years of college, I saw people change and stay the same. I met Sam, a quiet Korean man, when I volunteered at the University Lutheran shelter my first two years of college. He was young and clean-shaven, quiet and polite and looking for work. After I stopped volunteering at the shelter, I saw him in an alcove near the Garage, a mall on the corner of JFK and Mount Auburn Streets, in the same spot every morning. I smiled at him as I rushed to work or class, my backpack filled with books and a coffee-to-go mug clutched tight in my hands. He smiled back, sometimes saying good morning because he recognized me from the shelter. His hair had grown to his shoulders, and he looked tired and cold, but he was always in that spot, standing there with his cup held out for change. My last year of college, he slept on different benches around Harvard Square. His hair was now turning gray and frizzed, his skin dry and too tan, wrinkles forming around his eyes. His eyes were half-open slits by now, and he barely looked at me. Sometimes I looked away, not wanting him to feel ashamed that I saw him in this desperate condition. He struggled to stay awake, whereas before he was bright-eyed. He even slept standing up inside Holyoke Center, across from his usual bench. He couldn't sit because a Harvard policeman would tell him to move on.

In college, I came to know many others of the homeless people in the Square. They were my neighbors: Stacey, Wayne, Sam, Alger, Smitty, and Daniel. Smitty was never without his stuffed toy leopard, white with black spots. Daniel had my biorhythm chart ready for me each time that I saw him. Wayne loved to cook breakfast at the shelter and was in and out of the hospital. Stacey saw me on Monday mornings and said, *Good morning, tired one, how are you this morning?* because she remembered that Friday morning I had been hungover and tired from dancing at ManRay (a local club) the night before.

The week before graduation, Stacey saw me approaching down the busy brick sidewalk, amidst the zoo of people. I was bent over and sweating, lugging a big bin. (Why couldn't I ever do anything the easy way?) When she saw me, she interrupted her monotonous request for spare change to say—*Are you leaving, too?* A little sadness in her voice.

No, cheerfully. *I'm just going to Quincy, the other end of the Red Line. . . . You'll still see me.*

Quincy? she said, but I was already gone.

I got past the crowds, down the T elevator with its irritable operator, who asked grouchily over the intercom, "What do you want?" when I pushed all the buttons in a hurry. On the subway, people looked strangely at the big teal-colored bin and me. I finally got off at Quincy Center and hoped for a shopping cart. Usually I was in luck and there would be one waiting for me near the station or a block or two away, just when I thought my back would break from bending over dragging the heavy bin.

Exultantly, I'd lift the bin into the cart and be on my way: so fast! and easy, with a loud rattling of the wheels. Why am I so ridiculous, I would think. Doing things the hard way, spending all day every day going to and from Quincy, now that classes were over. Why can't I be normal and have boxes and someone with a car to move me? Some of the ways I thought about and did things had changed in four years, but some of the facts of life had not.

I wanted to be self-sufficient but didn't have family here with a car. This was the only way I knew to move, crazy and arduous as it was. I laughed at myself once as I actually wheeled a cart from my house to the Quincy T, hoping it would still be there later that night when I returned with another full bin. It was so ridiculous.

I laughed also, remembering once when I had three big bags to bring back to school after Christmas. Diane and I put them in a shopping cart we found near where we lived. We were wheeling away, when suddenly we heard *Get your own cart!* A homeless man with a felt hat and shaggy beard appeared from an alley between houses: *Get your own! That's my cart!* he huffed angrily. *Merry Christmas to you, too!* he muttered. We hadn't realized that the few cans in a plastic bag in the cart were someone else's. Fortunately, there was another cart a few steps away, so we transferred the bags to it and rolled noisily along, convulsing with laughter: *That's my cart! Get your own!* We giggled at each other.

So that's what I thought of as I rolled a cart back to the T. I thought that if anyone —especially most Harvard students— knew this part of my life, they would not possibly understand it, the necessity of having a cart waiting for you.

There are countless other complications, problems that can take your mind off the more academic and esoteric matters of life and bring you back crashing into the noise of laughter mixed with cart wheels against pavement.

Here I am supposed to be writing about graduation, and getting lost in the noisy memories of laughter and shopping cart wheels, noises that at that time took my mind off a future when I would be no longer a Harvard student but someone else instead, who might ironically and bashfully identify herself as a Harvard alumna.

Graduation day was wonderful in a way I had not expected it to be. From the moment my alarm clock woke me to the sight of the black cap and gown still in their bag, I knew this was it! The day! Graduation day had a hyperreal, surreal sense of elation and joy for me. My roommate for three years, Alena, and I stuck together the whole time in line, in the traditional march of the seniors through the sunny streets of Harvard Square. We ran across Mass Ave behind a flock of the black-gowned graduates, clutching at our caps when the wind blew. And what mattered to me most was that this was the last day—really—that I would spend next to Alena as her roommate and friend, the last day before we were out in the world—me still in Boston and she in Los Angeles.

We followed our classmates around the Yard, entering

through a back gate near Memorial Church. We crowded into the church, filling pews and floor, packing in sixteen hundred people. I kneeled on the floor, holding my cap, a church program, and a muffin from breakfast in case I got hungry during the long speeches.

My friend Rob Durbin was notorious for his exploits during wrestling trips (once we had to get him out of jail for going out on the field during the Orange Bowl), so when I looked around the church and saw all his roommates but not him, I knew something was up. I mouthed to them, *Where is he?* and they told me that he had still been in bed when they left, saying, Don't worry he'd meet them there later. So like Durbin it was, to casually sleep late on graduation day and saunter into the Yard when he felt like it. I smiled to myself; I would miss him.

After we had all been blessed in a strangely religious manner, considering how secular most of our education had been, we diffused from the church, unpacked ourselves like sardines from a can into the sunny morning of Harvard Yard. None of us were used to being up this early. We had all spent the past four years staying up until five every morning, talking and studying, drinking coffee and then sleeping through the next day. The early morning sun shone upon us like the bizarre light of an unfamiliar planet.

Alena and I and the other seniors were expected to loiter in the Yard for the next hour, grouped according to our undergraduate houses. I headed for the large white sign that read ADAMS in red capital letters. In previous years I had been one of the workers who posted these signs in the ground at five on graduation morning. I had been through three commencements, setting up and taking down chairs and signs, napping through long hours of grandiose speeches, but this was the first time that I played the role of graduate.

A photographer from a national magazine with a very large camera was taking pictures of me from every angle, while I tried not to pay too much attention to him. He asked me many times, "Is your mother here? Have you seen her?" "No, I don't know where she is," I told him. There were fifteen thousand people in the Yard. Anyone's mother would have been hard to spot. He kept asking me if I felt sad or was disappointed that I couldn't see my mother. He seemed to suggest that my mother was the kind of person who might abandon me. It was very much like my high school graduation, when camera crews had followed me around under big blue and white umbrellas in the pouring rain.

Cabot House, where my first-year roommate Maggie lived, was grouped next to Adams, so I went over and gave her and Jenny and Abena big hugs.

After a while of standing around, a parade of alumni and professors came processing down the concrete pathway. We graduates had to part and clear the path, lining up on both sides. The old men of the sixtieth reunion looked so cute with their canes and straw hats and bushy eyebrows. Alena's boyfriend JP elbowed Guy. "That'll be us in sixty years, oh yeah."

"I can't wait," replied Guy, rubbing his hands together in anticipation and smirking. "I wanna be in a parade."

The old men walked with little smiles, slow as turtles that know they have won the race. Then came the professors, with all different colors and stripes on their robes. We wondered what each color and decoration signified. Looking at our own plain black gowns, we realized that the degree we were receiving on this day could be considered barely a start, that we were babies in the world of graduates.

The hours passed quickly from 8:00 A.M. to noon. We were somehow directed to make our way over to the "Theatre." Tercentenary Theatre was the space between Memorial Church and Widener Library. Fifteen thousand folding chairs were set up underneath the trees, and the porch of Memorial Church was a stage adorned with microphones, large speakers, and podiums. By this time, some of us really needed to use a bathroom, because of all the coffee and champagne and orange juice that morning. My friends Jason and Guy were in especially dire need, because they had both carried champagne bottles with them. All the undergraduates were settled in their seats, and we decided to make a break for it. Jason, Noah, Guy, and I stumbled over rows of graduating students and ran across the front of the Theatre near the stage. Looking back into the mass of people, I knew that my mom and dad and Mr. Mac and Diane were out there, although I couldn't see them amidst all the faces. I saw my friend Ashley's mother with a video camera, but no one else that I knew.

Later, my mother told me that she saw us getting up and walking across the front, but she didn't know that it was us. "That was you?" she said, laughing. "I looked for you, but I couldn't find you."

We ran in a mad dash to the right side of the Yard, to Sever Hall basement, where the bathrooms were. It was so fun racing around, an informality in the midst of formality that made the day seem more festive. It was so funny to see Guy and Noah and Jason tripping over themselves in their gowns, drunk or happy both, getting lost behind me in the sea of people. It was a familiar space transformed into something entirely different and that made it a big party. In line for the bathroom a woman asked me, "Aren't the undergraduates already seated?"

"Yes," I said, "but we had to go."

By that time we were safely back in our seats. The graduation was under way, with the usual Latin orations of funny-sounding, bombastic words. I was sure that Mr. Mac was getting a big kick out of them, his face lighting up behind the glasses which make his eyes look bigger and kinder and more intense. He loved Latin and would Latinize any word or phrase by reversing the word order and adding -us to the end of every word. "Bookus gettus" was a favorite phrase, and everything was a "frasmus theatre" to him. "Cakus facus" was the term for getting cake smashed into your face when you least expected it.

All the speeches were about how great Harvard is and why we were so lucky to be becoming Harvard Alumni. One of the speeches could have been titled "How I Got Used to Being Around Black People in My Four Years at Harvard." My roommate and I didn't know what to feel or how to react to that, so we mostly laughed but didn't stand up or clap. Nothing new here.

More than the speeches I remember the people sitting around me. Familiar faces that I had come to know so well, faces and people I had come to love. People that I saw differently now that I knew I wouldn't see them as much anymore.

A few months before, I had been in a panic, unsure what I would do when I got out. Many of my classmates had thrown themselves into "recruiting"—signing up with investment banking (I-banking) and consulting companies. It was an easy ticket to making lots of money in a short time, although many would have to work eighty hours a week. I had no interest in such a scheme, and couldn't conceive of doing anything "for the money." Others were applying to law or medical school. For them, it was the logical next step. But I had never not been in school. I wanted a chance to relax. I just wanted to be free. What I really wanted to do was write a book. My thesis adviser had given me leads to literary agents, but that wasn't really a concrete plan. However, I felt confident that I now had a college education and would not go back to the circumstances my mother and I had lived in before. I could stand on my own. Harvard had opened me up to a larger universe, worlds of wealth, many different kinds of passionate, strong, intelligent people. Some would follow traditional career paths—doctors, lawyers, and professors—but I also met others who believed they could change the world through ideas and action in nontraditional careers.

Later Alena and I and our blockmates wandered back to Adams House, climbing over wooden folding chairs that were now in disarray, trying to navigate through the crowd of people that was slowly dispersing in all directions. I remembered from other years how much I hated cleaning up after commencement, filling bags with trash and lamenting that the grass pathways between the chairs had become trampled mud in such a few short hours. But today I would not be there for the aftermath in the Yard, because we had yet another smaller graduation ceremony to attend at our house. At this ceremony, in the courtyard of Adams House, we would actually have our names read and our diplomas given to us.

Alena found her parents and sister in the Adams House Courtyard. Alena's sister Yvette told me that her parents were upset with each other because her grandmother who was in a wheelchair had gotten lost, and her parents had spent the morning looking for her and worrying.

I was looking for my parents and for Diane when Mr. Mac swooped upon me with a big rib-crushing hug and thrust a bouquet of beautiful orange and yellow roses in my face. The magazine photographer started taking pictures right away, with a camera that had an even longer and more protruding lens than the one he had been using before. His assistant trailed him with the camera's big suitcase. I smiled genuinely because I was thrilled to see Mr. Mac in his suit and tie, and then I smiled weakly, because I was tired of having so many pictures taken, and because I was worried that none of my family had shown up yet and I knew they had probably gotten lost. Mr. Mac had to get back to school to prepare for Heritage night—the annual awards ceremony. Mr. Mac is like a bodhisattva; he has the amazing capacity to be in a seemingly infinite number of places in one day, because of his boundless compassion for all beings.

The photographer kept asking me, "Where's your mom? Do you see her? Where is she?"

"I don't know," I said, somewhat irritably, distracted, looking past him, searching for someone I knew and not seeing anyone.

The day was sunny but very cold for June. The wind blew right through my gown and dress and left a cold spot at the base of my spine.

It turned out that both my mother and father had gotten confused about where the second ceremony was being held. My mom and her friend Janeth ran into my dad and Dawn in the street and convinced them that if they all went up to my dorm room, they might find me there. During most of the ceremony, they were all up in my fifth-floor room, surrounded by boxes, plants, and bags of trash. Finally they heard the noise of applause and whistling from far below. They rushed down the stairs just in time to see me get my diploma. Diane had been there the whole time, standing next to a tree in the back.

I managed to lose the photographer and ran up to my room. I wanted to find my family. My dad's bag and some of my mom's newspapers were in my room, so I knew that they had been there. I threw on jeans underneath my dress and gown—so I'd be warmer—and ran down to the dining hall, where I saw first Diane and then everyone else sitting around a table. It was a relief to see everyone together and just be happy about graduation.

I hugged my mom, and I don't think she wanted to let go. In the end, Harvard did not distance me from my mother but made me closer to her. My studies of poverty and homelessness helped me understand how and why my mother's life was as it was. It increased my conviction that change is needed. Going to Harvard made me feel more comfortable in worlds of both poverty and wealth. I kept my openness to all people and relished time spent outside the company of intellectuals. I hadn't metamorphosed into a typical Harvard student. I was still me.

Moments are lost, unreturnable. I am not the girl who lay on the concrete in Santa Barbara staring at the blue-clad policeman. I am not the little girl who read *The Hobbit* front to back, continually. I am not either the ideal Harvard student, the fulfillment of the American Dream. But there is still a bit of the girl who ate hundreds of green peas so that she would grow up big and strong. I journeyed further out of myself, into the academy, into the world, into relationships with other people and their ideas. But I reclaim my own story. I write from the place where I stand, from the bus window I look out of. In doing so, I gently separate myself from the myths, reasons, and theories that people would like to place around and inside me. With these new tools I also dive further in, back into my mother's womb, into my childhood, into my particular body.

ABOUT THE AUTHOR

LAURALEE SUMMER received a B.A. in Children's Studies from Harvard University in 1998. She currently lives with her partner in Oakland, California, and is earning her master's degree at the University of California, Berkeley, School of Education.